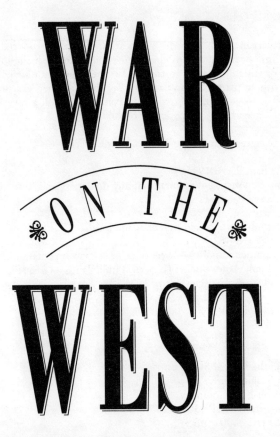

WAR ON THE WEST

GOVERNMENT TYRANNY ON AMERICA'S GREAT FRONTIER

William Perry Pendley

REGNERY PUBLISHING, INC.
Washington, D.C.

Copyright © 1995 by William Perry Pendley

Library of Congress Cataloging-in-Publication Data

Pendley, William Perry, 1945
   War on the West : government tyranny on America's great frontier / William Perry Pendley.
     p.   cm.
   Includes bibliographical references and index.
   ISBN 0-89526-482-X
   1. Environmental policy—West (U.S.) 2. Environmental policy—Great Plains. 3. Public lands—West (U.S.) 4. Public lands—Great Plains. 5. United States. Endangered Species Act of 1973.
   I. Title.
   GE185.W47P46 1995
   333.7'17'0978—dc20   95-24314
                                       CIP

Published in the United States by
Regnery Publishing, Inc.
An Eagle Publishing Company
422 First Street, SE, Suite 300
Washington, DC 20003

Distributed to the trade by
National Book Network
4720-A Boston Way
Lanham, MD 20706

Printed on acid-free paper.
Manufactured in the United States of America

10 9 8 7 6 5 4 3 2

Books are available in quantity for promotional or premium use. Write to Director of Special Sales, Regnery Publishing, Inc., 422 First Street, SE, Suite 300, Washington, DC 20003, for information on discounts and terms or call (202) 546-5005.

Contents

Dedication		vii
Acknowledgments		ix
Foreword by U.S. Senator Kay Bailey Hutchison		xiii
Preface		xvii
Chapter 1	The Good, the Bad, and the Ugly	3
Chapter 2	It Grows on Trees	27
Chapter 3	Whiskey's for Drinkin'—Water's for Fightin'	49
Chapter 4	Home on the Range	67
Chapter 5	The Pit Bull of Environmental Laws	85
Chapter 6	Parks and People	99
Chapter 7	Where Man is a Visitor	115
Chapter 8	Energy to Burn	127
Chapter 9	If It Can't Be Grown, It Has to Be Mined	141
Chapter 10	The False Hope of Tourism	157
Chapter 11	"Takings" Time: "Private Property" for "Public Use"	169
Chapter 12	Fighting Back: The Growth of Grassroots Opposition	187
Appendix A	What Can You Do?	211

Contents

Appendix B   What You Need to Know   217
Appendix C   What No One Knows About the West   225
About the Author   231
Notes   233
Index   303

Dedication

TO ALL THE BRAVE MEN AND WOMEN who stand at the front lines of this battle this book is dedicated. Their endeavors have enriched the West and the nation they love. Their embrace of the cause of freedom has encouraged others to step forward, to speak up, and to be heard. Their endurance under fire has emboldened their friends and their neighbors.

I have been on their farms and fields, on their ranches and ranges, in their mines and mills, in their forests and factories, in their cities and counties, in their homes and hotels, in their conference centers and courthouses. I know they wanted to learn something from me, but I was always the one who learned from them. I learned about their world and what makes it work and why they love it and have given their lives to it.

Even more important, I learned something about humanity, about faith, family, friends, and the fundamental principles that have governed through the ages. I feel blessed to have known them all and honored that they call me friend.

Acknowledgments

NO ONE DESERVES MORE CREDIT for the reality of this book than my family. For their support, understanding, patience, and generosity of spirit, I am forever indebted to my wife, Lis, and to my sons, Perry and Luke. With incredible goodwill they have endured my absences camped out at the computer, my inattentiveness to them as I focused on this work, and my agitation as I worried over this project, one more in a long and growing list. I only hope to be deserving of such love and consideration.

Lis deserves a special note of thanks for listening to me talk endlessly about this work and for providing me not only with a sympathetic ear but with wise counsel. Lis not only encouraged and supported me but also diligently read each page over and over. In the final days, as the deadline approached and time grew short, it was Lis who spent hours with me, not only ensuring that the 'i's were dotted and the 't's were crossed, but obtaining yet one more obscure cite to some impossible-to-locate source. I would never have finished without her.

There are hundreds of people whose names deserve to appear here, but I hesitate to attempt to list all who have been of such tremendous help to me. I know that despite my best efforts, I will omit someone who should be featured prominently. For this, I apologize. However, I must acknowledge publicly and thank those who made it possible for me to complete this book. What virtues this work may have are the result of their generous contributions. Its defects are mine alone.

There are many I should thank but cannot because their names have faded with time. What has not faded are the stories they told me, the information they shared with me, and the lessons they taught me. In my years on Capitol Hill and in the executive branch in Washington, D.C., and as an attorney, both in Washington, D.C., and throughout the West, I learned the most when I went out into the real world and met with the men and women who make it work. Days in the Library of Congress or hooked up on a computer simply cannot compare with a few hours walking through a forest or farm, a mine or mill, listening to and learning from experts. Over the years hundreds of people have been kind enough to give me their time to explain what they know better than anyone else. I am grateful for all they have given me. If you have ever taken me on such a tour somewhere out West, or approached me after a speech and told me the way things are, or met with me and rolled out the maps and charts to show me the way it is on the ground, you have my appreciation and my acknowledgment that you helped make this book a better product.

During my preparation for writing this book, I reached out to many people who provided documents and materials without which I could never have completed this work. In addition, I called out to many throughout the country who were all too willing to respond with information, ideas, and inspiration.

One individual in particular gave generously in helping me to report what is happening throughout the West: my good friend Bruce Vincent of Libby, Montana, who knows from personal experience about the war on the West and the antipeople sentiment that drives it. Bruce, one of the nation's best known and most effective speakers on this issue, devoted a substantial amount of time and thought to assisting me. I am forever indebted to him.

Others who answered every question I asked and helped me unselfishly deserve special mention: Joy L. Reinhart, Jerry Haggard, Jack Gerard, Con Schallau, Jim Petersen, Gary Langely, Kathleen Marquardt, Todd Welch, Steve Lechner, Joanne Herlihy, Paul Seby, Jenan Wood, Gloria Walker, Bev Jacka, Janice Alvarado, Kathy Penington, Cindy Zepin, Ruth Kaiser, Keith Knoblock, J. Burton Eller, Jr., Red Cavaney, Richard Lewis, Denise Bode, Barry Russell, Charles DiBona, Ron Arnold, Christine Kadlub, John Alan Morgan, John A. Knebel, Richard L. Lawson, Dean Kleckner, Charles S. Cushman, E. Edward Bruce, Laurie Zallop, Andrew N. Greene, G. Reeves Brown, Allan R. Kirk, Susan Ponce, C. Larry Mason, and P. J. Vincent.

I am also grateful to a long list of others who were there for me: Jim Sanderson, Shepard Tucker, William G. Myers III, Joseph T. Prendergast, Allen Howe, Wil Dare, Jim Burling, Brian McDonald, Jim Streeter, Robert J. Muth, Ernest J. Stebbins, Genevieve Laffly, Tom McDonnell, Mike Dail, Jim Craine, Jonathan H. Adler, William G. Myers III, Steve Hodapp, Don Zea, Jim Streeter, Bruce Fein, Esq., Gary G. Ellsworth, Clive Strong, Allen Tubb, Michael Brown, Donna Hufford, Mark Pollot, David A. Russell, Dan Kniffen, Robert G. Paul, and George Enneking.

Finally, a special note of thanks that helps explain how this book came to be. In the spring of 1992, my good friend Willa Ann Johnson told me that the Heritage Foundation, through the Heritage Lectures, provides conservatives a forum to address others regarding what Ronald Reagan once called the "reality" that surrounds Washington, D.C. Thanks to that information and inspiration, and thanks as well to the generous assistance of Bob Huberty, as well as Ed Fuelner, Ed Meese, Tom Atwood, and Adam Meyerson, on June 17, 1992, I delivered an address I called "Whither the West." In addition to discussing the attack upon the economic foundations of the West, all in the name of saving the environment, one of my main theses was that my conservative, libertarian, free market friends in the East did not understand that what was happening in the West was not about protecting the environment, it was about kicking people off the land. In short, it was about freedom. The Heritage Foundation published and circulated that speech as Lecture 417: "Whither the West: A Call to Action."

Subsequently, my good friend and fellow Reagan administration alumnus, Al Regnery, wrote me about my speech, noting prophetically, "As they say, you ain't seen nothing yet." Of course, he was right. Seeing what was coming, he asked me to consider expanding that speech into a book. After I agreed, Al helped to ensure that what needed to happen did happen by his patient prodding and steadfast support. Al was ably assisted by Kaari Reierson, Jamila Abdelghani, Jennifer Reist, Richard Vigilante, David Dortman, and Trish Bozell, who worked with me in finalizing the book you hold in your hands. I owe most to Trish, who worked patiently with me to ensure that I said what needed to be said—in my words—and no more.

To Willa Ann Johnson, Bob Huberty, my other friends at the Heritage Foundation, and to Al Regnery and his colleagues at Regnery Publishing, my deep thanks for making this happen.

William Perry Pendley

Foreword

BY KAY BAILEY HUTCHISON
UNITED STATES SENATOR

AT THE HEART OF WILLIAM PERRY PENDLEY'S *War on the West* is the concept of private property—one of the central ideas incorporated by our Founding Fathers into the U.S. Constitution. The critical position this principle occupies in American tradition and American law cannot be exaggerated.

Private property, under our Constitution, is sacrosanct. The Fifth Amendment is unambiguous regarding property rights. It reads, "No person shall... be deprived of life, liberty or property without due process of law; nor shall private property be taken for public use, without just compensation."

Yet despite this prohibition, federal environmental regulations have been used to take the property of Americans without "just compensation."

Private property has come under increasing attack in recent years from those claiming to want to "protect" the environment (inevitably at someone else's expense) and from the federal government itself.

Government encroachment has been urged and abetted by environmentalists who glibly dismiss the idea of "progress," along with the idea of private property, while driving cars, working on computers, and ensuring that their children are vaccinated.

That a spokesman for the Department of the Interior could, in 1994, refer to private property as an "outmoded concept" without evoking a massive public outcry shows how far down the road we've traveled toward abandoning that original principle.

Environmental protection, when taken to extremes, threatens the entire concept of private property. Critical habitat designation, in the name of environmental purism, is being used in a way that puts unjust limits on the use, market value, and transferability of property.

Pendley's *War on the West* is a compelling document that sets out the case for reversing that trend. For generations, Americans in the West have worked to provide food, clothing, and shelter to their families. For generations, they have been responsible stewards and the nation's most motivated protectors of the environment—their livelihoods have always depended on it. Farmers and ranchers across the West have tilled the soil and grazed the rangeland—and if they had a good year, they tried to provide for their futures by putting their money back into the land.

This land is their wealth—their property—which our government was formed to protect just as it protects our homes from burglary and our money in banks from theft.

In August of 1994, more than five thousand concerned Texans marched through the state capital in Austin. Not surprisingly, Perry Pendley was there to deliver a stirring speech to his Texas friends. They were protesting the erosion of their private property rights by federal government agencies' overly zealous enforcement of environmental laws.

Westerners are fed up with and frightened of a government that gives snakes, bait fish, and salamanders a higher priority than it gives human beings and constitutional guarantees. Under the guise of protecting species that might be endangered, the federal government has crossed a boundary erected, not by Congress, but by the U.S. Constitution.

In the Texas Panhandle, the addition to the endangered species list of a protected bait fish called the Arkansas River shiner could keep both agriculture and municipal utilities from having access to an adequate supply of water. The fish in question isn't even native to the river but was introduced there forty years ago.

In Travis County, families who, in good faith, purchased lots on which to build their dream homes are being penalized. In addition to the cost of their lots, some of which were acquired for $50,000 or more, they are being forced to pay a fee of from $1,500 to $5,000 to provide more protected habitat for a certain bird—in an area where 20,000 acres are already set aside for that purpose.

There are thousands of other examples all over the West of agricultural, residential, and recreational private property being, in effect, seized and held for ransom by federal agencies such as the U.S. Fish and Wildlife Service.

This is wrong, and it must be stopped. We have an obligation to reintroduce balance and common sense to the regulatory process.

Property owners in the West should not have to get permission from the federal government—from a bureaucracy in far-off Washington—in order to build a new house, put a fence around their ranch, or till the soil their forefathers left to them. Nor should they have to hire lawyers to convince bureaucrats that they are entitled to build a house on their own property or that their farming and ranching methods are in compliance with rules that relegate agricultural pursuits to second-class status.

Truth be told, most people and most property owners are less interested in being "compensated" than in having the government leave them alone. Government ought to seize control of private property only in the rarest of instances: when there is a compelling public need that cannot be accommodated any other way.

William Perry Pendley's *War on the West* marks a significant milestone in the march to restore our private property rights and bring balance back to the regulatory process.

Preface

THE WEST HAS BEEN THE NATION'S most enduring symbol. While the scenic beauty of the West is well known—the stuff of postcards, television commercials, popular movies, and breathtaking "purple-mountains-majesty"-style montages—it is not the pictures of the West, but its people who have captured the nation's imagination. Westerners—the loggers, the miners, the cowboys, the real people of tiny towns and communities—are part of Americana.

There is something special about the West. A vast, seemingly untamed region, it is well known for the hospitableness of its summers and for the harshness of its winters. Unlike most of America, life in the West continues much as it did more than one hundred years ago. Towns are few and far between. People often live in neighborly isolation—alone but not lonely, sharing a kinship that binds them more closely than neighbors in distant cities.

Westerners earn their livelihoods much as they did in the early days of the West, grazing cattle and sheep, growing crops, harvesting timber, mining for ore, exploring for and producing petroleum products, harnessing and utilizing waterways, and serving the visitors who come in the warm days of summer.

Today, the American West is a battleground. The men and women whose families settled the West, who have lived on the land for generations, find themselves besieged by environmental elitists sitting in their glass towers in New York City and San Francisco, their ivory towers in prestigious colleges and universities, and their marble towers along the corridors of power in Washington, D.C. These "strangers" to the West and to Westerners seek to turn everything from the 100th meridian to the Cascade Mountains into a vast park.

The battle now raging in the West is often couched as a fight between environmentalists (the "good guys") and anti-environmentalists (the "bad guys"), as powerful environmental organizations rant about ending the abuses of the past in mining, grazing, forestry, and the use of Western water. However, the battle is not about the quality of the human environment or about safety or survivability or sustainability.

The War on the West is about whether Westerners will have an economy, or property rights, or the ability to engage in economic pursuits that sustained their forefathers and that the nation still requires. The War on the West is more. It is about laws and culture and whether the freedoms guaranteed by the Constitution will survive. Today, the War on the West is important for millions of Westerners and for those who care about the traditions and culture of the West. It is also important to anyone who loves freedom and fears tyranny. For the War on the West is only the first skirmish in what will soon become a national campaign by environmental extremists.

Since its beginning as an outgrowth of the faltering antiwar movement of the early 1970s, the environmental movement has been on the outside looking in. Although almost always popular with the dominant liberal media and certainly with the politically correct since the first Earth Day in 1970, environmental extremists have never been in power. The federal laws they have strived mightily to enact and litigated aggressively to enlarge have had a significant impact on Westerners, but those laws have not been administered directly by the environmental movement itself.

That changed with the election of Bill Clinton and Al Gore.

Today, the war being waged against Westerners seems to come from all sides and all at once. Although I have devoted a chapter each to matters such as timber, mining, oil and gas, and ranching, each could easily have filled a book. In doing so, I have sought to bring Westerners together. My hope is that Westerners will finish this book with the realization that they are not alone.

On November 8, 1994, the nation made a dramatic shift to the right. Nowhere was that shift more pronounced than in the West. The state of Washington is a particularly interesting example given the agony of timber-producing communities, the result of lawsuits by environmental extremists and Clinton's betrayal of timber workers. U.S. Senator Slade Gorton, an unabashed supporter of timber communities, was slated for defeat by environmental groups while liberal Democratic members of Congress, such as Congresswoman Jolene Unsoeld, appeared to be in their ascendancy. Yet it was Senator Gorton who won and Unsoeld and five of her colleagues who lost—including Speaker of the House Tom Foley, whose lukewarm support of miners, loggers, and gun owners was a prime factor in bringing his three-decade career to an end.

Another example of Clinton's impact was Wyoming. Two-term Democratic Governor Mike Sullivan had an excellent chance of winning Republican Malcolm Wallop's Senate seat, given his statewide popularity and personal charm. In the end, it wasn't even close. Sullivan lost by 20 percent—mostly because of Sullivan's friends, Clinton and Secretary of the Interior Bruce Babbitt, and their anti-West policies.

Republicans picked up governorships in New Mexico, Idaho, and Wyoming and a U.S. Senate seat in Arizona. In addition to the six-seat congressional pickup in Washington, Republicans gained two seats in Arizona, three seats in California, and one each in Idaho, Utah, Nevada, and Oregon.

But the war is far from won. Although Republicans now control the U.S. Senate and the House of Representatives for the first time since 1952, the margins are far from veto-proof. Clinton has already vetoed one budget-cutting proposal, in part because it contained a requirement to salvage diseased, dying, and dead timber in the nation's forests. Much of the balance of power, moreover, rests with Eastern moderate Republicans—many skeptical about Western issues. And although Westerners chair the natural resources committees in the Senate and House, legislation reforming the laws that have been so vexatious to Westerners—the Endangered Species Act, for example—is months, if not years away.

Finally, it is the executive branch that implements the laws and manages the federal lands of the West. Secretary Babbitt appears undaunted by the change in the political landscape, as he presses on with his agenda. And environmental extremists still have access to the federal courts—where they have enjoyed their greatest victories— and the power to compel federal action against Westerners.

Thus the War on the West goes on! No wonder Westerners are afraid. No wonder Westerners are angry.

WAR

ON THE

WEST

THE GOOD, THE BAD,
AND THE UGLY

"THE GOOD"

IN 1976, ONE OF SAUL STEINBERG'S most famous drawings appeared on the cover of the *New Yorker*. In the foreground, Ninth and Tenth avenues are depicted in some detail. Across the Hudson River lies "Jersey," to the left Washington, D.C., and in the middle distance Chicago, Kansas City, and Nebraska. To the right and left respectively lie Canada and Mexico. And in the midst of a vast open expanse sit three towering mountains, to the left of which lies Texas, and beyond which are Utah, Las Vegas, and finally Los Angeles.

I have a framed, poster-size copy of the Steinberg drawing hanging in my office. Affixed to the glass is an arrow pointing to the three towering mountains. Beneath the arrow I've taped, "You Are Here." If ever you need proof that a picture is worth a thousand words, this is it.

For most Americans, the West is somewhere "out there," out

beyond the Washington, D.C., beltway, or maybe Chicago, somewhere short of California and the Pacific Ocean. As the saying goes, they haven't been here, but they've "seen pictures."

Even those who have been here aren't quite sure what they've seen. I met a coed at Washington University in St. Louis who appeared befuddled when I told her I was from Cheyenne, Wyoming. She admitted that every winter her family flew to Aspen to ski but she wasn't quite sure where Wyoming was. I told her, "go to Denver and take a right."

Out West, it is a long way from point "A" to point "B." The drive from Washington, D.C., to Boston, Massachusetts—through Maryland, Delaware, Pennsylvania, New Jersey, New York, Connecticut, and Rhode Island—is shorter than the journey from Cheyenne, Wyoming, to Old Faithful Geyser in Yellowstone National Park, during which one never leaves Wyoming.[1]

This can be a shock for Easterners. During my wife's and my first year at the University of Wyoming College of Law, I asked one of our professors, who had recently arrived in Laramie from Washington, D.C., how his wife was taking to the high plains of southeastern Wyoming. He admitted that she was a little disappointed. When they came West, he said, they weren't quite sure where Laramie was, but they figured it was close enough so they could go shopping each weekend in San Francisco.

It isn't just the distances that amaze people, it is the wide open spaces, the miles and miles and miles of nothing but countryside—a vista that goes on forever, prairies that roll away as far as the eye can see, mountains that reach for the heavens, a limitless sky, and almost no people.

The population density of the West is the lowest in the nation. Wyoming, the most sparsely populated state in the lower forty-eight, has 4.7 people per square mile. Montana has only 5.5.[2] While some Western cities are large, they are the rarity.[3] Drive out of any Western city and in no time you're in the middle of nowhere, out somewhere "where nobody lives."[4]

Except someone does.

It may not look like it, speeding down Interstate 80 at 65 miles per hour through Sweetwater County, Wyoming, past miles and miles of nothing, but there are people who live, work, and play there, and have been doing so for generations. Like many Westerners they depend for their livelihood on the land and its resources—timber, ore, energy, and forage. Westerners love what they're doing, as did many of their families before them, and want to keep on doing it.

It is not an easy life. The West is a land of searing heat and terrifying blizzards. The environment in which many Westerners live and work is harsh and remote. You can't spend any time in the West, in the tiny coffee shops and truck stops, in the out-of-the-way cafes and isolated gas stations, without hearing tales of human strength and courage in the face of environmental challenges most people only read about—a flash flood rips down through a canyon, with a wall of water sweeping everything in its path; a logging crew high in a mountain forest dives under their equipment as a fire, ignited by lightning, roars over them; a late spring blizzard hits as cowboys move their herd into what should have been summer pasture. Westerners often use such events to measure time: "the blizzard of '49," "the fire of 1910," "the Christmas floods of '64," "the 1921 blow."

The West is a region of great extremes. In Wyoming, the highest ever temperature of 114°F was recorded at Basin, with the lowest ever temperature of –63°F set just 150 miles away at Moran. Montana's highest recorded temperature was 117°F at Medicine Lake, near the North Dakota border, and the lowest temperature in history was –70°F at Rogers Pass northwest of Helena.[5] Certain mountain areas see the first killing frost before August 30, most of the West experiences it before the end of September.[6] Not surprisingly, for a region once referred to as the Great American Desert, most of the region receives less than 20 inches of rainfall a year.[7]

All of this—the isolation, the distance, the climate—only heightens Westerners' love for this part of the world. We take pride in the land's harshness and in the toughness it takes to do what we do. We love the wide open spaces and the endlessness of it all, not just in the gentle warmth of the summer but in the bitter wind of the winter. Despite the distances and the isolation, there is a spirit of comradeship, of being Westerners, of being different, of being part of a special breed.[8] But we also like our isolation and the distance that separates us.

Several years ago, I was in Harney County, Oregon, meeting with a rancher about problems he was encountering with the Bureau of Land Management. As we drove out upon his land, he spotted a herd of antelope clustered along the fence line. "We'll stop here," he said. "They're trying to get across the road and if we keep going they'll just worry themselves." So we stopped out in the middle of nowhere and waited for the antelope to cross over to wherever it was they were headed.

"How long you been here?" I asked.

"I came in from New Mexico about five years ago," he said.

"Why'd you leave New Mexico?"

"Too many people."

And yet. I remember reading a story in the *Reader's Digest* years ago about a reporter from the *New York Times* who drove across Wyoming, meeting folks and writing about them. Once in Bill, Wyoming, she got to talking to an old cowboy. She said that she just couldn't get over how friendly everyone was. After staring at the ground for several moments, the cowboy looked her in the eye and said, "Lady, we're not friendly. We're lonesome."

Maybe that's why, when you drive along any two-lane road in the West, without having seen a soul for hours, and you see an approaching vehicle, you lift a hand slightly off the steering wheel and wave to someone you will have glimpsed for the first and last time.

"THE BAD"

Westerners still wave to others driving by, but increasingly they find themselves looking in the rearview mirror. "You're not paranoid," folks will say, "if they really are out to get you." Westerners know who "they" are: environmental extremists and their allies in the federal government.

For the environmental extremists' vision of the West is of a land nearly devoid of people and economic activity, a land devoted almost entirely to the preservation of scenery and wildlife habitat. In their vision, everything from the 100th meridian to the Cascade Range becomes a vast park through which they might drive, drinking their Perrier and munching their organic chips, staying occasionally in the bed-and-breakfast operations into which the homes of Westerners have been turned, with those Westerners who remain fluffing duvets and pouring cappuccino. They are well on their way to achieving their objective:

♦ They have declared war on the federal mining law that permits the development of the rich mineral resources of the West; if successful this will put an end to 44,000 jobs and cost the federal Treasury more than $422 million annually.

♦ They have declared war on the life's blood of the arid West, its scarce water resources, demanding that its waters be used not for people, but for wilderness areas and for fish and birds.

♦ They have declared war on the most enduring symbol of the American West—the cowboy—seeking to price and regulate the rancher off federal grazing lands and out of business, destroying the economy of rural areas.

♦ They have declared war on the harvesting of the West's most abundant and renewable resource—timber—already costing a projected 100,000 jobs in the Pacific Northwest while condemning millions of acres of Western land to devastating forest fires.

♦ They have declared war on economic activity throughout the West and, while offering tourism as an alternative, have declared war on that too.

♦ They have declared war on the multiple use of the feder-

al lands of the West, locking millions of acres in single use
set-asides, off limits to economic activity and to motorized
recreation.

♦ They have declared war on the use of the national parks of
the West by tourists, which, if successful, will cost more
than 1,200 jobs and $250 million in Arizona and Nevada
alone.

♦ They have declared war on developing the West's rich
energy resources, which has cost more than 15,000 jobs
over the past decade in Wyoming.

♦ They have waged war by means of the Endangered
Species Act—what they call the "pit bull of environmental laws"—seeking to halt all economic activity wherever
any such arguable species is to be found, regardless of its
impact upon people.

♦ They have done all this and more with little concern for
Westerners—declaring that the creatures of the West are
more important that its human inhabitants and dismissing
the men and women of the West as unworthy of concern.

Environmental extremists have been able to engage in such a breathtaking assault because of yet another important difference between
the West and the rest of the country. The U.S. government owns a
vast amount of land in every single Western state, as it has since the
opening of the Western territories. The federal government owns
more than 80 percent of Nevada; nearly two-thirds of Idaho and
Utah; as much as half of Oregon, Wyoming, Arizona, and California;
more than a third of Colorado and New Mexico; and more than a
quarter of Washington and Montana.[9] These lands are owned and
managed by the U.S. government under a variety of federal laws and
through a number of federal agencies, each with its own particular
mandate and constituency.[10]

For many decades these agencies—the National Park Service, the U.S. Forest Service, the Bureau of Land Management, the Bureau of Reclamation, the Fish and Wildlife Service, the Department of Defense—and others maintained a largely cooperative relationship with Westerners who worked and lived on the land. Yet the enormous might of the federal government always meant that the life of the West was in the hands of strangers living thousands of miles away. Like the weather that can sweep down upon Westerners and change their lives in an instant, the federal government has always loomed as a distant threat.

Yet as pervasive and powerful as is the federal government, today there is another force nearly as pervasive and certainly as powerful: the environmental juggernaut.[11] The two cannot be considered apart, however, theirs being the strangest of symbiotic relationships. The movement would not exist had the government not given it substantial authority to operate, not simply as a body of citizens united for a common purpose, but almost as an arm of the federal government itself. Ironically, the servant has become the master. Today, the federal government is a slave to the "environmental" policies, programs, and procedures that it has fostered over the past two decades.

As a result, in the West, environmental groups possess unprecedented power. Armed with a wide variety of weapons, sustained by an overflowing war chest, capable of mobilizing a paid and volunteer army in the millions, and enjoying the impassioned support of the nation's media, academic, intellectual, and cultural elite, environmental groups can do battle as can no other political force in America. Former Secretary of Agriculture Clayton Yeutter described environmental groups as constituting "the most powerful political force in America."[12]

Environmental organizations probably wield their greatest power in litigation.[13] They have been given the right to sue by a provision contained in nearly every federal environmental statute, and they have found friendly faces in the judiciary. As a result, environmental groups have been able to delay or stop almost any activity in the West. Every major federal project anywhere in the West has been subjected to time-consuming litigation. There is hardly a national forest or a single Bureau of Land Management district that has not been slapped with appeals and/or lawsuits involving grazing, oil and gas exploration, timber harvesting, or off-road vehicle activity.

This all serves to heighten the power of environmental groups, driving federal bureaucrats to the bargaining table and corporations to their knees. In the meantime, environmental litigation is big news, which helps fill the coffers.

During the Natural Resources Defense Council (NRDC)'s carefully orchestrated attack on Alar and apples, the money flowed into the organization. David Fenton of Fenton Communications reported that his work with NRDC during the Alar scare yielded "substantial, immediate revenue" for the organization.[14] Of course, when it turned out that the "crisis" was overblown, NRDC did not return the money.

Today, environmental activism is big business. Although it varies from year to year, the annual budget for just the major national environmental organizations exceeds half a billion dollars. The accompanying chart demonstrates the huge financial resources of the top national environmental organizations and their millions of members.[15]

And this is not all. Scores of other organizations come in at just under the million-dollar-a-year funding level, and virtually hundreds of local environmental organizations pepper the countryside.

As a result, when environmental groups take on an issue somewhere in the West, they do so from a position of almost overpowering strength. When the National Wildlife Federation decides to challenge grazing on the Beaverhead National Forest in Montana, their attorneys fly in from Portland and Seattle, with the financial backing of the second most powerful environmental organization in the country. On the other side, the ranchers fighting for their very survival are represented by lawyers operating mostly *pro bono* (without pay)—men and women dedicated to assisting the people who are the backbone of much of the rural West.

There is great irony in the contrast between the financial support received by the environmental groups and by Westerners. Although environmental groups deprecate the local grassroots, property rights, wise use, and multi-use advocacy groups as "the tools of industry," these Western groups receive almost no funding from corporate America. Environmental groups, on the other hand, can count on the generous support of the largest and most successful corporations in this country. Grants in the tens of thousands of dollars are the rule and not the exception.[16] Environmentalism, after all, is the most politically correct of public virtues.[17] No other political movement has its own day of celebration, as do the environmentalists with their Earth Day and the accompanying tidal wave of media and Hollywood hoopla and organized public support from schools and other government institutions.

While local leaders in Montana walk door to door with leaflets to fight wilderness designation, environmental groups take out full-page advertisements in the *New York Times*. While local foresters and a handful of grassroots advocates negotiate with regional federal officials for enough timber to sustain local economies, Daryl Hall, John Oates, and Carole King take to the airways to condemn logging in Montana.[18]

The West is particularly vulnerable to the forces that environmental groups can exert. The primary reason of course is that the federal government owns most of the land of the West. Thus the local or state government does not make decisions regarding land use. Instead, federal officials and environmental groups play a major, if not the major, role in how those decisions are made.

While at one time the objectives of environmental groups may have been to ensure clear air, clean water, and safe lands, that has long since ceased to be the case. The environmental debate, particularly in the West, has moved from matters of safety, survivability, and sustainability to matters of aesthetics and values. Environmental extremists, for example, believe that a clear-cut is ugly and that as far as management of timber resources is concerned, nature's way (fire) is better. Many environmental extremists, moreover, see the West as

the last chance to stop mankind and put an end to modern civilization—preserving forever "the wild places."

Their policies often have a very human dimension, as in the case
of John E. Shuler of Dupuyer, Montana.

John Shuler raises sheep for a living far out on the prairie of western Montana. Late on a snowy September night in 1989, as he sat
watching television, three dark shapes sped past the window and John
heard the sounds of bones being snapped. On his way to the sheep
pen he grabbed his rifle from the front porch.

The sheep were in wild panic. Three grizzly bears were just outside the pen. But he did not shoot them; he stepped forward and fired
into the air. The bears disappeared.

But when John Shuler turned to go back to his ranch house he
found himself face-to-face with the mother of the three he had just
frightened away. She roared, rose up onto her hind legs, towering
above him, and spread her huge forepaws. Fearing for his life, John
Shuler shot and killed the bear.[19]

The Fish and Wildlife Service charged John Shuler with the illegal "taking" (killing) of a grizzly bear and slapped him with a $7,000
fine. John Shuler objected, citing the circumstances under which he
had killed the bear, and demanded a hearing. Such hearings are held
not in a real court but before an administrative law judge empowered
by the federal government. The judge ruled that in interpreting the
self-defense provision of the Endangered Species Act, he would use
the test that is applied when self-defense is claimed in the death of a
human being. Thus for the first time in legal history, the criminal law
self-defense standard was applied to an animal.

The judge applied two principles from criminal law—that self-
defense cannot be claimed by a person (1) "who was blameworthy to
some degree in bringing about the occasion for the need to use deadly force" or (2) "who provokes an encounter as a result of which he
finds it necessary to use deadly force to defend himself."[20]

Applying those rules, the judge held that John Shuler could not
claim self-defense, because when Shuler left his front porch and

ENVIRONMENTAL ORGANIZATION INCOMES

ORGANIZATION	REVENUE	EXPENSES	ASSETS	FUND BALANCES
The Nature Conservancy (fiscal 1993)	$ 278,497,634	$ 219,284,534	$ 915,664,531	$ 855,115,125
National Wildlife Federation (1993)*	$ 82,816,324	$ 83,574,187	$ 52,891,144	$ 13,223,554
World Wildlife Fund (fiscal 1993)*	$ 60,791,945	$ 54,663,771	$ 52,496,808	$ 39,460,024
Greenpeace Fund, Inc. (1992) { (combined different years)	$ 11,411,050 $ 48,777,308	$ 7,912,459	$ 4,047,761	$ 23,947,953
Greenpeace Inc. (1993)	$ 37,366,258	$ 38,586,239	$ 5,847,221	<$5,696,375>
Sierra Club	$ 41,716,044	$ 39,801,921	$ 22,674,244	$ 14,891,959
Sierra Club Legal Defense Fund (1993)	$ 9,539,684	$ 9,646,214	$ 9,561,782	$ 5,901,690
National Audubon Society (fiscal 1992)	$ 40,081,591	$ 36,022,327	$ 92,723,132	$ 61,281,006
Environmental Defense Fund (fiscal 1992)	$ 17,394,230	$ 16,712,134	$ 11,935,950	$ 5,279,329
Natural Resources Defense Council (fiscal 1993)	$ 20,496,829	$ 17,683,883	$ 30,061,269	$ 11,718,666
Wilderness Society (fiscal 1993)	$ 16,093,764	$ 16,480,668	$ 10,332,183	$ 4,191,419
National Parks and Conservation Association (1993)	$ 12,304,124	$ 11,534,183	$ 3,530,881	$ 769,941
Friends of the Earth (1993)	$ 2,467,775	$ 2,832,772	$ 694,386	<$120,759>
Izaak Walton League of America (1992)	$ 2,036,838	$ 2,074,694	$ 1,362,975	$ 414,309
Total	$ 633,014,090	$ 556,359,986	$1,234,824,267	$1,030,377,841

NOTES: All figures most recent reporting available. Some organizations had not filed for either calendar or fiscal 1993 as of September 1, 1994. Calendar year used unless noted. ◆ The Nature Conservancy obtained $76,318,014 of this amount from sale of private land to the government and $20,402,672 from government grants. ◆ National Wildlife Federation fiscal year 1993 ended August 31, 1993. ◆ World Wildlife Fund fiscal year 1993 ended August 31, 1993. ◆ Greenpeace Fund (a 501 (c)(3)) and Greenpeace, Inc. (a 501(c)(4)) have substantial financial interactions annually. Most recent Form 990 year available for Greenpeace Fund, Inc., is 1992. Greenpeace, Inc. Figures are from 1993 financial statements. ◆ National Audubon Society income includes $93,623 in mineral royalties from natural gas wells on its Rainey Wildlife Sanctuary and $505,850 from government grants.

entered his sheep pen, he "purposefully place[d] himself in the zone of imminent danger of a bear attack." John Shuler was found guilty and fined $4,000.[21]

Bizarre? Not really. For the federal government is well on its way to adopting the view of many environmental fanatics, namely, that human beings are no more than coequal inhabiters of the planet, no better than any other creature.

In September 1992, David Brower, former executive director of the Sierra Club, declared: "Loggers losing their jobs because of spotted owl legislation is, in my eyes, no different than people being out of work after the furnaces of Dachau shut down."[22] This comparison of loggers to the monsters who ran the death camps of Nazi Germany drew not a murmur of protest from environmental groups. Pretty strong rhetoric from a movement supposedly concerned about such warm and fuzzy issues as clean water and abundant wildlife. But it is not uncommon.

A few years back, then-Senator Al Gore's book, *Earth in the Balance*, topped the *New York Times* best-seller list for a number of weeks. Gore embodies the pantheistic, antihuman philosophy that runs rampant in the fanatic wing of the environmental movement:

> Many people seem to be largely oblivious of... the addictive nature of our unhealthy relationship to the earth. But education is a cure for those who lack knowledge; much more worrisome are those who will not acknowledge these destructive patterns. Indeed, many political, business, and intellectual leaders deny the existence of any such patterns in aggressive and dismissive tones.... But there is a way out... our civilization can change—must change—by confronting the unwritten rules that are driving us to destroy the earth.[23]

Gore is typical of environmental extremists in holding outlandish views that are at odds with our culture and heritage with a fervor that brooks no compromise, no concession.[24] Antihuman zealots are

sprinkled throughout the environmental movement. While project-
ing the charade that the goals they seek and the policies they pursue
are for the betterment of mankind, their rhetoric reveals otherwise.
At its core, the environmental view is that mankind is at best irrelevant, at worst an evil to be eradicated.

"Mankind is the most dangerous, destructive, selfish and unethical
animal on earth," says Michael W. Fox, vice president of the Humane
Society of the United States.[25]

Ingrid Newkirk, national director of People for the Ethical Treatment of Animals, sees "[m]ankind [as] the biggest blight on the face
of the earth,"[26] and makes this shocking comparison: "Six million
people died in concentration camps, but six billion broiler chickens
will die this year in slaughterhouses."[27]

David Brower, already quoted above, believes that "the death of
young men in war [is] unfortunate, [but] no more serious than the
touching of mountains and wilderness areas by humankind."[28]

Such comparisons are possible only if one believes there is no fundamental difference between human beings and other life forms on
the planet. For many environmental extremists, *including some
employed by the federal government*, there is no difference.

David M. Graber, a research biologist with the National Park Service, once declared:

> Human happiness and certainly human fecundity are not as
> important as a wild and healthy planet. I know social scien-
> tists who remind me that people are part of nature, but it isn't
> true. Somewhere along the line—at about a billion years ago
> and maybe half of that—we quit the contract and became a
> cancer. We have become a plague upon ourselves and upon
> the Earth ... some of us can only hope for the right virus to
> come along.[29]

If environmental leaders' prime concern were preserving our natural beauty, they would be grateful to ranchers whose irrigation and

tending of the land have caused wildlife numbers to grow dramatically, or to loggers who have so vastly increased the amount of forests in past generations as well as prevented devastating forest fires.

The ultimate goal of environmental extremists, however, is not about the safety of human beings, the survivability of species, or the sustainability of economic activity. It is not even about aesthetics. True, they object to the sight of a clear-cut, or a mine site, or a dam. But it makes no difference that the clear-cut has been revegetated, or that the mine will be reclaimed, or that the dam prevents floods while creating wetlands and recreational opportunities—in other words, that the aesthetic objections have been overcome. The problem for environmental extremists is that none of those things are natural, which they equate with good; they are evidence of the presence of mankind, which to them is evil.

These same environmental extremists will wax poetic over such calamities as wildfires, like the one that incinerated a million acres of Yellowstone National Park in 1988, or floods, like the waters that turned hundreds of counties in the Mississippi River Valley into disaster areas during the spring of 1993—aesthetic devastations that make man's efforts appear puny by comparison. But then, such devastation is okay, because it is "nature's way."

"THE UGLY"

Today, millions of Americans are discovering that the assault on constitutional liberties, private property rights, and economic activity is taking place, not just in the West, but throughout the country. And the results aren't pretty:

♦ In Texas, where 95 percent of the land is owned by private citizens, the city of San Antonio is tied in knots because of a federal judge's ruling that 60 percent of the Edwards

Aquifer, which supplies the city and its rich agricultural industry with water, must be set aside in times of drought to preserve three endangered species, one of them a salamander.[30]

♦ In Louisiana, the Fish and Wildlife Service has proposed that 2 million acres of private property—stretching from the northeast corner of the state to the Gulf of Mexico—be set aside as "critical habitat" for the black bear.[31]

♦ In Florida, environmental extremists plan to set aside nearly half of the state as wilderness, connected with vast areas ("buffer zones and corridors") in which little or no human activity will be permitted.[32]

♦ In New England, environmental groups are demanding that 26 million acres of privately owned forest land be placed under federal control to be managed as a vast Eastern-style wilderness.[33]

♦ In southern Indiana, timber harvesting in the Hoosier National Forest came to a halt when environmental groups objected, driving a number of small, family-owned timber companies out of business.[34]

♦ In Illinois, protests by environmental extremists caused years of costly delay when the Forest Service attempted to conduct a tiny timber sale in the Shawnee National Forest, the second smallest national forest in the country.[35]

Then there are the people:

♦ In Maryland, longtime environmentalist Bill Ellen was sent to jail for "wetlands" violations—because of his attempts to create new wetlands.[36]

♦ In Pennsylvania, John Pozsgai, a refugee from communist tyranny in Hungary, was imprisoned for wetlands viola-

tion when he tried to clean up a junkyard and dump he
had purchased.[37]

♦ In Florida, Ocie Mills and his son were jailed for trans-
gressing federal wetlands policy when they placed a few
truckloads of clean sand on their land—land that the state
of Florida had declared was not "wetlands."[38]

And on and on.

People who once placed the "environmental" battle far off somewhere in the West have been jolted. Many are starting to realize that
the target of the environmental war is people and economic activity
everywhere. Many are starting to realize that the War on the West is,
in fact, a war on Western civilization. Many are starting to realize
that Vice President Gore was serious when he called for a "wrenching transformation of society."[39]

David Lucas is one of the millions of non-Westerners who has discovered that he is not immune from the assault by environmental
extremists on individual liberty and economic freedom. He learned
the hard way that these people do not only target cowboys, miners,
loggers, and farmers. David Lucas ran afoul of environmental laws in
South Carolina when he attempted to use his own property. His suit
to recover "just compensation" was ultimately successful, following
his victory before the Supreme Court.[40] Lucas has since become a
popular speaker at private property rallies throughout the country. At
a "Save Our Western Ways" rally in Boise, Idaho, in January 1994,
David Lucas closed with this remark: "In the future, don't look to the
East as a source of your enemies, look to it as a source of your
friends."

The same struggle that is taking place in the West may be found,
in microcosm, wherever the federal government has large land holdings, such as western North Carolina, northwestern Pennsylvania,
southern Indiana and Ohio, and southeastern Missouri, especially
when the federal lands have an abundance of rich natural resources
such as timber, oil and gas, and minerals. Loggers in Kane, Pennsyl-

vania—where 26 percent of the land is owned by the federal government—have more in common with loggers in Kane County, Utah—where 84 percent of the land is owned by the federal government—than with their fellow Pennsylvanians.[41]

Regions are not even safe when the federal government is not (yet) a major landowner. In these areas—particularly in rural America—environmental extremists have mounted campaigns to increase federal ownership, or at least federal power, to determine what kinds of economic activities the locals can pursue. One example: "The Wildlands Project (North America Wilderness Recovery Project)," described in detail by *Wild Earth* magazine, would lock up vast areas in "core wildernesses surrounded by buffer zones and connected by corridors."[42]

Many non-Westerners, who have relied for over two hundred years on the protections afforded their property by the Constitution, have come to realize that environmental extremists honor neither the Constitution nor people, but only their naturalistic ideology.[43]

In short, what is happening to those of us who live in the West is happening to people throughout the country.

That is why the property rights movement has spread like wildfire across the nation. That is why consideration of a "takings" case by the Supreme Court elicits national attention; why property rights proposals in the Senate and House of Representatives have broad, bipartisan support; why state after state is pondering a property rights protection statute.[44]

Even those with no property are increasingly concerned about the nature of this war. For what is at stake is not simply the right of one landowner to use his or her property, but the viability of the Fifth Amendment to the Constitution. If, under the rubric of an "environmental crisis," environmental extremists can demand that we ignore such a fundamental right, and if the federal government carries out those demands, then not one of us is safe; no freedom is secure.

Many Western battles do not involve the Constitution, of course, since much of the land in the West is not privately owned. Yet the statutes that relate to the use of federal lands are clear, their legislative intent beyond question.

The Clinton/Gore administration, having adopted the agenda of environmental extremists, is ignoring, if not the express provisions of these statutes, at least their intent. Secretary of the Interior Bruce Babbitt refuses to comply with the requirements of the General Mining Law, former Secretary of Agriculture Mike Espy disregarded federal law regarding the management of the nation's forests, and federal officials wink at the fact that the Clean Water Act—under which "wetlands" are regulated—does not contain the word "wetlands."[45] When laws are scorned by government, citizens beware. If they can do it to us, they can do it to you.

Fear of an all-powerful federal government dates back to our Founding Fathers; that same fear permeates the lives of millions of Americans today.

What is happening out West, moreover, is happening not just to fellow Americans, but to fellow human beings. We are witnessing a human tragedy. When a federal judge can view the killing by John Shuler of a ferocious grizzly bear in self-defense as concomitant to his having killed another human being, it is a tragedy for humans. When after a young mother is killed by a mountain lion in California, the mountain lion's cubs receive more money from the charitable public than the orphaned children, it is a tragedy for humans.[46]

When Son of Sam was in the midst of his murderous spree in New York City some years ago, no one ever suggested that New Yorkers who were out after dark deserved what they got. Yet today environmental extremists demand that hundreds of grizzly bears—perhaps the most fearsome creature known to man—be placed in Kootenai Valley, Montana, where ten thousand people make their homes. That these peoples' lives are at risk is irrelevant. "They can always move," some say. "They just need to be more careful," others say. "That's what they get for living in a place where we want to put grizzly bears," is the general thinking.

To put creatures, no matter how cute and cuddly, unique or special, on the same plane—or above—fellow human beings is to place our society on a slippery slope. A crucial component of our Judeo-Christian culture is that human beings, all human beings, are special because they alone of all creatures have been created in the image of God. Our society and our laws are founded upon this primary precept. When human life has little or no value, civilization itself comes unraveled.

There is yet another troublesome matter involved here: the degrading remarks that are aimed daily against loggers, ranchers, and other Westerners—remarks that would never be permitted if leveled at an ethnic or religious group. Denigrating or demonizing human beings allows them to be treated in an inhuman manner. When people are stripped of their human qualities—made into demons or monsters—they deserve what they get. So when those outside the West hear phrases like "tree killers" (loggers), "welfare cowboys" (ranchers), "the rape, ruin, and run boys" (miners), they would do well to start wondering when they too will become subject to such an assault. If they can do it to us, they can do it to you.

Since the West is rich in the natural resources essential to the modern world, not just Westerners are hurt when those resources are locked up. Others suffer too—all consumers. The loss of much of the West as a source of wood fiber is just one example.

Since the controversy over the northern spotted owl resulted in drastic reductions in the amount of timber being harvested in the Pacific Northwest, the price of lumber has skyrocketed. Other "environmental" impediments to harvesting timber—such as the grizzly bear, the Mexican spotted owl, and a variety of salmon—have contributed to the growing scarcity of pine and have driven the price higher and higher, not just in faraway forests, but in the nearby lumberyard.

Then there is the matter of oil and gas. An abundance of oil and gas, the fuel of our modern society, lies beneath the lands of the West, placed out of reach because of the demands of environmental extremists. Thus our oil-rich country finds itself dependent on foreign sources, friendly and not-so-friendly. Our dollars flow overseas to purchase what we have within our own shores, unnecessarily inflating our devastating trade deficit, burdening all Americans.[47]

Similarly, extracting ores from federal lands in the West benefits not just Westerners, but all Americans; it creates jobs throughout the country—high-paying jobs producing and providing the goods and services that flow from the mining industry. Like oil and gas, every ounce of ore produced in the United States is an ounce of ore that is not imported; it preserves our domestic economic activity while offsetting our foreign trade deficit.

For those who view the West, not as some environmental purist's set-aside, but as a beautiful recreation spot, the War on the West has other serious consequences. Land lockup—declaring federal lands off limits—does not just exclude the logger and miner, but the vacationer as well.

Ski resorts depend on the goodwill of the federal agencies that manage the land upon which they operate. They are not exempt from the attack on uses of federal land, either for economic or environmental reasons. Recently, for example, a Colorado ski resort was visited by employees of the Fish and Wildlife Service searching for an endangered species—a frog.[48] As everyone knows by now, the discovery of a species covered by the Endangered Species Act is a show stopper. Even if the species does not permanently close down the resort, any long-term solution could involve millions of dollars, driving a ski vacation out of reach for many Americans.

National parks are also becoming less and less appealing—or even available—to humans because of a raft of restrictions. These have been adopted, allegedly, because of "overcrowding," possible harm by humans to "delicate ecosystems," or the special needs of certain species, such as the wolf. Off-road vehicle trails are becoming increasingly rare, and forest roads are being closed, making fewer national forestlands available to campers, hikers, hunters, berry pickers, bird-watchers, and others.

Nor is it just the federal lands and their recreational value that will suffer. One of the charms of the West is our tiny towns, the idyllic rural communities. When they lose the timber mill, when the ranchers are driven off, when oil and gas exploration is prohibited, the towns begin to die. The young people move away, the stores close down, and instead of a part of Americana, the town becomes a part of history—one more Western "ghost town" through which the touring family hurries on its way to the next gas station or small café.

A "nature's way" approach to managing federal lands, an attempt to "return to the wild," has ramifications for tourists as well. The sight of millions of acres of once verdant forests converted to barren moonscapes with blackened minarets is hardly appealing. Confronting a grizzly bear on horseback or a wolf on foot is not the stuff of tourists' dreams.

Economic and recreational self-interest are not the only reasons for all Americans to be concerned about the war being waged in the West. Those who care about the quality of the human environment should view what is taking place in the West with great alarm.

For starters, Western lands will suffer serious environmental consequences if the West loses its ranching families, the stewards of the range. Western ranchers protect their own land as well as the federal lands upon which they graze their livestock. They maintain the watering holes that are used not only by their own stock, but by wildlife— one reason why wildlife has been thriving throughout the West. Ranchers' livestock also control vegetation, which otherwise would grow tall, brown up in the summer heat, and provide fuel for wildfires.

Equally important are the rich agricultural meadows upon which most private ranches are located. These meadows by themselves cannot sustain ranches, but combined with nearby federal grazing lands, a livelihood can be eked out by those who love the life. These meadows also slow the surging spring waters, allowing them to seep to bedrock, irrigating the soil and providing lush forage and wetlands for wildlife and fowl.

Should ranchers leave, the meadowlands will either revert to their original state or be subdivided into lots for vacation homes. In either event, the water will be carried elsewhere, perhaps to some fast-growing resort community. Deprived of water, the land will no longer be able to nurture wildlife.

Of all the environmental consequences of a "nature's way" approach to Western lands, the one most recently etched into the consciousness of the American people occurred in the summer of 1994, when millions of acres of timberland disappeared in flames. Many of the forests that Westerners use for their livelihood and recreation, peace, and solitude were destroyed. The fires many Westerners had predicted publicly were coming—and had prayed privately would never get here—descended in the dreadful summer of 1994—the worst since 1910. Along with the 1.7 million acres of incinerated forest lands, America lost 34 brave men and women who stood in the breech between the inferno and the inhabitants whose lives and homes were threatened.[49] Today, many Western forests look like defoliated deserts, pockmarked with black silhouettes that stand as ghostly reminders of once-thriving timberland.

Huge expanses of the West have been sacrificed upon the altar of "nature's way" and "aesthetics." The transformation of a lush, green forest into a charred moonscape of blackened spires involved more than mere aesthetics. As those fires burned, thousands of metric tons of carbon dioxide, once trapped by photosynthesis in the pines of the forest, were released into the atmosphere.[50] Ash from the fires polluted the streams and lakes, killing the fish that had survived the rising temperatures. The ground, covered with years of unharvested debris, was scorched and in many places sterilized.

In time the forest will recover. Yet that recovery will take decades, not years as with land that has been harvested and reforested. More damage is in the offing. When the snows melt and the spring rains come, there will be no ground cover to slow the runoff and the water will speed downhill, carrying with it the topsoil. Hillsides and gullies will become muddy quagmires, the streams murky torrents, as mud mixes with ash and debris. More fish will die as spawning areas silt over. In some areas, until the soils and the grasses recover, these events will occur spring after spring. Devoid of grasses and other edible materials, bereft of shelter, these burned-over areas will be avoided by wildlife.

These ravaged areas will not only scare off wildlife, but humans too. This unattractive landscape—barren, bleak, burned, a bog in the spring and baked clay in the summer—will be dangerous. The charcoal sticks, once mighty trees, will rot from within, eventually toppling in the winds or of their own accord.[51]

Those outside the West should be concerned about the War on the West because it puts constitutional freedoms at risk and because it is being waged by an increasingly tyrannical government that abuses federal laws. They should be concerned because the War on the West will hurt the economy of the entire nation, decrease the quality of the human environment, and obliterate recreational resources. Most of all, they should all be concerned because the War on the West is being waged, not just against fellow Americans, but against fellow human beings.

You can join the battle for the West. Or you can get one of those Saul Steinberg posters of the view from New York City and pretend that the West is a vast wasteland that is "somewhere out there, where nobody lives."

IT GROWS ON TREES

MIKE WEIDMAN HAD SEEN THE FIRE STARTING. As a thunderstorm passed through the Wallowa Whitman National Forest in northeastern Oregon, lightning struck high along a ridge of pine, dry from an unrelenting drought. Mike, like his father before him a logger who knows the woods well, saw the hit and the plume of smoke as it curled out of the forest and up into the ominous sky. Mike knew something else. The forest wasn't just dry. Years of neglect, years of appeals of U.S. Forest Service (USFS) decisions by various environmental groups to stop timber harvesting, had allowed the forest to become clogged with diseased and dead trees, fallen branches and brush, what foresters call "fuel buildup."

Mike knew that if the fire got a good start it would be almost impossible to stop. He immediately called the Forest Service and told them of the strike. "If they had come then," said Mike, gazing up at the ridge line where it all started, "none of this," his hand swept the blackened forest around him, "would have happened."

But the Forest Service failed to respond to Mike's call. When the fire swept down off the ridge, Mike called again to warn Forest Service officials that the blaze had become much more serious and that unless they moved quickly, thousands of acres would be lost. Incredibly, the Forest Service again failed to come.

If the Forest Service had responded to Mike's first call within a few hours, the fire might have been stopped right there on the ridge line. If the Forest Service had responded to Mike's second call within a matter of minutes, the fire might have been stopped. By the time they did arrive, it was too late.[1]

In the summer of 1989, I walked through the scorched forest with Mike, one of the most resolute leaders of the Oregon Lands Coalition—a grassroots organization then representing nearly fifty statewide natural resources groups with more than fifty thousand members.[2] The earth was charred beneath our feet. Once healthy trees that towered in the sky and swayed in the wind were ghostly black silhouettes, stiff and brittle like burned matchsticks. As far as we could see, up and down the rolling valleys and down the dirt roads that wound away from us, the forest was still a smoldering disaster.

As we walked among the charcoal poles, Mike pointed out some harvestable wood. "See this," he said, stepping over to one tree and pulling away some of the blackened bark to reveal untouched wood beneath. "If the Forest Service moves quickly and authorizes a salvage sale, there's a lot of good wood here. But it will have to move fast." He stepped over to another tree and pointed high up the trunk. "Some of these have already started to check—split—because of the fire. Before long they'll all do it, and in the end, the checks will go all the way to the core of the tree. Then all these trees will be good for is pulpwood, if that."

I asked if he thought the Forest Service would move fast enough.

"No, I don't. With all the studies, appeals, and lawsuits, and opposition from enviro groups, it'll probably never make it."

Mike Weidman was right. The scorched, dead trees left after what became known as the Canal Fire in the Wallowa Whitman National Forest were never salvaged.

One area we passed hadn't burned. Like an oasis in the midst of a scorching desert, here was an island of emerald grass and tall cordoba-colored trunks with fresh green needles, seemingly oblivious to the destruction all around them. As we walked onto the cool grass, Arleigh Isley—then Oregon State University Extension Service agent, now county commissioner—explained why the area had been spared.

"This is managed forest. Notice the separation between the trees and the absence of fuel buildup on the ground. We've harvested in here. Trees can grow bigger, with less competition, and since there is less fuel buildup, when the fires come, the trees can survive. The grass is kept relatively short because we turn the cattle out here and we don't have long grasses that brown up in the summer only to burn." He turned to look out of the oasis into the burned area on the other side of the road.

"When the fire came in this direction it was flying from tree to tree, burning the dead trees, going down the trunks into the dry wood on the ground, scooting along the ground and then up the next tree. Then it got here and stopped. It couldn't jump from tree to tree here, and there was nothing on the ground to burn. The fire just passed this area by."

"Why wasn't the entire forest like this?"

"We haven't been able to log in here for years. It's all been locked up in appeals and lawsuits. Now it's gone."

Better than any amount of words and explanations, that walk in the woods and close-up view of the burn that swept through the Wallowa Whitman National Forest demonstrated what is happening to the forests of the West and to the men and women who depend upon them.[3] Extremists in the environmental movement have shut down the forests of the West, and timber communities are dying. The forests are too.

USE IT OR LOSE IT

As almost everyone knows, the national forest system was created by Congress in 1905 through the efforts of Gifford Pinchot, who became the first chief of the Forest Service and coined the word "conservationist."[4] Conservation means simply "the wise utilization of a natural product."[5] Pinchot wanted to ensure that the nation's federally owned forests would be used in a manner consistent with good management practices. The key concept here was use. The national forests were not national parks or even wildlife refuges, although the latter ensue naturally from a healthy forest—the result of good management practices.[6] The national forests were meant to be managed to meet the nation's need for wood products. The law that governs the manner in which the national forests are to be managed—the Organic Act—speaks of using forests to meet the nation's and the local community's needs, for instance, requiring that the national forests "furnish a continuous supply of timber for the use and necessities of citizens of the United States."[7]

Notwithstanding this clear mandate, there is today a full-scale assault against the use of the abundant timber resources of the national forests throughout the West. It is having, and will continue to have, devastating consequences. National forests make up a substantial portion of the Western states: California has 20.5 million acres or 21 percent of the state; Idaho has 19.9 million acres or 38 percent of the state; Montana has 15.8 million acres or 17 percent of the state; and Oregon has 15.6 million acres or 25 percent of the state.[8]

In the past these forested lands have been used not only for recreation, oil and gas exploration, grazing, mining, and wildlife habitat, but also to help meet the nation's ever-growing need for wood fiber. Mills throughout the West have supplied jobs, added revenues to local governments (25 percent of the money paid to the federal government for harvesting federally owned timber is returned to the local county), paid taxes, and otherwise contributed to the nation's economic well-being. At the same time, forested lands have been managed to safeguard the health of the forests.

Nor is the controversy just over the battle on behalf (allegedly) of the northern spotted owl. Wherever the forest is, environmental groups can come up with a similarly bogus excuse for putting an end to timber harvesting. In the Pacific Northwest, it is the owl, the marbled murrelet, and the salmon. In Montana, it is the grizzly bear. In Wyoming and Colorado, it is the so-called "below-cost timber sales" and "old growth." In Arizona and New Mexico, it is the Mexican spotted owl.

The U.S. Forest Service is a virtual sitting duck for environmental groups making nit-picking appeals regarding the endless USFS documents required to harvest timber: forest plans, new forest plans, interim forest plans, proposed timber sales, proposed salvage sales, and on and on.[9] Under USFS rules anyone can appeal a decision of the USFS, and it appears that almost anyone does.

According to the USFS, 1,291 appeals were filed in 1989 and 1,991 were filed the following year. While total appeals dropped in 1991 to 1,386, the decline was attributed to fewer sales and a decrease in the release of forest plans.[10] Though the vast majority of such appeals are denied, the matter is not ended. The appeal can simply be taken to a senior official within the agency or to court.[11]

Environmental groups actually conduct courses on how to file appeals, with two simple bottom lines: anyone can and should file an appeal and, in filing an appeal, throw in everything conceivable; the good stuff will stick, the bad stuff will be discarded. All the while, time marches on. For the environmental groups, that is all to the good. For the men and women who depend on timber jobs, time is the enemy.

That is particularly the case for the small mills in the Sierra Nevadas of northern California, where more than a dozen of the thirty-six mills that have closed throughout California are located.[12] The supply of timber from federal lands has simply run out. For example, Eldorado National Forest timber sales were 148 million board feet in 1992 and 160 million board feet in 1993, but the target for 1994 was only 75 million board feet. Even that minimal target was optimistic since appeals and threats of lawsuits have required additional studies on twenty-four "green" sales. Hopes for getting the bulk of the 1994 volume from salvage sales of 40 million board feet, and thereby keeping some mills open, were dashed by appeals. Said Pete Himmel, former general manager for Mich-Cal: "Radical groups using legal technicalities have caused a virtual shutdown of the Forest Service timber sale program."[13]

Appeals come from all over the country, not just from the area around the national forest, as was the case in Camino. With the proliferation of computer software on national bulletin boards, programs for appealing USFS decisions are within easy reach of every college student in the country. Bruce Vincent of Libby, Montana, reports that a young man from Brooklyn, New York, appeals every single timber sale in the Kootenai National Forest in northwestern Montana. Folks in the tiny towns of Libby, Eureka, and Troy doubt that their New York adversary has ever crossed the Hudson or the Mississippi River, let alone the Flathead, but his enmity has been felt as surely as if he were sitting in the regional office of the USFS in Missoula.

Anything can serve as the basis for appealing a decision by the USFS: not enough data considered; wrong data considered; improper data admitted into the record; not enough alternatives considered; not enough public hearings held; public hearings not held in the right place; insufficient time for the public to comment; and on and on—a list that is limited only by the imagination of those filing the appeal.

Even when it is over, it isn't really over. Unsuccessful appeals can become lawsuits. Most environmental statutes—such as the Endangered Species Act, the Clean Water Act, and others—allow private citizens to file lawsuits if they believe the U.S. government is not performing its job under the federal statute. Needless to say, with the abundance of "feel good" language that has clogged our federal laws to satisfy the demands of the various environmental groups, there is almost always a statutory basis for asserting that the law is being flouted.[14]

Once again, process is also a cause of action. Under the Administrative Procedure Act, failure to attend to the minutest detail is a basis for litigation. If a federal judge determines that the agency's action was "arbitrary, capricious, or otherwise not in accordance with law," then it's back to square one for the agency.[15] Similarly, the National Environmental Policy Act (NEPA), which requires the agency to set forth its decision-making process for "major federal actions" that "significantly affect the quality of the human environment," has become the source of endless delays, appeals, and successful lawsuits.[16] Even if the judge rules that the agency has complied with federal law, the clock has been running—not for weeks and months, but for years.

EVERYTHING OLD IS NEW AGAIN

What is it that environmental groups seek to achieve by their attack on Western timber harvesting? Bruce Vincent argues that the aim of environmental extremists can be summed up in two words: "Stop it!"[17] "Once they have said that, they have nothing else to say," says Bruce. "Unfortunately, we need more than that but they don't."[18]

C. Larry Mason a former small mill owner near Forks, Washington, agrees: "As to their plan, they don't have a plan or a vision. All they have is a strategy, a strategy to lock up more and more land. What views they do have," Larry Mason adds, "are not grounded in reality. They talk about returning major portions of the forest to 'presettlement conditions.'"[19]

Remarkably, the bizarre fantasy that is "presettlement conditions" was included, at the demand of the environmental leaders who wrote it, in President Clinton's extremely controversial "Option 9" decision regarding the northern spotted owl controversy.[20] Back-to-nature utopians believe that, but for the existence of man, a vast and verdant forest would stretch from the eastern edge of the Rocky Mountains to the shores of the Pacific Ocean and flourish for hundreds of years to come. The fantasy is based upon a flawed assumption—that the forest is static, unchanging, that trees don't die, and that if left undisturbed by mankind, they will be green and beautiful forever. In Larry Mason's words, "They forget that two hundred years ago forest fires burned from the mountains to the seas and that, by the way, 250 million people didn't live in America."[21]

More than two hundred years ago, the Spanish fleet sailed far from what is now the Oregon coast to escape the burning embers that the fires in the forest had thrown for miles out to sea.[22]

In the 1800s, the journals of the famous explorers Lewis and Clark describe the great plumes of smoke rising from the forests. Not only did (and does) nature destroy decayed, dying, and dead trees, but so too did the Native Americans, who set fire to them, among other reasons, to promote the growth of fresh tender plants and grasses in order to attract big game.[23] In the Black Hills of South Dakota, settlers were greeted with scattered patches of mangled pine, all that remained of the forest of years before. The area is now thick with the forests that surround Mount Rushmore and the monument to Crazy Horse.[24]

An Osborne photograph taken October 30, 1929, from Lava Butte, Oregon, shows scattered pines and open prairie that contrast sharply with the present view: a sea of green forest.[25] An even more startling contrast is between the August 24, 1935, Osborne photograph of a section of the Olympic National Forest on the Olympic Peninsula, and what the visitor sees today. The 1907 fire in this area burned 12,800 acres, starkly evident in the 1935 black-and-white photograph. Today, what appears to be "a blanket of old growth" is a stand of timber less than sixty years old.[26]

When environmental extremists call for "presettlement conditions," to what time before the white man moved West would they like the forest to be returned? Ten years after a major fire? Some midpoint in the growth and maturation of the forest? The forest at old age? The forest just before or during a catastrophic burn? After the smoke has cleared and the ground is cool enough to walk on?

Evidently, all of the talk about presettlement conditions is a smoke screen, like virtually every other alleged concern in the environmental debate. Realizing that the majority of the public is unaware of the life cycle of a forest, the call for presettlement conditions, like the call for "saving the northern spotted owl," or "protecting old growth," or "preserving ecosystems," or "biological diversity," is a public pose of seeking what appears to be a desirable goal while obscuring the consequences.

BURN, BABY, BURN

The consequence of a return to presettlement conditions—that is, an abandonment of the managed forests—means only one thing: fire! It means fire that will burn hot and long, sweeping across vast regions, taking out almost everything in its path. One of the popular misconceptions—not held in most of the West—is that the fires in Yellowstone National Park in 1988, which burned over a million acres, were good for the ecosystem. At the time, no one ventured the opinion that they were a good thing. Thousands of fire fighters put their lives on the line, day after bone-weary day. Wildlife was destroyed, hillsides were denuded, and the ground scorched white. It was, in short, a disaster.[27]

It was only when the snow began to fall and the heat of the flames had been forgotten that environmental extremists and other advocates of a return to "nature's way" began to assert that the fires were the best thing that had ever happened to Yellowstone National Park. The following spring, proponents of "let it burn" asserted that the park was better than ever—a wild distortion of the facts. Even today, some of the ground is black and barren, the soil still suffering from the sterilizing fire that scorched the land. Yet the myth survives.

Even were it true, Yellowstone National Park is not the Kootenai Valley in Montana, or Trinity County in northern California, or the Blue Mountains of Oregon. These areas are not parklands, but national forests, and they are not meant to be managed for "cleansing fires" but, among other things, to generate wood products. The most important difference is that people live in Libby, Troy, and Eureka,

Montana; and Hayfork, Peanut, and Wildwood, California; and in Dale, Granite, and Austin, Oregon.

In 1910, a monstrous fire swept through the Kootenai Valley in the northwestern tip of Montana. As had happened every eighty or ninety years for hundreds of years, the forest in the valley had become diseased, full of dying trees and dead wood, and ready to burn. More than 3 million acres went up in smoke in two days.

Today, as a result of the inability of the Forest Service to manage the forest properly, it is ready to burn again. And though much is as it was in 1910, there is one crucial difference. At present, more than ten thousand people live in the Kootenai Valley.

Today, huge sections of the national forests of the West are in a similar condition—diseased. As former Congressman Bob Smith (R-OR) has noted, "Were it not for the spotted owl issue, [forest health] would be a number one forest crisis facing the Forest Service and the nation today."[28] In the Blue Mountains of northeastern Oregon, some 6 million acres have been destroyed by bugs like the Western spruce budworm. Without intensive forest management, this will result in catastrophic fires. Umatilla National Forest Supervisor Jeff Blackwood sees it this way:

> What we have out here, in the way of dead material ready to burn, is probably equal to what there was in Yellowstone before it burned. If it burns, it will cook everything, including the soil. The impacts on air quality, and fish and wildlife will be widespread and significant. It may be natural to let a wildfire take it all, but I cannot imagine such a fire being acceptable in a civilized world. [29]

Forest health is an issue throughout the West. As *USA Today* reporter Linda Kanamine wrote: "Federal forests from Idaho to Mexico are so crowded and stressed that fiery disasters loom—unless at least half the trees are cut down."[30] Ironically, given environmental groups' apparent passion for protecting the habitat of the northern spotted owl, the spread of insects and disease and the bar on salvage activity threatens even western Oregon's Douglas fir forests.[31]

The Clinton/Gore administration appears to have no intention of managing Western forests to prevent the fires that Western communities fear. What would be required would be intensive management—thinning the forest—with salvage and other sales in areas that are overgrown and have not been harvested in years; it would include taking out one-half to two-thirds of the trees.[32]

Even more remarkable and frightening, the Clinton/Gore administration has failed to provide the Forest Service with the wherewithal to fight the fires caused by the irrational forest policy.[33] Whether out of a sense of false economies—the demand that the money be put into more trendy programs—or out of a cynical desire to let nature take its course, uncontrolled fires will be devastating in lives lost, private property destroyed, marketable timber consumed, and wildlife habitat eradicated.

Far from being deforested, America is being reforested. After four hundred years of exposure to human beings, forests cover 70 percent of the land that was covered in 1600.[34] Tree planting has been at record levels for more than a decade. In 1988, for example, a record 2.3 billion seedlings were planted on 3.4 million acres, and in 1990 more than four hundred trees were planted for every child born in the United States.[35] Timber growth, moreover, has exceeded timber removals for more than forty years, and in 1992 net growth was 21.6 billion cubic feet while harvest was 16.3 billion cubic feet.[36] Timber growth also exceeds removals on national forest lands and has since 1952. Today, growth exceeds harvests by 60 percent.[37]

Thus the timber resources are there, ready to be harvested in an environmentally sensitive manner and capable of being sustained for centuries. Yet the war on timber communities grows more fierce by the day.

◆ In Idaho, the timber sold in the Clearwater National Forest has fallen dramatically over three recent years—from

1991 to 1993.[38] In the most recent U.S. Forest Service plan, allowable sale quality has been cut by 31 percent.[39]

♦ The reductions in timber offerings from 1988 to 1991 resulted in a 27 percent reduction in timber production at sawmills in Fredonia, Arizona, and Panguitch, Utah— and a 31 percent loss of wages paid.[40] In early 1995, the Fredonia mill was forced to close, putting its 200 employees out of work.[41]

♦ Already the cutbacks associated with the Mexican spotted owl have compelled the Kaibab mill in Payson, Arizona, to close. Continuing cutbacks by the Forest Service portend a similar situation in the Kaibab mills in northern Arizona and southern Utah.[42] Should those mills close totally, the impact locally would be devastating. The region would suffer a $6.7 million loss in direct wages; a $3.5 million loss in indirect wages; a $7.9 million loss in direct local expenditures; a $12.4 million loss in indirect local expenditures; a population drop from seven thousand to five thousand; a Forest Service revenue loss of $470,711; a revenue loss to county governments and schools of $1,176,776; severance tax and property tax losses of $218,380; and a loss to the U.S. Treasury of $3.1 million.[43]

♦ In northern California, the Forest Service, fearful of lawsuits by environmental groups, cut allowable timber harvest by 500 million board feet in the Sierra Nevadas, so as to "protect" the California spotted owl—which was not even listed under the Endangered Species Act.[44]

♦ The great majority of northwestern Montana has been placed in a Critical Habitat One zone for the grizzly bear, virtually eliminating effective active timber management.[45]

♦ In Wyoming, timber harvesting in the Bighorn National
Forest was cut back to almost nothing as a result of a lawsuit filed by environmental groups. In the meantime, the
forest plan that had permitted the harvesting of 14 million
board feet a year was cut in half and then reduced further
to 2 million board feet.[46]

In Colorado, attempts to cut timber selectively in the San Juan
National Forest—to ensure the health of the forest and enhance the
growth of the remaining trees—was hampered and rendered
extremely expensive by representatives of the radical Ancient Forest
Rescue out of Boulder, Colorado. Although the timber was eventually harvested, it was done at great cost, not only to the timber company, the Forest Service, and the poor rural county, but also to those
performing contract work on the sale—people who could easily be
driven into bankruptcy by such actions. And this is not an isolated
occurrence. Other Westerners have had similar encounters.[47]

The issue of those who deny loggers their ability to earn a living—
either by civil disobedience or by acts of terrorism—is particularly
nettlesome. Despite their pretentious claim of being heirs to the
legacy of the civil rights leaders of the 1960s, environmental terrorists shrink from taking responsibility for their acts. They engage in
their activities under cover of darkness and, if apprehended, deny
responsibility. Although Congress has criminalized certain acts of
"civil disobedience" regarding some activities, interfering with the
ability of Westerners to harvest timber is not prohibited by federal
law.[48] To date, remedies have been limited, although a decision of the
Supreme Court may allow Westerners to bring legal action under a
powerful law written to combat organized crime.[49]

Those who oppose timber harvesting often assert that many
timber sales should not be conducted because the federal dollars
spent to sell the timber exceed the dollars gained. But like most issues
raised by the opponents of forestry, the below-cost timber sales issue
is a red herring, for various reasons.

First, the accounting is questionable: the government ignores the 25 percent of the revenue of the timber sale that is returned to the county in which the harvest occurs. Second, the ancillary benefits of road building—such as the access that hunters, fishers, bird-watchers, and others enjoy—is disregarded. Third, the multiplier effect of timber sales—the impact of the sale reverberating through the local economy—is also overlooked. Fourth, the restrictions placed upon the amount of timber to be harvested—and hence the money derived—in order to enhance recreational, wildlife, and other environmental values is disregarded. Fifth, the alternative cost to the federal Treasury of fighting a fire in an unharvested area—an all but certain occurrence—is not considered. Sixth, the Forest Service could make sales more profitable simply by introducing reasonable businesslike practices. Finally, the alleged cost savings is not a savings at all, since such past proposals have used the money previously spent on timber sales to increase recreational funding.[50]

Moreover, as usual, there is a fair amount of hypocrisy in the environmental groups' argument because their own practice of appealing or suing to stop every sale helps turn money-makers into money losers.[51] In the Shawnee National Forest, for instance, appeals, lawsuits, and protests have cost the public dearly. It all began as a simple purchase of hardwood lumber slated by the Forest Service for sale in order to prepare a site for oak regeneration in a part of the forest that had become overmature, increasingly unsuitable as wildlife habitat, and rife with maple, beech, and other undesirable trees. Although the oak, hickory, and pine on a 141-acre parcel of the Shawnee National Forest was purchased in 1985, it took until 1991, after five years of appeals, lawsuits, and protests, before the timber could be harvested.

While the environmental impact of the sale was positive, the economic impact to federal taxpayers was not. Originally, the Forest Service's projected costs had been under $20,000, compared with revenues of $50,762 for the sale—a profit of $31,000. In the end, the Forest Service spent more than $315,229, including bringing in rangers from other states to help control the protests. The sale lost money.[52]

THE ENDANGERED LOGGERS ACT

And then there is the northern spotted owl. It is a classic example of environmental gridlock, wherein environmental extremists have thrown impediment after impediment in the way of any resolution.[53] As a result an economic, emotional, and cultural disaster is exploding on hundreds of thousands of people in Washington, Oregon, and northern California.

It all started in the 1980s when environmental groups filed lawsuits in Seattle, Washington, and Portland, Oregon, to stop timber harvesting on Forest Service lands in those two states. In September 1989, Congress adopted legislation—the Northwest Timber Compromise—mandating that the Forest Service achieve a specific level of timber harvesting and increase protection for the owl.[54]

In April 1990, the so-called Jack Ward Thomas Report was released, calling for a set-aside of 8.4 million acres in three states to protect the northern spotted owl. No economic analysis was conducted to discover the possible impact of implementing the recommendation. Three months later, the Fish and Wildlife Service (FWS) listed the owl as "threatened" under the Endangered Species Act. No economic analysis was conducted to discover the possible impact of the FWS's decision. In September 1990, the U.S. Court of Appeals for the Ninth Circuit declared that the Northwest Timber Compromise legislation was unconstitutional.[55]

In February 1991, U.S. District Court Judge Thomas Zilly ordered the Fish and Wildlife Service to designate critical habitat for the owl. Three months later the FWS proposed the designation of 11.6 million acres in Washington, Oregon, and northern California as owl habitat—an area equal to a seven-mile swath stretching from Portland, Oregon, to Portland, Maine. The same month, U.S. District Judge William Dwyer enjoined 80 percent of the Forest Service's northwest timber program. In August, the FWS revised its habitat designation down to 8.2 million acres—an area the size of Massachusetts, Connecticut, and Rhode Island—and estimated that the designation would cause the loss of 2,400 jobs.

In January 1992, the Endangered Species Committee (the "God Squad")—the cabinet level committee empowered to grant relief from the Endangered Species Act's provisions—was convened in an attempt by Bureau of Land Management (BLM) Director Cy Jamison to conduct forty-four timber sales.[56] While the FWS was spending hundreds of thousands of dollars opposing the BLM's forty-four sales, it was also issuing its final designation of critical habitat—6.9 million acres in Washington, Oregon, and northern California, an area equal in size to Massachusetts or Maryland—an action it estimated would cost 33,000 jobs. The next month, U.S. District Court Judge Helen Frye issued an order temporarily barring the Bureau of Land Management timber sale program.

In May 1992, the God Squad divided the baby by exempting thirteen of the forty-four BLM timber sales from the Endangered Species Act requirements. At the same time, the Department of the Interior released its 5.4 million-acre draft recovery plan—estimating that it would cost 32,100 jobs—as well as its 2.8 million-acre owl preservation plan that put 14,990 jobs at risk. The same month, U.S. District Judge William Dwyer ruled that the Forest Service's environmental impact statement, based on the Jack Ward Thomas report, was inadequate and enjoined further timber harvesting activity.

In June 1992, Judge Frye enjoined the BLM timber sale program—including the timber sales exempted from the Endangered Species Act by the God Squad—and ordered an environmental impact statement on the northern spotted owl. The next month, Judge Dwyer permanently enjoined approximately 80 percent of the Forest Service timber sale programs in Washington, Oregon, and northern California; he also ordered the Forest Service to update its environmental impact study to consider the fourteen God Squad-authorized timber sales as well as the needs of thirty-two old growth species, none of which were listed under the Endangered Species Act.

In July 1992, the Western Council of Industrial Workers, the United Brotherhood of Carpenters and Joiners of America, and the International Woodworkers of America proposed that then-Governor Clinton convene a 1993 Timber Summit, a suggestion that Clinton accepted the following month. In September 1992, on a campaign trip to Oregon, Governor Clinton proposed a "no net job loss" policy on timber, and President Bush, on a campaign trip to the state of Washington, called for changes in the Endangered Species Act.

Also in September 1992, a federal judge ordered the Fish and Wildlife Service to list the marbled murrelet as "threatened" in its West Coast range under the Endangered Species Act. At the time the marbled murrelet population in Alaska was estimated to exceed 250,000. The West Coast range reaches 50 miles inland from southern California to the Canadian border. On October 1, 1992, the Fish and Wildlife Service listed the marbled murrelet as threatened.

Subsequently, a federal judge banned logging in marbled murrelet habitat, thereby voiding existing timber contracts as well as planned sales. The same month, environmental groups filed the first lawsuit seeking to prohibit logging on private land in the territory of the northern spotted owl.[57]

In December 1992, the U.S. District Court ruled that the Fish and Wildlife Service had violated the NEPA in designating critical habitat by failing to prepare an environmental impact statement. The next month, the Forest Service, on its own, announced conservation measures for the California spotted owl, a species not listed under the Endangered Species Act, thereby reducing timber harvests in the Sierra Nevada Mountains. In February 1993, the U.S. Court of Appeals for the Ninth Circuit ruled that the God Squad had been subjected to improper political influence by Bush administration officials.

Finally, in April 1993, with great fanfare, President Clinton, Vice President Gore, and a number of other high-ranking officials journeyed to Portland, Oregon, for the so-called Timber Summit. Unfortunately for the forest families of the Pacific Northwest, the Timber Summit was long on style—featuring Clinton's "I feel your pain" type of rhetoric—and very short on substantive solutions for getting men and women back into the woods and into the mills.

C. Larry Mason, one of the grassroots leaders who, with others, made a presentation to President Clinton, feels deceived:

> I thought that Clinton could not cut and run from his promise to labor that there would be no net loss of jobs in the Pacific Northwest. I admit that I was taken in personally. Clinton shook my hand, looked me in the eye, and said, "Larry, we won't forget about your people." What I didn't know was that the forest plan was already being written before I spoke with President Clinton.[58]

Unbeknownst to those who had taken President Clinton at his word, even as the summit was under way, Clinton's people were meeting behind closed doors of the U.S. Bank Tower in Portland to determine the fate of those they referred to as "timber junkies."[59] They called their meeting place, fittingly, "the tower of power," since they believed they were involved in "a major policy-making effort to revolutionize land management in the Pacific Northwest."[60]

The Clinton plan handed down on July 1, 1993, was a devastating blow to the men and women of the timber-producing communities of the Pacific Northwest.[61] Huge portions of the forests of Washington, Oregon, and northern California were to be set aside to protect the owl in preservation system "management," 16 million acres were to be returned to "presettlement conditions," multiple-use mandates were brushed aside, and federal law provisions regarding production of timber from O & C Lands (Oregon & California Lands Act lands) were ignored.[62]

In short, timber harvest goals on federal lands were to be cut back to a mere 25 percent of normal and the sum of some $1.2 billion was supposedly proposed for worker retraining. The results of such a cutback are staggering.[63] Yet even these few crumbs were not guaranteed. The Clinton/Gore administration neither took steps to ensure that even the paltry timber harvest targets would be achieved nor included any funds for retraining timber workers.

Thus no federal timber was offered for sale in the northern spotted owl region during 1994.[64] The FWS has asked the USFS to delay ninety-six timber sales until the agency searches for marbled murrelets and until environmental groups petition the FWS to list, under the Endangered Species Act, some eighty-three different kinds of snails that live in the forest. Meanwhile, federal officials are seeking to apply section 4(d) of the Endangered Species Act to private lands.[65]

Science has played little if any role in this process.[66] As Chief of the Forest Service Jack Ward Thomas—ostensibly appointed because he is a scientist—said recently:

> Whether [Option 9 is] enough protection is a matter of opinion. There isn't a magic number [of owls] that's enough as far as I know in science. All of these decisions in the end turn out to be moral decisions by a decision maker who has weighed those risks against production of goods and services and the community out there.[67]

Since 1990, 132 sawmills and plywood mills have closed, affecting more than 12,868 people, and the job loss continues to grow. At an August 4, 1993, hearing of the U.S. House Subcommittee on Public Lands, Dr. Brian Greber, a forest economist at Oregon State University, disclosed that although the Clinton/Gore administration has been asserting that, in the end, the job loss is a mere 6,000, the actual job loss will be more than 66,000.[68]

Perhaps the most thorough study of the cumulative impact of policies imposed in the name of the northern spotted owl is the one prepared by Dr. John H. Beuter, working with a team of professors from various universities. Dr. Beuter examined the likely impact of the spotted owl solution set forth by the federal Interagency Scientific Committee (ISC), or the Jack Ward Thomas proposal—a plan that was rejected as inadequate by Judge Dwyer and that has been vastly enlarged under President Clinton's Option 9. Dr. Beuter and his colleagues predicted the loss of 102,757 jobs and a total cost to the economy in the region of $3.8 billion.[69] Clearly under the Clinton plan, the loss will be greater.

With the loss of timber revenues, where will local governments find the money to provide for schools, hospitals, law enforcement? Dr. James Reinmuth, dean of the College of Business Administration at the University of Oregon, has calculated that some Oregon counties would need to increase taxes by more than 1,400 percent.[70]

Statistics on job losses and other financial burdens are a rough indicator of the tragedy occurring in the Pacific Northwest, but it is impossible to measure the human dimension—the brutal impact upon individual after individual. Billie Lawson, trauma specialist, Harborview Hospital in Seattle, noted:

> These people aren't just losing their jobs. They are losing their way of life. Loggers who were once seen as valued members of their community, and of society, are now being likened to baby killers. They feel abandoned, betrayed and unable to control their fates. In some ways, it is like what happened to Vietnam vets.[71]

There are other impacts as well, such as a dramatic reduction in the amount of timber available to American consumers. One expert estimates that a variety of environmental factors has caused timber harvesting on national forests to be reduced by more than 50 percent.[72] The northern spotted owl issue alone "could conceivably tie up the equivalent of nearly 12.5 percent of annual U.S. softwood lumber consumption—even more if the impact on private forests is included."[73] And the alternative?

Environmental extremists point to the forests of the South. But Southern forests are not more productive than those of the Pacific Northwest. Even more important, Southern forests are being subjected to the same environmental assault as Western timberlands. The issue of "wetlands" is of particular concern in the South, and an

Endangered Species Act species can as easily be found in the South as in the West. Already the red cockaded woodpecker is disrupting timbering in Texas, Georgia, and the Carolinas.

What of the substitutes for timber? As the miners say, "If it can't be grown, it has to be mined." If the studs in new houses are not wooden, they will be metal or plastic. How much energy is needed to produce these products? According to a report prepared by the Committee on Renewable Resources for Industrial Materials, a ton of softwood lumber requires 2.9 million btu's, a ton of steel studs requires 50.1 million btu's, and a ton of aluminum siding requires 200.5 million btu's.[74]

In the name of saving the planet, environmental extremists are killing the most environmentally friendly resource available, as well as jobs, communities, and healthy Western forests. They are also making America increasingly dependent on foreign timber—which is not harvested in accordance with this nation's high environmental standards—and on less environmentally friendly natural resources.

There is a bumper sticker seen frequently on the backs of Volvos. It reads "Think Globally, Act Locally." The environmentalists should take their own advice.

CHAPTER 3

WHISKEY'S FOR DRINKIN'—
WATER'S FOR FIGHTIN'

DENNIS AND NILE GERBAZ'S FATHER came over from Italy in the early 1900s. In 1919, he returned to Italy to marry his childhood sweetheart and bring her back to his new home in the American West, where he worked as a miner. Years later, he achieved his dream and bought the land that is now the Gerbaz ranch in western Colorado.

Dennis and Nile worked with their father from the time they were able to walk and, when he died in 1961, took over the ranch he had labored over and loved. They raised cattle, grew oats and barley and potatoes, and lived in peaceful harmony with the land.

Every spring, for years past, the Roaring Fork River has flowed high with the melting snows of the Rocky Mountains. As the Roaring Fork plunges past the Gerbaz ranch, the force of the flowing water sets the boulders that make up the river bed to tumbling, emitting the dull roar that gives the river its name.

In 1984 a neighbor requested a permit from the Corp of Engineers to perform some work on the Roaring Fork River. As a result, the river flooded about 5 acres of the Gerbaz ranch. The Gerbaz brothers asked for a permit from the Corps to correct the problem. The government not only denied the permit, it also refused to visit the Gerbaz ranch to see what was happening to the Roaring Fork River.

The following spring, rocks, trees, and debris created a dam that prevented the river from flowing in its historic channel. Instead, the river poured onto the Gerbaz land, flooding some 15 acres and washing away 5 feet of precious topsoil over a 2-acre area. The brothers went to a lawyer and learned that the law allowed them to take action without a permit in order to protect their land. So they did.

They took the obstruction out of the river, rebuilt the levee that had been washed away, and returned the river to the channel in which it had flowed for decades. Then one day the U.S. government came to their ranch and ordered them to report to federal court to pay a fine of $45 million—each.

The government never told the brothers Gerbaz exactly why it was suing them. Sometimes the government asserted that when the Roaring Fork River flooded the Gerbaz ranch it had created a "wetland" that could not be dewatered without a permit. At other times the government asserted that by rebuilding the fifty-year-old levee the brothers Gerbaz had limited the so-called "reach of the river." Then again it just said that the brothers Gerbaz were supposed to get a permit and hadn't.

One thing was perfectly clear. The government intended to make a national example out of Dennis and Nile Gerbaz.

Unable to afford the hundreds of thousands of dollars it would cost to fight the U.S. government, the Gerbaz brothers turned to Mountain States Legal Foundation (MSLF), a nonprofit public interest legal center, which agreed to represent them.

For nearly five years, Dennis and Nile, through the MSLF, have fought back. They know they could lose everything. But they fight on, backed by their belief in America and their knowledge that they have done nothing wrong. They know as well that for years past, tradition and the law have been on their side.

What is happening to Dennis and Nile Gerbaz is but one of many instances across the West in which the U.S. government has sought to seize control of the West's most valued resource: its water.[1]

The West is the most arid region of the country. This scarcity makes water an extremely valuable commodity, a commodity around which a voluminous, and vigorously developed, body of law exists to ensure that those who have water rights can exercise them. Under that law, the right to use water is a constitutionally protected property right, a right even more valuable than the land to which it applies, for without the water the land often has little economic value. As Westerners put it, "Whiskey's for drinkin', water's for fightin'."

The water that comes during the winter in the form of high mountain snows must be saved somehow and parceled out during the dry months of the summer and fall. The "somehow" is dams. The West is home to a huge collection of dams large and small, dams that make arid land useful and productive, generate electricity, and provide abundant recreational opportunities. Yet despite the role played by the federal government in providing the funding for these "water projects," the water behind them, as well as all of Western water, have been governed by Westerners. Today, that fundamental principle is under assault.

The first salvo came during the Carter administration.[2] On June 25, 1979, the solicitor of the Department of the Interior, Leo Krulitz, issued an opinion claiming that lands designated by Congress as wilderness areas under the Wilderness Act of 1964 possessed "federal reserved water rights." The "Krulitz Opinion" sparked public outrage—not only from Western water users and their representatives in Congress, but from legal commentators.[3] It was an audacious assertion of federal power over Western water, accomplished, not after careful consideration by Congress, but with the stroke of a bureaucrat's pen. Even worse, the opinion flew in the face of federal law: for when Congress adopted the Wilderness Act, it clearly stated that it had no intention of disturbing Western water law.

When the Reagan administration took over, it reexamined the Krulitz Opinion and issued its own views on the issue of Western water rights. Subsequently, the solicitor of the Department of the Interior, Ralph W. Tarr, issued an opinion that wilderness areas do not create federally reserved water rights.[4] But the attempt by environmental extremists to take over Western water rights and halt activities dependent upon those rights was far from over.[5] That attack began in earnest following the 1992 election of Governor Bill Clinton and Senator Al Gore as president and vice president.

BABBITTING

While it was not altogether certain that the Clinton/Gore administration would attack Western water, there were some troubling signs. First, Vice President-elect Gore, as senator from one of the wettest regions of the country, had joined in the attack by environmental extremists upon Western water rights and the prior appropriations doctrine upon which those rights are based. In his book *Earth in the Balance*, Gore "question[ed] the fairness of a relatively small group of farmers using the vast majority of [California's] water in a state of 32 million people," and looked covetously at "the watershed in Colorado."[6] Second, the Clinton/Gore administration appointed a host of environmental leaders to high positions, demonstrating that for Westerners the political wind in Washington, D.C., was blowing in the wrong direction.[7]

However, the most troubling sign was a speech delivered by private citizen, soon to be interior secretary, Bruce Babbitt before the Northwestern School of Law on November 13, 1992.[8]

Babbitt began: "In the rush to settle the West, the federal government divested water rights to the states." Actually what took place regarding Western water was hardly done in a "rush." As the West was settled, elaborate customary rules for the use of water were developed over many years by the settlers themselves. As Western rancher and constitutionalist Wayne Hage points out: "When the territory was admitted to statehood, its new legislature gradually formalized these informal property arrangements [and the] federal government soon recognized these informal property arrangements in an Act of Congress...."[9]

For Babbitt, those carefully worked out property rights undergirding the economy of the West were "mistakes" that cried out for federal regulation. Federal control needed to be asserted under which "public access" to private property "will be seen as a fundamental right, obtained either through the courts or dictated by legislation."[10]

When did Congress give the federal government power to assert such massive control? According to Babbitt, the nation's basic environmental legislation did just that, though Congress did not intend it at the time it passed those laws. "[T]he Clean Water Act... is a very important assumption of federal regulatory power because it reaches everything that is wet (and some things that arguably are not so wet)." Furthermore Babbitt said he was "certain that members of Congress who passed the Endangered Species Act did not fully understand the American West.... They did not understand the amount of endangered fish in the American West. Within five years," Babbitt continued, there "will be a massive fight, which in my judgment will make the spotted owl seem like a relatively gentlemanly discussion...." On and on he went with his vision for the West, until finally he took a shot at Western dams, both federal and nonfederal:

> Through some wonderful quirk of history... licenses [for nonfederal dams] are granted for terms not to exceed fifty years. Through another wonderful quirk of history, most of the dams were built in the 1930s and 1940s. This means that the renewal periods are coming up. This creates a policy planner's dream.... There are not going to be any more large dams in the West unless there is the most excruciatingly evi-

dent case made, or unless they are built for a Native American
tribe which has a special claim to water....[11]

A little more than a year following Babbitt's speech on Western water
law, his colleague, Attorney General Janet Reno, suspended the Reagan era ruling that the Wilderness Act had not given the federal government control over Western water. Subsequently, John D. Leshy,
Babbitt's solicitor, requested comments on a new opinion and
ordered federal agencies to "file claims for water rights in pertinent
designated wilderness areas when required to file water rights claims
by court deadlines in pending adjudications."[12]

Without putting too fine a point on it, the opinion ordered by
Babbitt and Reno flies in the face of the legislative history that pre-
ceded adoption of the Wilderness Act of 1964.[13] When Western senators, fearful that Senator Hubert Humphrey's wilderness bill would
overrule state water laws, announced their opposition to the bill,
Senator Humphrey took pains to reassure his colleagues by adding
this provision: "Nothing in this act shall constitute an express or
implied claim or denial on the part of the Federal Government as to
exemption from State water laws."[14]

This view was reasserted sixteen years later when wilderness legislation was adopted for lands in Idaho. As Senator Frank Church
explained:

> [We] desired to reiterate and underscore the jurisdiction of
> the State of Idaho over the water resources and fish and game
> within the wilderness areas and accomplished that by repeat-
> ing the provisions of the 1964 act which relate to these
> issues.[15]

This abundant legislative history notwithstanding, Babbitt and Reno
forged ahead.[16]

But their plans for grabbing Western water go far beyond rewrit-
ing the history of the Wilderness Act. Babbitt had hinted as much
when he announced that he intended to bring about the "New

West"—which would include much more than taking over water rights. As head of the League of Conservation Voters, he had asserted in a 1991 fundraising letter, "We must identify our enemies and drive them into oblivion."[17]

Babbitt began by launching a campaign to revise dramatically the rules for grazing cattle on federal land, a plan Senator Ben Nighthorse Campbell called an attack on "my neighbors and my friends."[18] When Babbitt's plan was stymied in the Senate, he sought to "compromise" by supporting language in legislation introduced in the Senate that would have given the federal government vast new powers over Western water.[19]

Under Babbitt's compromise language, the government could challenge every state-issued private water right on the grounds that since the federal government owns the land, it also owns the water. The language could even be used to challenge a water permit that had been applied for but not yet issued, even though the priority has been vested under state law.

Westerners also feared the new water language would be used to attack not just water rights used on federal land, but water rights developed on federal land, sweeping in virtually every water right in the West, including those for towns and cities. Moreover, the water language could be interpreted by federal courts as a congressional reversal of what has been a requirement of Western water law for years—a requirement specifically approved by the U.S. Supreme Court—that federal officials comply with Western water law and obtain permits from state officials.

Even worse, Congress would be preempting state water law by authorizing the federal government to "assert its claims to those [water] rights and exercise those rights to benefit those actions and the public lands and resources thereon." No longer would the federal government be required to comply with state water law regarding the purpose of use, the place of use, or the point of diversion of a state-granted water right.[20] Ultimately, as a result of a Senate filibuster in which Westerners were joined by non-Westerners,

Republicans and Democrats, Westerners prevailed, at least for now.[21]

THE ENVIRONMENTAL PRESIDENT

Democrats have not been the only ones indifferent to Western-ers' water rights. President George Bush's promise of being more sensitive to the environment than his Western predecessor had an immediate impact upon the West.

One of George Bush's first acts as president was to appoint William K. Reilly—a man who had been a career staffer to environ-mental organizations of one sort or another—as administrator of the Environmental Protection Agency (EPA). One of Reilly's earliest decisions was a brutal slap in the face of Westerners and Western water rights.

For nearly sixty years the people of Denver had planned to con-struct a dam at the confluence of the South Fork and the North Fork of the Platte River, within an hour's drive of Denver—a project that became known as "Two Forks." (The water decrees for the project are in fact some ninety years old.) As early as the 1980s, the city of Denver and its suburbs had taken steps to make the dam and the resulting reservoir a reality.

Since the project related to water in a Western state, the U.S. gov-ernment became involved through a number of its agencies, includ-ing the Forest Service, the Army Corps of Engineers, and the Envi-ronmental Protection Agency. In addition, a major environmental study under the National Environmental Policy Act was required. In the end, environmental studies for the project cost in excess of $42 million.[22]

Environmental groups came out strongly against the project. It was "not needed," "environmentally destructive," "the end of the last best 'Gold Medal' trout stream." Before Bill Reilly was even officially head of the Environmental Protection Agency, a number of environmental leaders met with him and demanded that he veto the project. Soon thereafter in 1989, Reilly announced he was taking jurisdiction of the permit that was yet to be issued by the EPA, thus removing the decision from the EPA regional administrator, who had been about to allow the project to go forward.

Reilly started the fact-finding process on Two Forks all over again. After announcing his own reservations about the project, he appointed a regional administrator from Atlanta, Georgia (which receives anywhere from 40 to 80 inches of rainfall a year), to decide if Denver really needed the water project. The Georgian concluded that Denver did not.[23]

In the end, despite the efforts of Denver and its smaller, less financially secure and water-poor suburbs, Reilly vetoed the project. There were better places to put the project, the EPA concluded, but it wouldn't say where. Start over, the EPA said, study another site— at a cost of tens of millions of dollars—and then we'll tell you if it's acceptable. Or, the EPA suggested, obtain the water from elsewhere without building a dam and a reservoir, like buying water from farmers in northern Colorado—never mind what that would do to *their* economy, the wetlands, and the wildlife habitat created by irrigation ditches and irrigated croplands in that part of the state. Or, the EPA continued, Denver could mine the water from underground aquifers in southern Colorado—and never mind the effect on that economy.

Reilly's usurpation of power was nothing more than an attempt to use the Clean Water Act to engage in an activity Congress had rejected consistently: land-use planning.[24] This was in clear violation of the Clean Water Act's provision "preserv[ing] and protect[ing]" state primacy over Western water rights.[25]

Yet another express provision set forth in the Clean Water Act ensured the sanctity of Western water rights; this one became known as the Wallop amendment:

> It is the policy of Congress that the authority of each State to
> allocate quantities of water within its jurisdiction shall not be
> superseded, abrogated or otherwise impaired by this Act. It is

the further policy of Congress that nothing in this Act shall be construed to supersede or abrogate rights to quantities of water which have been established by any State. Federal Agencies shall co-operate with State and local agencies to develop comprehensive solutions to prevent, reduce and eliminate pollution in concert with programs for managing water resources.[26]

Senator Malcolm Wallop, who sponsored the provision, explained the purpose of the amendment:

The conferees accepted an amendment which will reassure the State[s] that... the Clean Water Act will not be used for the purpose of interfering with State water rights systems....[27]

Federal courts have interpreted the Wallop amendment as Senator Wallop and his colleagues intended. In *National Wildlife Federation v. Gorsuch*, the court read the Wallop Amendment as a clear demonstration of the intent of Congress "to minimize federal control over state decisions on water (emphasis in original) *quantity.*" [28] In *Riverside Irrigation District v. Andrews*, the Court of Appeals for the Tenth Circuit found:

The Wallop Amendment does, however, indicate "that Congress did not want to interfere any more than necessary with state water management."... A fair reading of the statute as a whole makes clear that, where both the state's interest in allocating water and the federal government's interest in protecting the environment are implicated, Congress intended an accommodation.[29]

Thus it appears that the EPA, in vetoing the Two Forks project, defied Congress and ignored what several federal courts have deemed was the purpose of the Wallop amendment. Denver's Two Forks is not the only Western water project that has run afoul of the federal government's attempt to engage in land-use planning under the guise of protecting water quality.

In Sheridan in northern Wyoming, a vital project is in jeopardy because federal officials have refused on the thinnest of rationales to give the necessary Clean Water Act approvals. The Corps of Engineers failed to approve the attempt by Sheridan to expand its Twin Lakes Reservoir and instead urged the city to buy out nearby ranchers. At issue are 23 acres of alleged "wetlands"—23 out of some 2.8 million acres used by an alleged rare species of frog.[30] As in the case of Denver's Two Forks project, the federal government is saying "no" to storing water and "yes" to getting farmers and ranchers off the land.

During the Bush administration, even Secretary Manuel Lujan's Department of the Interior got into the act. In the summer of 1991, the Department of the Interior ordered dams in what is known as the Upper Basin States of Wyoming, Utah, and Colorado to release water flows in the spring and early summer, in order to enhance recreation (e.g., rafting on the Colorado) rather than using the water to generate peaking power.[31]

Of apparent little concern to Secretary Lujan and other officials at the Department of the Interior was the fact that these releases would dramatically alter the long-standing purpose of those dams: to provide water for irrigation in dry months, to generate electricity, and to provide recreational opportunities.

Glen Canyon Dam along the Colorado River in northern Arizona, for example, is capable of generating 1,300 megawatts of peak power; the dam provides 70 percent of the Colorado River Storage Projects Act hydroelectricity—electricity that is purchased by consumer-owned utilities. As a result of Secretary Lujan's order requiring "interim flows" and restricting the timing and amount of dam flows, electricity generated has been reduced by one-third to nearly one-half.[32]

Ironically, this policy all but compels the development of more coal-fired or gas-fired turbines as well as shifting from hydro-peaking to coal-fired and gas-fired peaking. The former means air quality problems for Colorado's Front Range communities that—given their meteorology and topography—could be pushed over the edge into air quality violations.

The shift that began during the Bush administration regarding the manner in which Western water projects were to be used and the role the West's dam builder—the Bureau of Reclamation—was to play has ripened in the Clinton/Gore administration. Allegedly as part of Vice President Al Gore's "reinventing government" campaign (Secretary Babbitt views the Bureau of Reclamation as a "dinosaur"),[33] the Bureau of Reclamation has undergone a "total makeover," abandoning its traditional role along with many of its employees.[34] As a result, the bureau will shift from dam building to environmental protection.[35]

One instance of the new job of employees at the Bureau of Reclamation—attacking the use of privately owned lands—was seen recently in northern California, where farmers were notified that in order to renew their irrigation leases, they would have to submit to an inventory of their private land to determine if their lands contained habitat for species listed under the Endangered Species Act. If such inventories—to be conducted by federal agents—were not permitted, the government would "presume" that the land contained protected habitat.[36] The government's action was challenged and federal officials have backed off for now.

BIG FISH STORIES

The attempt to use the Endangered Species Act as an excuse to change land use activities and challenge Western water rights is being pursued aggressively throughout the West,[37] not just in rural areas.

In northern Colorado, the Forest Service has asserted that full-blown environmental impact statements must be prepared prior to the *renewal* of permits to operate water storage facilities on federal land in national forests. To cope with such requirements, a city like Greeley, in northern Colorado, has spent hundreds of thousands of dollars and many years seeking renewal of its permits for two small reservoirs located in the Roosevelt National Forest. According to City Manager Paul M. Grattet, "Greeley's experience is relevant to all Coloradans because hundreds of existing water facilities will need permits renewed over the next five to ten years.... As far as we can tell, the evidence for [finding that the reservoirs adversely affect species under the Endangered Species Act] is almost as good as the evidence for UFO sightings. It is uncertain how much time and resources the federal government has invested in this process to date, although it appears substantial."[38]

What happens if the Fish and Wildlife Service can compel cities to give up water rights because of alleged harm to protected species? Already the city of Denver and its water-short suburbs face future shortages as a result of the loss of Two Forks and other water options.[39] If the U.S. government succeeds in compelling Coloradans to leave more of the water in the Platte River, to which they have legal rights, for transport to Nebraska, serious changes will take place, not just in the economy of northern Colorado, but in the climate of the area.[40] Even the casual observer of the cities that line the Front Range of Colorado's Rocky Mountains can see the stark difference between the treeless prairie that surrounds those cities and the verdant vegetation within. Such greenery affords not just physical beauty to the region but also shade in the summer and windbreaks in the winter. Should these water proposals win out, it would mean abandoning much of this vegetation and drastically reducing other uses of water—for people, for example.

While northern Coloradans fear for the future, people in the Pacific Northwest are already suffering from federal action—this time in the name of the salmon. In Washington, Oregon, California, and Idaho, the Forest Service and the Bureau of Land Management (BLM) are developing a massive land control program nicknamed PACFISH. Like its apparent namesake, the video game PACMAN, in which the yellow ball gobbles up everything in its path, PACFISH could, in effect, cripple most economic activity in the Pacific Northwest, threatening ranchers, farmers, miners, and timber workers, as well as the financial solvency of county and city governments.[41]

PACFISH includes the watershed for nearly 17,000 miles of streams in the four states. While the federal government asserts "only lands administered by the [Forest Service] and BLM" will be regulated, "[i]t is hoped... that private landowners eventually would join the effort to restore watersheds and improve water quality on their lands because watersheds do not end at Federal boundaries." This, of course, is the Bureau of Land Management and Forest Service speaking. Wait until the Fish and Wildlife Service gets involved and concludes that since "watersheds do not end at federal boundaries," what is occurring on private lands runs the risk of "taking" endangered and threatened species. That explains why the phrase "[o]pportunities for private landowners and other interested parties to become involved" has caused such anxiety among Westerners.[42]

Even the low ball, totally unrealistic government estimates of the likely impact on users of federal lands are frightening. The federal government's preferred alternative predicts a 42,000 animal unit month—42,000 cows and their calves or 210,000 sheep or a combination thereof—reduction in grazing, a loss of 58 million board feet of timber, and the elimination of 789,000 recreation visitor days for a total cost of $20 million. The most expensive of the ranges of options costs $54 million and further decreases grazing, timber harvest, and visitor days. Remarkably, given this assessment, the federal government has concluded that the proposed strategy is *not* "a major federal action significantly affecting the quality of the human environment."[43]

Even without PACFISH, impacts are already being felt in Idaho and elsewhere because of federal plans to "save the salmon." In early May 1994, federal officials began the spilling of water over the eight Snake and Columbia River dams, ostensibly as an emergency procedure to help spring chinook salmon. (In fact, such spills more than likely hurt the salmon.) Such releases are also, of course, detrimental to other water users and in violation of various water rights. As Senator Larry Craig said on the floor of the U.S. Senate on May 11, 1994, the day after the spills began:

> With no forewarning, the National Marine Fisheries Service (NMFS) has ordered the Bonneville Power Association and Corps of Engineers to dump large quantities of water over the spillways in a poorly-researched attempt to aid salmon. Instead of helping the salmon, this action will place them in dire jeopardy due to the gas supersaturation in the water, an unavoidable result of heavy spilling. Gas supersaturation is a well-known phenomenon in fisheries biology, and it is lethal to fish above the 120 percent saturation level. It causes problems similar to the "bends" in humans. The order, directed from the White House, would raise gas supersaturation to more than 130 percent.[44]

What PACFISH illustrates is the manner in which the water of the West, like the land, may be locked up, to be used only as federal officials permit.[45] Yet ever since gold was panned in California, the hand upon the water faucets throughout the West has been that of a Westerner, governed by state, not federal law. Now federal officials, using federal laws such as the Endangered Species Act, are coming into the region and declaring that Westerners are not fit to control their own water. From now on the hand on the faucet will be a bureaucratic hand, which responds not to the call of Westerners "upon the river," but to the call of environmental extremists.[46]

Yet another Babbitt target—as he predicted in his water law speech in November 1992—is the construction of water projects. The Animas–La Plata water project, which resulted from an agreement between the United States and the Southern Ute and Mountain Ute tribes, is now back on the drawing board after more than ten years of research and planning by states, water districts, counties, and tribes. When environmental groups sued, the U.S. government quickly confessed error, agreed to return to the planning process, and asked that the lawsuit be dismissed. It was.[47] It will likely be years before the project will again be ready for implementation—at which time expect yet another lawsuit by environmental groups. Secretary Babbitt says that the difficulties can be worked out and that Native Americans are a special case. It is unlikely that environmental groups will ever be willing to sign off on Animas–La Plata or any other water project.

The opposition of environmental groups to Animas–La Plata should put an end to their attempts to exploit the so-called "environmental justice" issue. Notwithstanding their assertion that they are protecting minorities by their appeals and lawsuits, minorities and other economically disadvantaged individuals are the ones who suffer the most when projects are stopped.

Thus it is with the campaign of environmental groups against Animas–La Plata. For the Animas–La Plata water project will inject more than $20 million into the Four Corners area of Utah, Colorado, Arizona, and New Mexico, creating more than a thousand jobs during the project's construction. Total annual benefits from agricultural, municipal and industrial, recreational, and fish and wildlife uses will exceed $31 million. In addition, revenues generated by the sale of power will more than pay for the cost of construction, with interest.[48]

For now, at least, Animas–La Plata has the tacit approval of the U.S. government.[49] Other nonspecial case water projects—that is, those for non-Native Americans—will have a much harder time of it. A case in point is a water project long planned for southern Wyoming—the Sandstone Dam.

In south central Wyoming, just north of the Colorado border along the Little Snake River where the land is still rolling and green, lie the small towns of Baggs, Dixon, and Savery. There, five generations of Wyomingites have operated their ranches, run their sheep and cattle, and cultivated and harvested their fields of native hay and alfalfa. One of those ranches—the Banjo Sheep Company—is run by Pat and Sharon Salisbury O'Toole.

Years ago, the state of Wyoming sent 21,000 acre-feet of water out of this river basin to provide the state capital with a long-term water supply. In return, Wyoming promised to construct a water project along the Little Snake River for the people who live here. Originally, the plan was to construct a 52,000-acre-foot dam both in return for the water delivered to Cheyenne and for the long-term water development of Wyoming. But then the EPA vetoed that proposal. Today, the plan is for a dam holding 23,000 acre-feet, nearly half of which will go to irrigators, with the remainder serving the long-term needs of Dixon and Baggs.

Currently, the project—to be paid for in its entirety by the state of Wyoming—is undergoing environmental review under Section 404 of the Clean Water Act. Pat O'Toole knows what is taking place. In his words, "It makes me sick to drive through Greeley and see farmland in the second most agriculturally productive county in the country lying fallow because the water that was once used to irrigate it has been sold to the city of Thornton. That's all because of the veto of Two Forks. They've got to get the water from somewhere. Told they couldn't impound the water they own, they bought it from the farmers."

The EPA's involvement in land-use planning is not Pat O'Toole's only worry. "We know the Fish and Wildlife Service is going to use the Endangered Species Act to say that our project will hurt the humpback chub, the boneytailed chub, the Colorado Squawfish, and some sucker I can't even remember. The great irony is that the government tried to kill all of these fish years ago 'cause they're trash fish. Now they're saying the fish are endangered and they are going to try to save them on the backs of the people of Wyoming."

Pat O'Toole, the Western rancher, the man selected by Democratic Governor Mike Sullivan to represent Wyoming at the Clinton/Gore administration transition, knows what this is all about. He knows it is about property rights, but he knows equally that it is about the ability of a proud and resilient people to continue to live on and take care of the land as they have for generation after generation. He knows what all Westerners know—if people from somewhere else can control the water, they can control the land.

HOME ON THE RANGE

IN THE EARLY 1970S, shortly before the creation of the Environmental Protection Agency, the U.S. government declared that the poison 1080 (sodium monofluoracetate), which had been used for years by Westerners to kill coyotes that were devastating sheep herds, could no longer be used for predator control. Instead, declared the federal bureaucrats, the government was making available to wool growers a chemical substance that would render coyotes sterile.

Following this far-reaching and controversial decision, federal bureaucrats traveled West to explain the new policy and to tell Westerners that they "were there to help." One such appearance took place in Gillette, Wyoming, before a standing-room-only crowd at the elementary school. After the formal presentation by the Washington, D.C., official, the floor was opened for questions.

After several long minutes of silence, a weathered old fellow in jeans and a cowboy hat, who had been leaning up against the back wall, walked slowly to the microphone in the middle of the room. He had about a three-day growth of beard on his face and appeared to have been up most of the night, perhaps to drive into town from a distant ranch. When he got to the microphone he took off his hat, stared for a moment at the floor, looked up at the bureaucrat on the stage, and spoke. "Sonny, I don't think you understand the nature of the problem. You see, the coyotes, well, they're killing and eating the sheep, they ain't raping them."[1]

Quite simply, the environmental extremists' vision of the American West does not include the rancher.[2] They believe the lands upon which ranching families have grazed for generations should be returned to the "wild." But since such a naturalistic view is not shared by the majority of the American people, these particular environmental extremists have gilded their assault as a battle over economics (to prevent the "unfair" federal grazing "subsidy") and over the environment (to stop the "ecological devastation" of Western lands).

Like most issues embraced by environmental extremists, the fight is neither about money nor the buzzwords of environmental policy— safety, survivability, and sustainability. The fight is over who will control millions of acres of Western land. Environmental extremists, who know that Western ranching families stand at the forefront of the fight against turning everything in the Mountain West into a vast open space, displayed their true intent in a bumper sticker: "Cattle Free By '93."

If the ranching families of the West can be driven off their federal grazing allotments, if their private holdings can be rendered uneconomic and they are forced to sell those lands, if water rights become unusable and the lands worthless, then vast expanses will be snapped up by the federal government and given over to "presettlement conditions"—to nature. Economics and the environment—like the northern spotted owl—are only window dressing for the real goal: to drive people off the land.

MORE THAN GRAZING THE SURFACE

Western ranchers settled years back in a high, cold, semi-arid region, where killing frosts could hit any month of the year. It is a region of deserts, snowbound mountains, and rugged geography with very short growing seasons. Ranches were developed along valley floors, where the rushing flow of the melting snow during spring and early summer could be harnessed and used to irrigate meadows. Because of the short growing season—three and a half to four months at best—the grazing cattle had to be turned off the meadow for the summer, in order to conserve feed for them come early winter. Thus the cattle were turned out upon the surrounding federally owned land. On such land—land managed by the Forest Service and the Bureau of Land Management (BLM)—the livestock could graze during the summer and early fall and return to spend the winter in the meadow near the ranch, to fatten up on hay that had grown in their absence.

Contrary to popular belief—a belief perpetuated by environmental groups and their allies in Congress—these federal grazing lands are hardly on a par with privately owned lands, for a variety of reasons. First, they are not considered prime real estate. At one time, all the land of the West was available, under federal law, to those who wanted to settle it—to grow crops and raise stock. Although a great deal went to homesteaders, much was not settled because it was unsuitable.

Second, renting federal grazing land is a lot like renting an unfurnished apartment—one without walls and a front door. It is up to the rancher who grazes his livestock (not the federal government) to provide the roads, the fences, the gates, the water wells, and the repairs on all the above. If something goes wrong while the rancher's livestock is on federal land, the federal government is not held liable, unlike the analogous situation where the private landowner is generally held responsible for damage or loss.

An excellent example of how this works involves Ray Weber, who runs a cattle ranch near Baggs in south central Wyoming. Mr. Weber runs his herd during the winter on 640 acres of land that he owns, and he leases 80,000 acres of federal land for summer grazing. The allotment he uses lies 25 miles north of his ranch on land for which he has provided the fences (including 96 miles of fence line), gates, and water sources. Repairs on the fence line alone often consume two weeks each summer. As Dr. Fred Obermiller, economist with Oregon State University, puts it regarding Mr. Weber's grazing lease: "[What those who criticize federal grazing fees] don't realize is that [Weber's] nonfee costs associated with management and maintenance and gathering and taking off and death loss out there on the allotment are considerably higher than they are on private lands on average."[3]

The rancher benefits, of course. But so too does the federal land and, more important, the wildlife upon that land. Today, as a result of the careful management practices of thousands of Western ranching families, federal lands are in the best shape ever.[4] According to the Bureau of Land Management, the amount of land rated as excellent to good has doubled.[5]

More noteworthy, wildlife numbers throughout the West are at all, time highs.[6] Since 1960, antelope numbers are up 112 percent, big horn sheep up 435 percent, deer up 36 percent, elk up 800 percent, and moose up almost 500 percent.[7] The abundance of wildlife demonstrates two facts. One, the rangeland of the West has become increasingly better, good enough to sustain more and more wildlife. Two, much of the credit is due to Western ranchers, not just for helping to improve the quality of the range, but for developing and tending to the water sources upon which such wildlife thrive. Stop at almost any watering site on federal grazing lands—a freshwater source created and maintained by private enterprise—and the tracks most often seen belong to wildlife.

Similarly, on the rancher's privately owned lands, the fast-flowing waters of spring and early summer are slowed and channeled to irrigate the land, which benefits not just the rancher, but wildlife. Dr. Quentin Skinner, University of Wyoming range scientist, has noted that the diversion of water across adjoining dry land allows the water to sink into the soil, down to bedrock, at which point it returns slowly to the stream. Thus the rancher increases his riparian area, increases the water table, and increases the vegetation, ensuring more and more wildlife and greater biodiversity.[8]

Bill Heicher, regional manager of the Colorado Department of Game and Fish, calls private ranchlands "critical winter range" for wildlife, especially in Colorado's high country.[9] When waist deep snow covers what little forage there is in the high country, the low-lying meadows are essential for vast herds of wildlife. Mr. Heicher states that "without those livestock producers... [you] end up... with condominiums, town houses, houses packed in. There's very little habitat here for deer and elk to make it through the winter so you lose animals...."[10]

The loss of such privately owned lands, at least less densely occupied ranchlands, would result if Western ranchers were priced or regulated off federal grazing lands. Unable to take their herds from their privately owned meadowlands during the short but vital growing season and onto federal lands, they would be forced to reduce their herd size in order that at least a portion of their private lands could be left to grow feed for the approaching winter. Given the slender margin upon which Western ranchers already operate, such cutbacks would likely doom their operations.

Raising grazing prices or stiffening regulations could put half the ranchers in the West out of work. Today, most ranching families live day to day, with little or no vacations. Here in the West, they tell the story of the rancher who won the lottery. When asked what he was going to do with all his millions, he replied, "I guess I'll just keep on ranching until it's all gone."

Ranching, however, is a way to become rich in spirit and blessed with a sense of well-being that comes from hard work in beautiful open country. It is not just a living, but a way of life, an attitude, an optimism. It encourages families to stay together, as several generations work the land side by side. This is not a place where the elderly tend to be turned over to rest homes. They live out their days with their loved ones on their beloved land.[11] As Kathleen Sun of Wyoming remarks, "If you don't wake up at four in the morning anxious to get started on your work, you're in the wrong business."[12]

Today, something is disturbing the sleep of ranchers, and it isn't work. It is what is happening in Washington, D.C., within federal agencies, and what is happening in the courts of the land as environmental extremists search out ways to drive Western ranchers out of business.

Secretary of the Interior Bruce Babbitt was barely sworn in before the radical federal lands policies advocated by some environmental organizations became part of President Clinton's first budget document. On February 17, 1993, the Office of Management and Budget announced its proposed budget for fiscal year 1994.[13] Among the proposals: to increase grazing fees, over a three-year period, from $1.86 to $4.28 per AUM—a 230 percent increase.[14]

Shortly thereafter, in May of 1993, just when the rhetoric on the issue had begun to lighten up, Secretary Babbitt's now infamous "Straw Man Memo" became public,[15] disclosing the political strategy on grazing fees: "We realize you want to use price increases as a straw man to draw attention from management issues," Babbitt's staff wrote to him. "But there are other ways this might be done," including "leaks, press releases, op-eds, whatever," as well as a proposal "to adjust expectations" prior to issuing new regulations.[16] The release of this cynical memorandum galvanized opposition in the Senate, providing the forty senators needed to debate the administration's proposals to death.

After Secretary Babbitt's defeat at the hands of the Senate filibuster, he embarked upon a series of meetings throughout the West, ostensibly to achieve a compromise on which all could agree.[17] Most notable was the so-called Colorado Roundtable, at which ranchers, environmentalists, and others sat down to reach agreement. Although neither the process nor its product was accepted universally—both ranchers and environmentalists voiced suspicions—the Colorado experience had the appearance of a fair and equitable approach to a controversial issue. Thus ranchers were greatly disappointed that Secretary Babbitt,

on March 25, 1994, issued a major rewrite of Bureau of Land Management grazing regulations, his so-called "Rangeland Reform '94,"
which repudiated much that ranchers thought had been agreed to in
Colorado.[18]

The bottom line, according to Senator Pete Domenici (R-NM), is
simple: "These proposed changes would cause permanent and ever-
lasting harm to many ranchers and initiate an irreversible movement
and in many cases eliminate small family ranchers from the public
rangelands."[19]

According to a recent study, the economic loss to the eleven Western states, as a result of the ruin of those ranchers who could not
absorb the increased grazing fees, would exceed a third of a billion
dollars annually. Even without the administrative changes included in
Range Reform '94, 57 percent of ranchers in rural Montana said they
would be driven out of business if grazing fees were increased, costing the Montana economy $82 million annually. In New Mexico,
44 percent of ranchers say they will have to leave, costing the economy $43 million a year. In Wyoming, 31 percent say they will quit
ranching, costing a state already hard pressed because of the loss of
timber and oil and gas jobs $39 million each year.[20] Other states, it
is forecast, will have similar economic losses.[21]

The loss of such a sizable portion of the Western economy will be
devastating. Communities will become virtual ghost towns. One
need only look at the devastation of the timber communities of the
Pacific Northwest to forecast the trauma to the people who lose all
that they know how to do, lose the ranch that has been home to them
for generations, lose their reason for being, lose hope.[22]

Moreover, the government itself admits that its increases in grazing fees cannot be justified by sound economic data. According to the
government's own grazing appraisal:

> In using the results of these analyses, it must be understood
> that the appraisers have not made an appraisal on a westwide
> basis and do not purport that the numbers which result are

estimates of the fair market value of grazing public rangelands. [23]

A Pepperdine University report on the government's method of raising fees determined, "The probability that the data used to draw final
conclusions accurately reflects the data collected is less than 1 percent."[24] All of which caused the Pepperdine University report to
conclude

> It is staggering in this era of escalating fiscal deficits to reflect
> upon the millions of federal dollars and countless hours of
> federal employee time devoted to the studies of questionable
> accuracy and worth. But, it is even more sobering to reflect
> on the fact that the public policies of Congress on matters
> relating to the publicly-owned grazing lands in the West
> might be built upon a foundation of massive studies support-
> ed by pillars of statistical sand. One can only conclude that,
> at best, the Congress has been ill-served or, at worst, it has
> been misled.[25]

The fundamental difficulty, as the Pepperdine University report
makes clear, is that "the question of comparability of private vs. public lands is never answered... cast[ing] a dark shadow over" the federal government's attempt to set federal grazing fees based upon fees
charged for grazing on private lands.[26] To put it bluntly, federal land
is generally inferior and not as valuable for grazing purposes as private
land. An analysis comparing Montana ranches using federal forage
with Montana ranches that do not use federal forage concluded that
the livestock operator who uses federal land generates less revenue per
animal unit; incurs higher labor and feed costs per animal unit; has
higher fixed costs per animal unit; has a higher annual culling rate of
his herds; requires a higher ratio of bulls in his breeding operation;
has a lower net operating income per animal unit; and enjoys a significantly lower economic rate of return on his investment.[27]

Even the federal government's own 1993 Grazing Fee Task Force is in agreement: "The government is not collecting the full market value for grazing public lands, but ranchers are paying full value through the current fee, non-fee grazing costs, and the grazing permit." [28]

One aspect often overlooked in the attempt to compare public and private grazing rates is the relationship between the grazing rancher and the federal government. Unlike the private landlord, the U.S. government has a plethora of interests and concerns that are, in turn, imposed upon the grazing lessee. For example, there are requirements to own base property, to construct and maintain improvements, and to provide for public access, as well as restrictions relating to multiple use, forage use, and watershed and wildlife issues, not to mention time-consuming meetings with federal agencies and officials as well as interested members of the public. [29] Just when that aspect of grazing on federal lands looked as if it could not get any worse, along came Range Reform '94.

Range Reform '94 might fittingly be subtitled "A Thousand and One Ways to Get Ranchers Off Federal Land." Although nearly every provision seems to contain a dagger pointed at the rancher's throat, one stands out: the proposal to abolish the Grazing Advisory Boards and Councils (GABs), which are empowered to promote proper grazing practices and are peopled by ranchers, and create in their place the Multiple Resource Advisory Councils (MRACs), [30] which are empowered to alter radically the approach to grazing and are peopled by some of those opposed to livestock grazing on federal lands.

MRAC members could be nonresidents, most likely members of national environmental groups. [31] The local rancher, on the other hand, because of conflict-of-interest rules, is prohibited from weighing in on grazing issues. (Environmentalists, of course, never have conflicts of interest on this issue.)

Range Reform '94 greatly augments the ability of nonlocals and even opponents of ranching to challenge federal grazing decisions on an allotment-by-allotment basis. Even more important, the regulations would change the special relationship that has existed in the past between the rancher and the federal government by extending that relationship to other parties. Under these regulations, it is possible for the federal government to choose not to deal with the rancher but with the other "interested parties."[32]

There is even a proposal to change the landowners in the West from ranchers to those who would not use their allotment for grazing. Ranchers fear the proposal is an opening for huge, financially powerful organizations such as the Nature Conservancy to buy up ranches and their grazing permits.

The new regulations set forth a variety of vague new "objectives" for which grazing lands are to be managed, such as "to preserve [public land] resources," and to "maintain the public values provided by open space and integral ecosystems."[33] These new "objectives" adopt an antagonistic approach toward ranching and a guilty-until-proven-innocent attitude toward the rancher. Other proposals set ill-defined and arbitrary standards for lease renewal. Yet other provisions would allow anyone to cross ranchlands—for example, prohibiting any "locked gates" and "signs." Water rights developed for stock on federal allotments, according to one provision, would be turned over to the federal government—the price for obtaining a grazing permit. Such a provision not only threatens Western water law—previously managed by each state—it also helps to ensure that no new water sources will be developed, which is bad news for wildlife. It may even violate the Fifth Amendment.[34]

HANG 'EM HIGH

Perhaps as disturbing is a new regulation that permits the Bureau of Land Management (BLM) to enforce nearly all federal laws—even those over which the BLM has no jurisdiction—against a rancher with a grazing permit. Such violations, moreover, may be grounds for cancelling the grazing permit itself. Thus BLM officials—without any delegated authority from the entity responsible for enforcing the law in question, without implementing regulations, and without notice about when the BLM might choose to enforce such a law—could become super environmental cops.

Increasingly, federal officials can be spotted on federal lands with their guns drawn. In Rigby, Idaho, a rancher was in the midst of constructing a fence along a preexisting fence line on property he had purchased from a neighbor. With an unusual show of caution, he had even checked out his title with the county land office. None of it was enough to help him when Bureau of Land Management officials showed up asserting that the land was federal land.

When he insisted that it was not and continued constructing his fence, the BLM issued the rancher a citation. What between private parties would have become a sit-down meeting with maps, charts, and legal documents, or at worst a quiet title action, became instead a federal criminal case. The rancher was charged with criminal trespass. After his conviction and sentencing, lawyers discovered that he had been denied his right to trial by jury. His conviction was vacated, and a new trial ordered.[35]

Such cases occur throughout the West wherever the federal government's "hang 'em high" mentality has become all too apparent. Even when the federal government loses, it has achieved two goals: to strike fear into all ranchers and to empty their all-too-scanty pocketbooks.

In western Colorado, an inholder, a landowner whose property is surrounded by Forest Service land, was charged with criminal trespass for constructing a culvert upon the only road accessing his inholding. Charges were dropped when federal lawyers were told that a federal appeals court decision prohibited criminal proceedings in such cases.[36]

In northern Montana, a miner removing obstructions on the road to his patented mining claim was surrounded by several vehicles loaded with armed federal agents brandishing their weapons. After an attorney was brought into the case by the Montanan, the Forest Service admitted he had a legal right to use the road.

The best-known example of federal enforcement gone wild in order to remove ranchers from the range involves Wayne Hage of

Tonopah, Nevada.[37] Hage, whose outspoken advocacy on behalf of Western ranchers and their legal rights sometimes put him crosswise with high-ranking federal officials and environmental extremists, had for years run an exemplary cattle operation in the Monitor Valley near Tonopah.[38] Like all ranchers, he had at times disagreed with those regulating the federal lands on which he held grazing as well as water rights and various rights of way. But not even Hage would have believed that when he went out for his routine stray round-up operations he would be surrounded, not once, but twice, by federal officials armed to the teeth. Some thirty agents of the U.S. government (including members of the military) held rifles, automatic weapons, and other military armaments on Wayne Hage and his cowhands. To the surprise and dismay of the federal agents, Hage came armed—not with a gun, but with a 35-mm camera.

The federal government seized his cattle and terminated his grazing permits, thereby destroying his ranch. As if that were not enough, the government forbade him from cutting down or removing any trees, once considered nuisances by the federal government, that were blocking rights of way owned by Hage. When Hage persisted, the government charged him with destruction of government property.

The federal government's legal action against Hage followed, by only four months, Hage's suit against the government for the unconstitutional "taking" of his property—his grazing permits and water rights having been rendered useless.

Wayne Hage and his lawyers won a reversal of his criminal conviction before the U.S. Court of Appeals,[39] beat back an effort by the National Wildlife Federation and several other environmental groups, representing themselves and the attorney general of Nevada, to intervene in Hage's "takings" case, and defeated the federal government's motion to dismiss.[40] Still pending is the federal government's motion for summary judgment, after which, if that motion is denied, Wayne Hage and his lawyers can return to discovery—the process of learning the facts involved in a case to ensure that there are no surprises during the trial.

Discovery has already yielded some amazing information—including the fact that federal officials planned the "raid" on the Hage ranch to coincide with an upcoming vote on federal grazing fees! The federal officials, moreover, briefed key senators and members of Congress—including then-Congressman Mike Synar (D-OK), but not the members of the Nevada delegation—prior to the raid. All of this took place during the "kinder, gentler" administration of President Bush.

Yet another action that continued, although not initiated in such "kinder, gentler" days, was the attempt to deny inholders, primarily Western ranchers, access to private lands. Under a variety of federal laws, as well as several aspects of common law, inholders have absolute right of access to their lands.

Nevertheless, beginning in the Carter administration, various federal officials insisted that inholders held no such rights, neither as descendants of original homesteaders nor as inholders protected by the provisions of the Alaska National Interest Lands Conservation Act (ANILCA).[41] While holding the access denial gun to their heads, federal officials told ranchers that they must execute agreements to cede all rights of access. Many have had the courage to refuse to sign and to go toe to toe with the U.S. government.[42]

Despite the federal government's defeat in a major decision by the U.S. Court of Appeals for the Ninth Circuit, it refuses to recognize access rights.[43] The federal government petitioned successfully for a rehearing and denied a ranching family access to its ranch in Arizona.[44] The U.S. government insists that it has the right to demand payment for and to regulate and even revoke access.

The obstacles that federal officials put in the way of ranchers gaining access to their private inholdings is in sharp contrast to the ease environmental groups experience gaining access from those same federal officials to the administrative process and litigation against ranchers. Not unlike their colleagues in timber, mining, energy, and recreation, ranchers are finding their activities increasingly influenced by litigation undertaken by environmental extremists.

Once again, relatively innocuous language inserted into a federal statute has been expanded to permit open season on Western ranchers. The Federal Land Policy and Management Act (FLPMA) provides that those having "affected interests" must be involved in federal grazing decision making.[45] It is through the "affected interests" language that litigation was undertaken in southern Utah challenging the process that issued grazing permits.[46] Similarly, "affected interests" were granted appeal rights involving grazing permits in southeastern Oregon, the Beaty's Butte case.[47]

Several recent decisions of the U.S. Supreme Court have required parties to demonstrate clear evidence of injury in fact when they challenge federal agency action.[48] The Bureau of Land Management administrative appeal regulations have been interpreted in the same manner.[49] Despite these interpretations, the federal government has been weak in turning back such challenges. For example, a challenge of a grazing permit by someone residing more than 45 miles away from the site, whose concern about the allotment was that he "found cowpies everywhere" and didn't like the "smell and insects," was granted "affected interest" status.[50] In another example, in a recent "affected interest" challenge to a Bureau of Land Management grazing allotment regarding the Southern Ute Indian Tribe, the federal government declined to take a tough stand against such gadfly legalizing.[51]

The willingness of federal lawyers to roll over and play dead in the face of lawsuits by environmental groups is becoming increasingly apparent and raises concerns that such responses to "sweetheart" litigation are unethical. Recently, the California Cattlemen's Association fired off a strong letter to the regional forester for Region 5 protesting the decision of government attorneys to exclude the association, which had filed an *amicus curiae* brief—in aid of the federal government—from settlement discussions. The association concluded that the federal government "considers this to be a 'friendly' environmental lawsuit and apparently the Forest Service will only work with and talk to groups who bring legal action against the agency."[52]

Perhaps the best example of what can result when the demands of environmental extremists are coupled with the desires of federal land managers is the one that involved grazing in the Glen Canyon National Recreational Area in southern Utah. In the rugged canyon lands where the Escalante River empties into the Colorado River, grazing has gone on for more than a hundred years. For the past fifteen to twenty years it had been the target of environmental protests and environmental terrorism. In 1990, twenty-six head of cattle belonging to Ivan and Arthur Lyman, father and son, were found shot to death upon the federal allotment in the Glen Canyon National Recreation Area. Two of their line cabins—historical structures dating back to the early 1900s, and used by hikers and campers—had been burned to the ground. Although a reward was offered and law enforcement personnel alerted, the terrorists were never apprehended. Despite the shocking nature of the attack on private property, environmental groups were slow to condemn the action, asserting instead that the act just showed the need to remove cattle from the area. The cattlemen had had enough of the harassment, intimidation, and name-calling. They sold out to the Nature Conservancy and moved their cattle elsewhere.

Today, according to Commissioner Louise Liston of Escalante, who knows the area well, the trails through the canyon are overgrown with creek willow, Russian olives, Chinese elms, and cottonwoods, making hiking nearly impossible. What was once a showpiece of multiple use—permitting both cattle grazing as well as hiking and camping—now boasts neither.[53]

Utah State Representative Met Johnson is not surprised. A longtime rancher, although he no longer runs cattle on federal lands, Johnson reports, "It's just astonishing to look down the fence line that separates federal lands where grazing has been removed from federal lands where grazing continues. The difference is startling, like down next to the Grand Canyon near Tuweep. On lands managed by the National Park Service where grazing is prohibited, the weeds have grown up and the plants and the grasses have died. It's

just unbelievable. Then on the side of the fence where there's grazing, the plants are healthy, they're strong, they're productive, they're
holding the soil. It's like night and day. It's a shame what we're doing
to the land in the name of preservation."

Of equal concern is the number of federal professional land managers who have been driven out because of the policies they've been
asked to implement—policies that are supported neither by good
management practices nor by a strong statutory foundation.[54] Congressman Bill Orton reports that nine of the eleven Western state
BLM directors have "resign[ed] or retire[d]" because of Secretary
Babbitt's effort "to instill his philosophy and policies into the largest
federal landlord agency in most of our public lands states."[55]

Each day seems to bring a new foe, a new agency that, under the
mantle of environmental protection, has declared war on the Western rancher. The newly created National Biological Survey, for
example, with its commitment to survey the nation's land for species
and ecosystems, is a clear threat to Western ranchers and property
rights, as is the continued aggressive enforcement by the Fish and
Wildlife Service of the Endangered Species Act.[56]

Yet another threat to Western ranchers is the Environmental
Protection Agency (EPA) proposal to embark upon a national, even
international, "Ecosystem Protection" program.[57] The EPA wants
to adopt "a broad national vision for change," for which "EPA
should be a catalyst...."[58] Targeting such "[s]ignificant man-made
stressors [sic]" as "over-grazing, unbridled commercial and residential development, over-population, pollution and a host of others,"
EPA proposes to "reinvent our governmental and societal approach
to... ecosystems and natural resources."[59] The EPA is quite well
aware that the shift to ecosystem management is a new role for it:
"Historically, EPA has primarily focused on the protection of
human health...." However, in this new age, "EPA must make
ecosystem protection a primary goal of the Agency, on a par with
human health...." It calls such a shift—equating the protection of
ecosystems with the protection of human health—a "cultural

change." No doubt most Americans would regard it as such. Hence the barriers the EPA sees to achieving its goal of a "broad national vision" include "political [as opposed to ecological] boundaries,"[60] "lack of knowledge regarding ecosystem issues,"[61] "ecosystem level data [that are] unavailable or difficult to access,"[62] "primacy of state enforcement,"[63] and "EPA [having] little influence over state and local politics."[64]

In other words, to overcome the little difficulty that most Americans value human health more than "eco-systems management," the EPA will need a lot more power to tell Americans what to do and a lot more protection from democratic government when more citizens protest.

CHAPTER 5

THE PIT BULL OF ENVIRONMENTAL LAWS

MENTION THE NAMES FRANK AND DEBORAH POPPER in almost any rural Great Plains or Western community, and you are likely to freeze from the icy glare. In Nebraska and Kansas, Wyoming and New Mexico, Colorado and Montana, thousands of rural Westerners have heard quite enough, thank you very much, of the Professors Popper and their very serious proposal for the "Buffalo Commons."[1]

The professors have concluded, from their vantage point in one of the most congested areas in the world—Frank teaches at Rutgers in New Brunswick, New Jersey, Deborah at New York University in New York City—that mankind was never meant to live upon the Great Plains. The Poppers believe that sooner or later most of the folks living on the Great Plains will be gone. The Poppers don't want to wait that long. To hasten the process, they advocate a massive government program to "deprivatize" 110 counties in nine states in which 400,000 people live so that the buffalo may return to roam freely across a vast area of once private land.

The audacity of the Poppers' proposal stems not only from the effrontery with which it is offered—that is, without regard to the people who populate the region—but also from the Poppers' conclusion that "the Great Plains' experience has implications for much of the rest of the Western and rural United States."[2]

Notwithstanding their repeated conclusion—that the exodus from the region is already occurring—the facts do not bear them out. The Center for the New West, for example, has concluded that just the reverse is true—although the Professors Popper have given up on the Great Plains, others have not.[3]

How do the Poppers propose to "reinvent" the Great Plains? They have an assortment of weapons in their arsenal: designating vast areas for single use; purchases by the federal government's land agent, the Nature Conservancy; outright purchases by the government; regulating cattle and sheep off federal lands; and using the Endangered Species Act (ESA) to lock up land. Despite their assertion that the free market is helping to achieve the Buffalo Commons, the Poppers admit that, of the "potential building blocks for the Buffalo Commons, most of them [are] federal."[4] The weapon of choice, of course, is the ESA, or as it is called by environmental extremists, "the pit bull of environmental laws."[5]

The Endangered Species Act didn't start out as a "pit bull" or even as a land-use planning tool. While not a pussy cat either, it was supposed to achieve what almost everyone seemed to think was a good idea, preserving genuinely endangered species. Certainly, support for the ESA was bipartisan, with Democrats and Republicans in clumsy competition to be considered the more devoted defenders of wildlife. In 1973, the Senate passed the act with only eight "no" votes, the House of Representatives with a scant four votes in opposition.[6]

It was not the first federal law to address the matter of disappearing species. In 1966, Congress had adopted the Endangered Species

Preservation Act.[7] Then in 1969, Congress passed the Endangered Species Conservation Act.[8] But neither seemed to do the job.

The House of Representatives Committee on Merchant Marine and Fisheries noted: "There is presently in effect a series of Federal laws designed to protect species of fish and wildlife which may face extinction without that protection.... [A]t the time [these laws] were enacted, they were adequate to meet the demands as they then existed. Subsequent events, however, have demonstrated the need for greater flexibility in endangered species legislation, more closely designed to meet their needs."[9] The Senate Report concluded: "It has become increasingly apparent that some sort of protective measures must be taken to prevent the further extinction of many of the world's animal species. [Today], the rate of extinction has increased to where on the average, one species disappears per year."[10]

How many species were in trouble? While the numbers varied, by most accounts they were relatively small and seemingly easy to handle. The Merchant Marine and Fisheries Committee reported that "100 species of fish and wildlife" in the United States were "threatened with extinction."[11] Internationally, the numbers were more startling: "375 species of animals [are] imminently threatened with extinction throughout the world and another 239 species of animals [are] not as yet threatened with extinction but requir[e] additional controls over their trade."[12] Senator Ted Stevens (R-AK), one of the five Senate managers of the conference bill that became law, noted that "109 species and subspecies of wildlife—14 mammals, 50 birds, 7 reptiles, and 30 fish species—[were] threatened with extinction" and advised his colleagues that the list included "such animals as the black-footed ferret, the whooping crane, the eastern timber wolf, the masked bobwhite, the ivory-billed woodpecker, and peregrine falcons."[13]

That was then. Today, Senator Stevens' list has blossomed into a virtual Who's Who of regulatory roadblocks to economic activity and the use of private property. This includes the red-cockaded woodpecker, the Texas blind salamander, the Lahontan cutthroat trout, the humpback chub, the Colorado River squawfish, and the Devil's Hole pupfish.[14] Senator Stevens could never have imagined that the Texas blind salamander would be used, some twenty years later, to lock up the greater part of the Edwards Aquifer that lies beneath the city of San Antonio. Nor could he have imagined that the red-cockaded woodpecker would be used, some twenty years later, to stop timber harvesting in Texas, Georgia, and North Carolina, on private as well as federal land; nor that the Colorado River squawfish would be used, some twenty years later, to threaten the growth of small communities in western Colorado.[15]

Yet surely some of the other ninety-one senators voting for the ESA—including conservatives like Hansen (R-WY), Helms (R-NC), and Hruska (R-NE) and liberals like Hart (D-MI), Hartke (D-IN), and Humphrey (D-MN)—might have seen it coming, despite the apple-pie atmosphere of the debate over the ESA in the Senate.[16] For example, Senator Gaylord Nelson (D-WI), the Senate's leading environmentalist—later of the Wilderness Society—spoke of "another danger to our wildlife, a threat that is unavoidable: the expansion of our cities and industries."[17] Senator Nelson had a solution: "Habitat acquisition... [to provide] a base for the construction of true sanctuaries, preserves free from harmful human intrusion."[18]

Another clue should have been picked up—the deceptively simple statement of Senator Harrison Williams (D-NJ) that "[c]itizen suits are also permitted...."[19] Over the next twenty years, this citizen suit provision was used aggressively by environmental groups to compel the listing and protection of various species, thereby delaying and even stopping economic activity.

The purpose of the Endangered Species Act has become the stopping of all activities of which environmental extremists disapprove. Timber harvesting is at the head of the very long list of activities condemned by environmental extremists. Thus forestry, specifically forestry near the hotbed of environmental activism in Seattle and Portland, was the first to feel the full force of the Endangered Species Act.[20]

Beginning in 1987 and continuing to this day, the environmental movement has waged an aggressive war of attrition against timber harvesting in Washington, Oregon, and northern California. Environmental groups from these states and elsewhere have sought to end forestry on federal lands through lawsuits filed before federal district courts in Washington and Oregon. Obtaining injunction after injunction, they must have succeeded beyond their wildest imaginings. They have virtually shut down logging on federal lands in the Pacific Northwest.

Although the northern spotted owl litigation is the best known and most egregious example of the abuses that have stemmed from the Endangered Species Act and of the manner in which that act is being used to wage war against Westerners,[21] that owl is only one of more than seven hundred species currently listed as "threatened" or "endangered."[22] Yet in the closing days of the Bush administration, Department of Justice lawyers settled a lawsuit filed by environmental groups by agreeing to triple the number of species listed under the Endangered Species Act.[23] Exactly how many more will there be? No one really knows. The Council on Environmental Quality once predicted that more than nine thousand species were eligible for listing; the vast majority of those species are clams, spiders, snails, mussels, insects, and other invertebrates.[24] How far such creatures are from the initial attractive list presented to the Senate during consideration of the Endangered Species Act is beyond imagining. In the vernacular of the trade, we have gone from the "warm and fuzzies" to the "cold and slimies." In short, Westerners are losing jobs and property not just to owls and grizzly bears, but to snails and flies.

The attack, moreover, has hit private as well as public property. The experience in Washington and Oregon differs only in magnitude from what is happening throughout the West:

♦ In northern California, a federal judge ordered the total shutdown of irrigation water to 141,000 acres of farmland, as well as wildlife refuges in the Glenn-Colusa Irrigation

District, to protect the endangered winter-run salmon. If left standing, that decision will devastate not only some 1,200 farming families in Glenn and Colusa Counties, whose crops have an annual value of $85 million, but wipe out 12,000 farm-related jobs and $255 million in economic activity. Already the unemployment rate in the area has soared to 31 percent.[25]

♦ In Riverside County, California, an endangered fly has stopped construction on the Ontario airport and stifled plans for an economic enterprise zone. The scientist who proposed the Delhi Sands flower-loving fly for listing asserts that it would be a mistake not to stop everything until more is known about this fly: "Organisms with an unknown value are like books on a library shelf you haven't read. Would you toss them out before you've read them? It's not wise to throw out nature's storehouse of information."[26]

♦ In northwestern Montana, the Fish and Wildlife Service (FWS) has proposed to use this rural area as a vast recovery zone for the grizzly bear, which would virtually eliminate timber harvesting—the lifeblood of this timber-producing community. Each year the Critical Habitat One area, as it is called, is increased in size. In one Forest Service timber sale area alone, the harvest level was cut back by 43 percent in order to achieve a 1 percent increase in grizzly bear habitat.[27]

Like the situation in northern California, where one decision under the Endangered Species Act led to other unintended consequences, the Forest Service's decisions in Montana will leave standing millions of board feet of timber that have been devastated by the mountain pine beetle. The hills around Libby, Troy, Eureka, and other Lincoln County homes and communities are thick with dead and dying trees that will serve as kindling for the cataclysmic fire the residents expect. With the fire will go not just the jobs and economic uses of the forest, but the environment the people of the area love *and* the habitat of the bear.

What will happen when bears turn to humans for food? If the decision of a Department of the Interior administrative law judge stands, people will not be able to use deadly force to defend themselves, especially if they have introduced themselves into "the zone of imminent danger" or have provoked the bear by carrying a weapon. The decision, as mentioned earlier, came in the case of John Shuler of Dupuyer, Montana, who, when confronted by a grizzly bear in his own yard, and fearing for his life, killed the bear. The ALJ ruled that he could not claim self-defense and fined him $4,000.[28]

♦ In Idaho, the listing of the salmon as endangered threatens to devastate not just timber harvesting but agriculture and the generation of power.[29] The people of rural Owyhee County have dodged the bullet, at least temporarily, by successfully challenging the listing of the Owyhee Bruneau hot springsnail—the matter is still on appeal by environmental groups—but there will be other threats to the rural, agrarian lifestyle the residents love.[30]

♦ In Utah, another snail, the Kanab ambersnail, was declared "endangered" in an emergency listing so that the FWS could force the property owner to turn his land over to the government. The owner's refusal to cede his lands to the FWS or to its agent, the Nature Conservancy, resulted in a cease-and-desist order that prohibited him from using his property.[31]

♦ In Nevada, the desert tortoise has all but destroyed any other use of the lands in Clark County because of a trade demanded by the Fish and Wildlife Service that permits building to continue in Las Vegas.[32]

♦ In Colorado, the Bureau of Reclamation was forced to return to the drawing board regarding a water project guaranteed to the Ute Indians by treaty, following a lawsuit filed by environmental groups alleging potential harm to the Colorado squawfish.[33] In northwestern New Mexico, the same fish is jeopardizing a major coal fire power plant from being built, with resultant loss of jobs and income for the Navajo Indian Reservation.[34]

♦ In Arizona and New Mexico, timber harvesting has been cut by 80 percent on Forest Service lands because of the presence of the Mexican spotted owl, a distant cousin of the northern spotted owl. As a result, around 2,400 jobs and $60 million in direct revenues might be lost forever.[35]

If this is the impact of a "mere" seven hundred species, what will happen when nine thousand are listed? If this is the impact when only federal lands are at risk, what will happen when the Endangered Species Act is applied to private land? If this is the result from a virtual handful of "recovery" plans to save species, what will happen when the FWS completes such plans and land set-asides for all species?[36]

There are a host of problems with the Endangered Species Act, most of them unfamiliar to the American people. Yes, the national news has reported what has been happening regarding the northern spotted owl and timber-producing communities of the Pacific Northwest. Until recently, however, that news has been remarkably one-sided—the conflict portrayed as a classic one of good guys (environmentalists) vs. bad guys (the timber industry).[37] Only recently have the media, specifically NBC, exposed what most knowledgeable observers have known from the start, that the spotted owl was only window dressing for the real objective—the end of timber harvesting. NBC's Roger O'Neil, for example, said, "Environmentalists... admit the spotted owl was part of a bigger strategy [to] stop the cutting of big old trees in the national forests.... Some biologists agree, now, that the politics of environmentalism got in the way of careful science."[38]

Yes, the national news has detailed a handful of outrages, such as the "20/20" report of homes that burned down in southern California because of the efforts by the Fish and Wildlife Service to protect the kangaroo rat.[39] Yet while this program brought to the nation's attention the potential for abuse of the Endangered Species Act and the absurdity of risking peoples' lives and property to insulate rats and their habitat, it did not expose a number of fundamental deficiencies in the statute itself.[40]

"Science" as used by the Endangered Species Act is a political tool to effect a specific aim.[41] As the late Dr. Dixy Lee Ray reported in her book, *Trashing the Planet*, Stephen Schneider, professor of biological studies at Stanford University, asserted that "We [scientists] have to offer up scary scenarios, make simplified, dramatic statements, and make little mention of any doubts we may have. Each of us has to decide what the right balance is between being effective and being honest."[42]

When the Endangered Species Act speaks of a "species," it is not a species as that term is commonly defined by the scientific community, which includes all animals able to breed with each other and produce fertile offspring, and none that cannot do so.[43] In effect, the ESA treats much smaller groups as species. As Dr. J. Gordon Edwards points out:

> "Species" are defined by biologists as being "reproductively isolated" and "genetically distinctive" natural populations of animals. This is a scientific requirement, and has no resemblance to the political definition that has been used by the environmentalists who developed the Endangered Species Act…. The political definition omits the requirements of the legitimate scientific definition of "species," yet it is the foundation upon which the entire Endangered Species Act is based. It considers ANY loose assortments of similar individuals to be so-called "species."[44]

The act is at its most amorphous in the matter of geographically distinct species.[45] Under this rubric the Fish and Wildlife Service protects a species in a particular location, even if that species thrives elsewhere. Thus, the wolf is listed under the Endangered Species Act throughout much of the lower forty-eight states, even though it is so abundant in Alaska that it threatens the wildlife herds Alaskans depend on for subsistence.[46] Another example is the marbled murrelet, nearly half a million of which live in Alaska, but which is considered "endangered" in Washington and Oregon.[47]

Perhaps the most egregious recent example of this abuse involved the ordeal of the University of Arizona when it attempted to build a world-class observatory atop Mount Graham in the Coronado National Forest in southeastern Arizona.

Two years after the university advised the U.S. Forest Service (USFS) in 1984 that it wished to establish, at a cost of more than $240 million, an international observatory on Mount Graham, the FWS listed the Mount Graham red squirrel as "endangered." As a result, hundreds of thousands, perhaps millions, of dollars were added to the cost of the observatory. In the end, it took an act of Congress, repeated negotiations among the USFS, the FWS, and the university, and several years of costly litigation before the observatory was able to go forward.

Was the red squirrel truly endangered? Not according to noted biologist Dr. Conrad Istock:

> The red squirrel is very widely distributed in North America and is able to flourish in a wide range of habitats. This includes Douglas [fir], Corkbark [fir], Engelmann [spruce], Ponderosa [pine], and a number of other coniferous and hardwood tree species....[48]

Nevertheless, the Sierra Club asserted in the opening sentence of its oral arguments before the U.S. Court of Appeals for the Ninth Circuit, "If this court permits this decision to stand, it will cause the extinction of the first mammal to become extinct since the adoption of the Endangered Species Act in 1973."

Perhaps the most disturbing aspect of the Endangered Species Act is its ability to force other federal agencies and private citizens to enrich the Fish and Wildlife Service. Since a "jeopardy opinion" (an opinion that a listed species will be affected adversely) from the FWS is a death sentence for any particular undertaking, people will go to any lengths to avoid the ruling. The Fish and Wildlife Service calls these lengths "mitigation," but most thinking people recognize it as a "kickback" and the "jeopardy opinion" as "blackmail."

At the height of the Las Vegas, Nevada, building boom in the early 1990s, the Fish and Wildlife Service listed the desert tortoise as "threatened." Since desert tortoises were found throughout Las Vegas' Clark County, building all but came to an end. Fearing an economic disaster, property owners, developers, and city officials began to scramble.[49] The Fish and Wildlife Service was delighted to come to the rescue. The solution offered by the FWS was a little-known section of the Endangered Species Act that provided for "habitat conservation plans" accompanied by so-called "incidental take permits."[50] That is, if the private parties agree to set aside other land as habitat conservation areas, they will be permitted to use their own land, even if that use results in the incidental loss (or "take") of the protected species. In short, covetous federal bureaucrats extorted a payoff.[51]

In the end, in exchange for permission to build on 22,352 acres in downtown Las Vegas, at least 400,000 acres were set aside for the Desert Tortoise Management Zone (DTMZ).[52] Eventually, in return for permission to build in the rest of the Las Vegas Valley, some 1.4 million acres may be placed into the DTMZ.[53] All other uses of this vast area, including ranching, mining, off-road vehicle recreation, hiking, and horseback riding would be placed off limits. In short, a million and a half acres of land in Clark and neighboring Lincoln Counties could be locked up to "save" the desert tortoise.

Meanwhile, in another Lincoln County, this one in Montana, a similar situation is being played out. There, the Noranda Mining

Corporation proposed to develop a world-class underground mine.
The mine would employ 450 workers at some of the highest non-
supervisory wages in the country in one of the most economically
hard-pressed regions of Montana. Although the adits, shafts, and
other facilities are all located on private land—old patented claims—
the road to the mine traverses lands managed by the Forest Service.
Since the Fish and Wildlife Service considers the area to be critical
habitat for the grizzly bear, it demanded $8 million worth of "miti-
gation" from Noranda. In a county where 78 percent of the land is
already owned by the federal government, the Fish and Wildlife Service is making the company buy $8 million worth of private land and
turn it over to the federal government.[54]

The matter of private land bears special mention, since the
Endangered Species Act was meant to be applied expressly to federal lands and federal activity. Congress recognized that private land
could be habitat to endangered or threatened species, but it concluded that it was better to acquire than to regulate these lands.[55]
Notwithstanding the clear legislative history, federal agents have
sought, through a variety of means, to restrict the use of private land.
The Fish and Wildlife Service, for example, defines "harm" under
the Endangered Species Act to include "habitat modification." As a
result, any use of private land that could be considered harmful habitat modification would be prohibited.[56] Furthermore, the Clin-
ton/Gore administration is currently proposing to impose a conservation duty regarding listed species upon private landowners, a duty
to be defined by the federal government.[57]

Clearly, Congress intended that the habitat of listed species was to
be protected, not through the regulation of private property, but by
means of federal land acquisition. Land acquisition, however, is difficult for the government.[58] Simply put, it doesn't have the money.

Environmental groups have asserted that the American people are
willing to pay any price and bear any burden to achieve environmental goals. For years, however, these goals have been achieved through
regulations that affect others and whose costs are almost unnotice-

able to the majority of the people. When the costs of these goals become known, environmental policies will lose their luster. The day the American people see line items in the federal budget to purchase land to preserve the habitat of the Kanab ambersnail or the Delhi Sands flower-loving fly or the Bruneau hot springsnail, public attitudes will begin to change.

Such a change is years down the roads. The Endangered Species Act is just now beginning to take over private land, and it will be years before the expected expenses will appear in the appropriation bills. What is becoming increasingly well-known—thanks to the work of a handful of experts—is the incredible, even incalculable, cost to the American people of the Endangered Species Act.

Westerners know all too well what the ESA is costing in terms of lost jobs, lost wages, lost revenues, lost projects, and lost land uses. Yet not even Westerners are aware of the total cost to the American people. The National Wilderness Institute (NWI) reports that "[t]he government has no idea of the true cost of the endangered species program [since cost] estimates in the recovery plans do not correspond to actual expenditures identified in ESA expenditure reports given to Congress."[59] The NWI estimates that the costs of implementing the ESA as being "in the multi-billion" category.

One reason the costs are so high is because of the gap between the government's estimate of the cost of "recovery" of a species and the actual expenditures. The recovery plan for the red-cockaded woodpecker was estimated at $8.3 million, yet nearly $15 million was spent from 1989 through 1991, an increase of 180 percent.[60] (Since cost figures were not required of the FWS before 1988, expenditures between 1970, when the red-cockaded woodpecker was listed, and 1988 are not included.)

There is more. As the National Wilderness Institute notes, federal cost figures don't include decreases in property values; lost jobs; reduced or terminated business activities; supplements in lieu of lost wages; governmental (federal, state, county, or city) cost of compliance; and loss of tax revenues.[61]

Now the government is moving even more aggressively to impose its will upon privately owned land. Secretary Bruce Babbitt proposes to conduct a biological survey of the entire country through his National Biological Survey. He then proposes to use the results to make decisions as to how land, public or private, may be used throughout the entire country. The government, moreover, will base its future decisions on the Fish and Wildlife Service's view of the Endangered Species Act. With these tools in hand the government will have total control over the land of the West—and the lives of its people.

CHAPTER

6

PARKS AND PEOPLE

IN MARCH 1994, THE NATIONAL PARK SERVICE (NPS) conducted a three-day public meeting in Flagstaff, Arizona. The meeting had been planned as a carefully orchestrated, "consensus creating" presentation. Unfortunately for the NPS, its assignment was a tough one: create a *public* mandate for *closing* Grand Canyon National Park to hundreds of thousands of annual visitors.

That NPS proposal is just one more example of why many Westerners believe the NPS is anti-people, arrogant, and out of touch, not only with the American people and with reality, but with its own mission. While the attitude of the NPS may not concern most Americans, it is a grave problem for Westerners, since the NPS manages huge portions of the eleven Western states.[1]

One of those states is Arizona, which holds the most famous park in the world—the Grand Canyon National Park, situated in north central Arizona. Running along the Colorado River and the majestic canyon that has cut deep into the sandstone over the course of millions of years, Grand Canyon National Park encompasses 1.2 million acres or 1,904 square miles, an area the size of Delaware.[2] Grand Canyon National Park is miles from nowhere; the closest major city, Phoenix, is 219 miles away.

Yet as remote as it is, much of Grand Canyon National Park is even more so since paved roads reach only a tiny portion of the canyon's 277-mile length.[3] Those wishing a better view have a number of choices: they can take a raft trip through the canyon, seeing what John Wesley Powell saw when he took the trip in 1869; they can ride burros down into the canyon for a camping trip along selected trails; or they can hike a small portion of the more than 400 miles of trails that trace the canyon walls, camping out in some of the sites along the way.

There is only one problem with these alternatives; they require time and a certain degree of hardiness. River raft trips may last five days or longer; burro rides, half a day or overnight; and hiking, for as long as one can carry the necessary supplies by backpack. Even then, these activities allow a view of only a portion of the grandeur that is Grand Canyon.

There is another way to visit Grand Canyon National Park, a way chosen by more than 800,000 visitors every year, as compared with the 30,000 who raft, ride, or hike. That unique experience is by air— by helicopter or by fixed wing—into areas of the park set aside for such viewing.[4] Visitors who overfly the Grand Canyon see a magnificent, unparalleled sight. More important, thousands of elderly or physically challenged visitors could see it no other way.

The National Park Service should be delighted that such visitors can enjoy the wonder of Grand Canyon National Park, especially given the NPS's repeated statement that national parks mean tourist dollars to the local economy. In this case, the air tour industry around Grand Canyon National Parks garners $250 million a year and employs over 1,200 people in Arizona and Nevada.[5]

The NPS is far from delighted. It is working hand in glove with environmental groups to put an end to air tours, on the grounds that the distant, faint hum of aircraft overflying the remote and isolated portions of Grand Canyon disturbs the "natural quiet" of the park. Yet Grand Canyon is a national park, not a wilderness area. Moreover, surveys show that only an infinitesimal number of Grand Canyon visitors object to overflights. Finally, parks are intended to serve a multitude of visitors and not just a handful of hikers, boaters, or burro riders. Nevertheless, the NPS pushes on.

The federal statute that created the first national park—Yellowstone National Park—set the land aside "as a public park or pleasuring-ground for the benefit and enjoyment of the people."[6] The Secretary of the Interior (the National Park Service was not created until 1916) was to publish regulations that "shall provide for the preservation, from injury or spoliation, of all timber, mineral deposits, natural curiosities, or wonders in said park, and their retention in the natural condition."[7] Most interesting, in light of the increasingly anti-people attitude of many in the NPS and most in the environmental community, is the unequivocal statement that Yellowstone was meant to be used while being preserved.[8] Such a view held sway more than three decades later when Congress created the National Park Service. Once again Congress saw parks as performing two missions: "to *conserve* the scenery and the natural and historic objects and the wildlife therein and to provide for the *enjoyment* of the same in such manner and by such means as will leave them unimpaired for the *enjoyment* of future generations" (emphasis added).[9] Note that Congress chose the word "conserve," not "preserve," to explain what the National Park Service was to do with the "scenery and the natural and historic objects and the wildlife." In other words, the National Park Service was to utilize those natural resources wisely, not place them off limits to the people.[10]

The National Park Service is currently busy putting a creative spin on the statutes under which it is supposed to operate. In 1976, for

example, the NPS contended that the Yellowstone National Park Act
was written:

> ...in 1872, at a point in this Nation's history when only a
> handful were convinced that America's natural resources
> were limited and that the public could not have its cake and
> eat it too. Today, with the Nation and the park facing an
> environmental crisis, it should be apparent that to have both
> is to have neither. In light of this, the original purpose must
> be translated in terms of contemporary connotations; as such
> it should read: To perpetuate the natural ecosystems within
> the park in as near pristine conditions as possible for their
> inspirational, educational, cultural, and scientific values for
> this and future generations.[11]

Thus in one fell swoop, without congressional approval, the National Park Service, at least in respect to Yellowstone National Park, eliminated the words "enjoyment," "public park," and "pleasuring-ground." The NPS's views coincide with those of environmental extremists, the self-proclaimed protectors of the nation's parks.

Connie Parrish, California representative of Friends of Earth, once told a Los Angeles reporter that "what Friends of the Earth, the Sierra Club, and other conservation groups have proposed is to phase out national park visitor accommodations." The Wilderness Society in 1975 urged in its *Wilderness Report* "that the National Park Service adopt and implement a firm policy of phasing out unnecessary concession facilities in the parks."[12] And Martin Litton, longtime board member of the Sierra Club, said, "The only way we can save any wilderness in this country is to make it harder to get into, and harder to stay in once you get there."[13]

What is at issue here, however, is not "wilderness." "Wilderness," as seen in Chapter 7, has a specific meaning as expressed by federal statute. Thus, what environmental extremists are trying to do is to manage the nation's parks like wilderness areas. The extreme nature of their views is at odds, not only with the wishes of the vast majority of the American people, but with the intent of Congress in creating parks and the National Park Service.[14] Even some of the most faithful congressional allies of the environmental movement know that a park is a park, not a wilderness. Morris K. Udall, former chairman of the Interior and Insular Affairs Committee of the House of Representatives and the man responsible for creating more parks and wilderness areas than anyone in history, said:

> The parks are not, unless they are otherwise so designated, wilderness areas. They are meant to be seen, enjoyed and experienced by people. To do that, we have to provide them with certain services—places to stay, places to eat, tours, interpretive facilities and the like.[15]

In 1965, Congress decided that the best way to ensure that the "places to stay [and] places to eat" were "enjoyed" was to allow such facilities to be provided by the private sector. To this end, certain incentives and assurances would be offered those who wished to own and operate visitor facilities. Congress knew that without security of tenure, without a right of renewal, and without a reasonable opportunity to make a profit, private concessioners would not be able to operate in the national parks.

Concessions in the national parks—especially in the wide open spaces of the West—are unlike any other free enterprise undertaking. Miles from nowhere, these facilities exist for only one customer—the visitor to the national park in which the concession is located.[16] Not only is the park visitor the concessioner's only potential customer, but the concessioner's relationship with that customer is ruled by the National Park Service. The NPS directs what services the concessioners provide and at what prices, how long the facilities remain open, when they start up and when they close down, what buildings are used, and when, where, and how those building may be constructed.

Needless to say, such authority—while certainly reasonable given that the facilities are within units of the national park system—has a direct and dramatic impact upon the ability of the concessioner to earn a profit. Recognizing that reality, Congress sought to ensure a positive, long-lasting relationship between the units of the National Park Service and the concessioners who served them by passing the Concessions Policy Act of 1965—an act that provided security of tenure and a number of other inducements and assurances.[17] As long as the nation's parks were to be "seen, enjoyed and experienced by people," and as long as the National Park Service sought to "provide [people] with certain services," the Concessions Policy Act worked well.

The relationship between NPS officials and private concessioners was one in which the two saw their fortunes tied together. NPS officials realized that the park unit's ability to provide a pleasant park experience for visitors depended, in part, on how well the concessioner did his or her job. The concessioner knew that any investment made in the concession facilities was a protected investment, not just in financial terms, but in terms of the goodwill of NPS officials. As a result, concessioners were only too willing to bear the financial burden of constructing new facilities within national parks, believing that they were there for the long haul and knowing that their investment was protected by law. For example, many of the grand structures that the American people associate with our national parks were built by the private sector.[18]

Such a relationship was bound to arouse the ire of the anti-people crowd. They believe that the only park experience is a wilderness experience, with mankind a stranger and his works unseen. Former Secretary of the Interior James Watt, on a trip to Yosemite National Park in California, was exposed to that philosophy firsthand when he mentioned the need to improve access to the nation's parks. Said one environmental extremist:

> You are not speaking to the real problem. The real problem
> is people and the degradation they bring to the National Park

resource. We have to prevent people from coming here, not make it easier for them.[19]

Of course, one sure means of keeping people away from the parks is to make them hard to get into and harder to stay in, which means targeting the concessioners. The assault against the presence of the private sector in the national parks by those who wished to discourage people from visiting them probably reached its height during the Bush administration, and from a most unexpected source: George Bush's Secretary of the Interior Manuel Lujan.

Lujan, after having been attacked by the media within hours of being sworn in was suddenly held up, by that same media, as a man of courage. The reason: Lujan's attack on national park concessioners. Secretary Lujan had discovered that concessioners were "ripping off" the National Park Service. "Why was it," *The Washington Post* was delighted to hear Secretary Lujan ask, "that concessioners pay three-quarters of a percent to 14 percent royalty in the national parks while vendors at the New Mexico State Fair pay 40 percent royalty?" The difference, of course, is between building and operating a seasonal facility in a national park where all prices are controlled and operating out of a state-owned stand for two weeks and charging whatever the traffic will bear.[20]

The assault against park concessioners, which had, at one time, been about keeping people out of the parks, had taken a different turn. Now it was about "ripping off the American people." It was about "getting a fair return." It was about "leveling the playing field." It was about nothing of the sort. Like the debate about forestry, or mining, or grazing, or oil and gas leasing, the debate over national park concessioners policy was not about money, it was about ending an activity opposed by environmental extremists.

During the last Congress, attempts to gut the Concession Policy Act of 1965 nearly prevailed. Had they succeeded, Congress would have replaced it with a system that would have ended concessioners as we know them today. Environmental extremists would have gone a long way in accomplishing their objective—to get people-oriented facilities, and people, out of the parks.

Yet the attack is not just against activities within the parks. The National Park Service and environmental extremists are agitating against tourist facilities *outside* the parks as well. Recently, the superintendent of Yosemite National Park in California signed a memorandum declaring that no tourist facilities should be constructed near the park:

> It is not our intent to adversely affect local economies. Rather it is to inform you that the National Park Service is no longer seeking development of outside accommodations to support park visitors. We cannot be responsible for economic dislocation resulting from future expansion and marketing of Yosemite based tourism knowing that a limit on park visitation to protect park resources will be implemented in the near future. [21]

The way the Wilderness Act of 1964—adopted to preserve a few special places untouched, and virtually untouchable, by mankind—has been expanded far beyond the intent of its original congressional proponents is taken up in the next chapter.[22] What bears mention here is the manner in which the Wilderness Act has been used by the NPS to make further inroads on limiting the ability of people to use the parks.

In early 1966, two years after the Wilderness Act was adopted, the National Park Service estimated that 22.5 million acres of parklands might become wilderness study areas under the legislation. Eventually, sixty-three units covering more than 28 million acres were designated for study.[23] Today, there are more than four million acres of officially designated wilderness within the national parks of the eleven Western states.[24]

It isn't only wilderness designation that can close national park lands to people. The same objective can be achieved by something

called Master Plans or General Management Plans, the documents
by which units of the National Park Service are managed. As the
Sierra Club Political Handbook instructs, the solution to winning
policy battles, Master Plans, or otherwise, is "hassling administrative
agencies,"[25] in this case by pushing for changes in the Master Plans,
behind the scenes, far from the scrutiny of most Americans:

> [W]hen environmentalists became familiar with the Master
> Plan idea, they realized it contained a framework for even
> more sweeping people-exclusions than the Wilderness Act.
> Master Plans could do what the Wilderness Act could not:
> They could eliminate concessions and crowds entirely. One
> excuse or another could easily be manufactured for down-
> grading one at a time Class I sites (where most concessions
> are) to Class II (where fewer concessions are). Then these
> Class II lands could be lobbied into Class III and IV (where
> only key concessions are) and finally Class V (where no con-
> cessions are). In the hands of politically savvy and ruthless
> lobbyists for the Sierra Club and Wilderness Society, the
> Master Plan was to become the Frankenstein monster of the
> 1970s.[26]

Although the NPS has always included those who saw visitors as a
nuisance, for decades official policy was to encourage park use.[27] No
longer.

In 1991, in Vail, Colorado, park officials and their allies gathered
to discuss the future of the National Park System. What came out of
that gathering is often referred to as the Vail Agenda. It is blatantly
elitist:

> While public access and enjoyment are essential elements of
> the purpose of the park system, it should not be the goal of
> the National Park Service to provide visitors with mere
> entertainment and recreation. Rather, the objective should

be to provide the public with enjoyment and enlightenment
attendant to those park attributes that constitute each unit's
special meaning and contribution to the national character.
This is use and enjoyment on the *park's* terms. It is enter-
tainment, education, and recreation *with meaning* (emphasis
in original).[28]

To this end, the National Park Service is committed to "minimiz[ing]
the development of facilities within park boundaries...." [29]

All kinds of tourists visit the national parks of the West. Yet for the
park purists only one kind of tourist is to their liking—those like
them, those who are into the "leave only footprints, take only pictures" approach. I have been there myself.[30] But one size does not fit
all. Parks are for all kinds of people, even those whom park officials
derogatorily refer to as "windshield tourists"—those who view the
parks as they drive through. In fact, such folks are in the majority. A
study in Glacier National Park reports that 94 percent of those who
drive into the park never stop, emphasizing the need to provide
accommodations that will entice them to pull over, at least for a few
hours.[31]

Yet another assault by the National Park Service on people-friend-
ly facilities is now underway in the isolated, economically hard-
pressed, southeastern part of New Mexico—home of the Carlsbad
Caverns. The caverns were discovered in 1901 by cowboys who
thought that the plume they saw in the distance was smoke from a
wildfire. Instead it was millions of bats leaving the caves. In time the
caves became a source of fertile bat guano that was mined for years.

The Carlsbad Caverns were made a national park in 1932 and
have been a popular tourist attraction ever since. Originally, conditions were so primitive that visitors were lowered into the caves in
barrels and proceeded cautiously with small hand-held lanterns.
Today, visitors descend down a long, wide asphalt path, step onto
another narrower, illuminated path, and end their journey at a large,
underground cafeteria, returning to the surface by elevator.

Unaccountably, the National Park Service has decided to close the underground cafeteria as "not appropriate," notwithstanding the surveys showing that visitors believe it should remain, and the opposition of the City of Carlsbad, the Eddy County Commissioners, the Eddy County Land Use Committee, the Carlsbad Department of Development, and the volunteers who clean the cave, all of whom believe that the trash in the cave will increase with the closing of a carefully regulated cafeteria.[32]

When NPS Associate Regional Director Ernest Ortega told concessioner George Crump of the park service's decision, Mr. Crump, twenty-five years at Carlsbad, asked about the opposition of the various governmental entities. The answer: "This is not a democratic process."[33] When he brought up the public opinion surveys supporting the cafeteria, he was told, "The public response was emotional and not substantive." Thus the underground cafeteria, which Mr. Crump put in at a cost of nearly $350,000, must go, and with it many of the tourists who visit the area.[34]

Another effort of the National Park Service to make the nation's parks more inhospitable is taking place in Colorado at the popular Rocky Mountain National Park. There, amidst the beauty and grandeur of one of Colorado's most popular parks, Rex Walker runs the High Country Stable Corporation at Sprague's Lake on Bear Lake Road in Glacier Basin. The stables have always been there, originally as part of the Sprague Lodge that was bought out by the National Park Service. In 1959, a concession was established to provide visitors with the type of horse ride that is indigenous to the area.[35]

During the Carter administration, the National Park Service attempted to drive Rex Walker's operation out of the park, alleging that his stables were contaminating the water supply, were an inappropriate use of parkland, and were a source of congestion. But, despite years of study, the park service was never able to demonstrate that his stables were a significant source of pollution.

More recently, the National Park Service has changed its tactics.

Now the park service says Rex Walker's stables are located in a "wet-lands." Although neither a private study paid for by Rex Walker at a cost of $10,000 nor an investigation by the Army Corps of Engineers found that the area was a wetland, the National Park Service stood firm. "They said they didn't care what the Corps of Engineers said; they thought it was a wetland," reported Rex Walker. What is happening to horseback riding is not about congestion, not about pollution, and not about wetlands. "The hidden agenda of the Park Service," says Rex Walker, "is the elimination of horseback riding in the parks and limited use by the public of the park."[36]

The examples could go on and on, but the point is clear. Although the National Park Service and environmental extremists—those who oppose natural resource activities like timbering, mining, oil and gas exploration, and ranching—assert that in the New West tourism is king, they do all in their power to inhibit tourism in the national parks.[37]

Moreover the NPS and its allies use the parks as "beachheads" to assert federal control over more and more of the West, regardless of who owns the land. Yellowstone National Park includes 2.2 million acres of land, an area almost twice the size of Delaware. But it is surrounded by another 16.8 million acres that covetous bureaucrats and environmental extremists classify as part of the Greater Yellowstone Ecosystem.[38] Much of this area is federal land managed by other agencies, but as much as 25 percent of it, nearly 5 million acres, belongs to private citizens.[39]

In August 1990, the National Park Service released its "Vision for the Future" document—what became known as the "Vision Document"—which proposed that all lands surrounding Yellowstone be managed more aggressively to "conserve the sense of naturalness," "maintain ecosystem integrity," "improve biological diversity"—perfect phraseology for land managers since, meaning nothing, those words can mean everything.[40]

Nor is it just the Vision Document. Another attempt to impose the NPS's "vision" upon its neighbors was the NPS's "let it burn" policy, which resulted in more than a million acres being burned in and around Yellowstone National Park in the fires of 1988, including national forests and private land.[41]

Just as the NPS operated with a blind eye to the natural result of its fire management policy, so it has behaved regarding wildlife. For example, the NPS refused to make any attempt to control the dread disease brucellosis in the park's buffalo population.[42] Similarly, the NPS, in cooperation with the Fish and Wildlife Service, has ignored the pleas of its neighbors—the private citizens as well as the officials of the states of Wyoming, Idaho, and Montana—in pressing forward with its $13 million plan to "recover" the wolf in the region.[43]

As the Yellowstone fires, the brucellosis epidemic, and the wolf plan demonstrate, one of the great difficulties with the NPS is that its borders are not real borders. Practically anything can be seen as affecting Yellowstone National Park. Examples include "integral vistas" and air quality demands.

"Integral vistas" means essentially that park visitors have a right to pristine views, not only if they are standing on the boundary of a park looking inward (which is reasonable), but even standing at the same place looking outward! During the Carter administration, Secretary of the Interior Andrus ruled the Alton coal fields in southern Utah could not be mined because that activity could be *seen* from 5 miles away atop Yovimpa Point in Bryce Canyon National Park. There were no problems of pollution, noise, or safety, just a break in the integral vista.

Air quality provides yet another tool that can be used to turn national parks into beachheads of federal power. The Forest Service and the National Park Service, for instance, have asked Colorado to adopt restrictive controls on emissions that may harm such resources as water, plant life, and lichen in parkland. The federal government's case is extremely weak on the facts. However, if the federal government is successful, it will be able to control essentially all lands in the West. Imagine a map of the Western United States, with large "buffer zones" drawn around units of the

National Park System, National Wilderness System, and every other kind of special land classification. This would show just how far the federal control could reach.[44]

The U.S. government owns one-third of the nation's land, which should be enough. It isn't! With little regard for the taxpayer or for the local community, the bureaucracy continues to take more and more land under federal control. Acquisition of private lands by federal agencies is one of the great untold stories of greed and rip-off.

One aspect of the federal government's land acquisition program that is especially troublesome—and has been the subject of an investigation by the inspector general of the Department of the Interior—is the manner in which federal agencies use a land-purchasing entity or agent as a go-between to obtain the land. In situations in which Congress has neither told the federal agency it can buy the land in question nor given it the money to do so, the federal agency makes a list of the most desired land purchases, to be acquired generally over a three-year period.

At that stage the federal agency approaches a land-purchasing agent that agrees to buy the land for the agency and hold it until the agency has the money to buy it.[45] In many cases, for example, the land agent buys the land at a greatly reduced price—the landowner having taken a charitable deduction for the difference between fair market value and the price received—then sells the land to the U.S. government at the "fair market value,"[46] or quite often an inflated version thereof, according to the inspector general's report.[47]

Although the inspector general's report disclosed loss of federal funds that have resulted from federal agency's land acquisition program, it did not address two fundamental questions: why does the United States government need a middleman to purchase land from its own citizens,[48] and what is the result of these land purchases?[49]

First, the property owner takes a tax deduction for the difference between the selling price and the fair market value. Second, the land agent sells the land to the government at its "fair market value." Third, the land agent is paid for "costs" and "expenses," which the inspector general faults as excessive, unnecessary, or even illegal. Fourth, the land agent is typically a nonprofit, public interest entity that pays no taxes on its multimillion-dollar enterprise. Fifth, the lands, now in the hands of the government, are off the tax rolls of the typically hard-pressed local government.[50] Sixth, the purchased lands, once in productive use and generating income (multiplied through the local economy), now lie fallow. Seventh, the government will be asked to make federal "payments in lieu of taxes" as a small recompense to the local government that now has less productive income- and tax-generating private property.

Today, land purchases by the government are a multimillion-dollar business. For fiscal years 1986 through 1991, the federal government spent more than $992 million taking land off the tax rolls.[51] In 1994, the Clinton/Gore administration planned to spend $348 million to enlarge the federal government's dominion even further and requested $299 million for 1995.[52]

The NPS does not always buy land outright. Sometimes it simply designates private property as a quasi unit of the national park system. One example is the National Natural Landmarks Program, which first came to the public's attention in a series of articles written by the late Warren Brookes.[53]

Under the National Natural Landmarks Program, the National Park Service designates property it believes should be so classified.[54] While the NPS insists that such a designation carries no special meaning, the National Natural Landmark designation exposes the land to local land-use restrictions and to local, state, and federal bureaucrats and environmental extremists. The NPS, for example, has used the designation of National Natural Landmarks to target future land acquisitions.

So far, more than 587 such landmarks have been designated throughout the country, and thousands more are in the crosshairs of the NPS's regulatory apparatus. In the process it seems National Park Service employees have violated the law by surveying private property without the permission of the landowner. A 1992 investigation revealed that "land may have been evaluated, nominated, and designated without the landowners' knowledge or consent."[55] According to one NPS document: "The question of secrecy and publicity is a hot topic which will undoubtedly come back to haunt us over the years if this document becomes generally available to the public."[56] While this particular program has been applied throughout the nation, Western landowners have been singled out for abuse, intrusions, and attempts to seize their property.[57]

Today, the national park lands of the West little resemble what those who founded and helped to form them intended—a haven from the pressures of the day and a pleasuring ground for people. Because of the anti-people ideology of environmental extremists and, increasingly, National Park Service employees, parks have become less and less attractive to the ordinary person and, perhaps worse, more and more a base from which environmental extremists and their bureaucratic allies wage war upon the people and the surrounding communities.

CHAPTER 7

WHERE MAN IS A VISITOR

A FEW YEARS AGO, MY SONS (Perry, ten, and Luke, eight) and I visited Lake City, Colorado. Early one morning, long before first light, we drove up an old mining road to the trail head for our hike to the top of Red Cloud, one of Colorado's Fourteeners, a mountain peak more than 14,000 feet high.

It was light by the time we parked and began our hike. Although we couldn't see the sun, its reddish glow lit up the snow-covered mountain peak behind us. It was one of those incredible September days—sunny, bright, warm, with not a cloud in the sky. The trail stretched before us past mammoth boulders, up a rock-strewn drainage, and through a bowl-like meadow ribboned by the trail to the top.

After we had traversed the meadow, we reached a 13,000-foot ridge and there we rested. In time, I turned to look up to where we had yet to go. I had never seen anything like it. A long thin spine of mountain, like the backbone of some huge beast, pointed almost directly into the sky. It resembled a surrealistic painting, framed by the cloudless blue sky, some artist's vision of the stairway to Heaven. We climbed that spine, four, five, maybe ten steps at a time. One thing that kept the boys going was the sight of Red Cloud before us, seemingly within easy reach. I didn't have the heart to tell them that what we were seeing was a "false peak," that the real Red Cloud was still further ahead and towering above us.

At the top we celebrated! Then I saw Sunshine—another Four-teener—just a mile and a half away across a gentle wide saddle. And so we went on.

In some ways the hike back was harder. A few yards toward Red Cloud from Sunshine we left the trail and slid feet first down a talus-covered mountainside. We finally reached the trail that led us back across a valley filled with boulders, and then along a streambed, and on to the car.

I thought of that climb and of other similar adventures when in May 1994, Colorado Congressman Dan Skaggs (D-CO) introduced legislation to designate Longs Peak, one of Colorado's most famous Fourteeners, and 91 percent of Rocky Mountain National Park, as a wilderness. His rationale: "I don't want us having a souvenir shop on the top of Long's Peak or anywhere else."[1] It does not appear as if Mr. Skaggs has ever been to the top of Longs Peak, or any other Colorado Fourteener. There must be some other reason for wanting to declare so much remote country a wilderness. There is.

By federal law, a wilderness is "an area ('[of] at least five thousand acres of land') where the earth and its community of life are untram-meled by man, where man himself is a visitor who does not remain." It is also an area that "retain[s] its primeval character and influence, without permanent improvements or human habitation... [which] appears to have been affected primarily by the forces of nature [with] outstanding opportunities for solitude...."[2] Thus, wilderness areas are off limits to any type of motorized vehicles; logging, mining, oil and gas exploration, buildings or other structures, commercial activities, and mechanized off-road vehicles are all strictly prohibited. In the past, federal agencies have declined even to fight fires in wilderness areas.

Environmental extremists want to shut off more and more land in the West from human activity—economic or recreational.[3] Designating an area wilderness does that, flat out. Moreover, wilderness designation is a wonderful weapon even when environmental extremists are unable to win a wilderness designation for a particular area. For the "wilderness process" means endless studies and reconsideration that can make a purgatory of delay for Westerners who wish to use the land.

When the Wilderness Act was adopted in 1964,[4] it applied to a few high alpine areas mostly in Western states, what were once called "primitive areas" by the Forest Service. Advocates of wilderness designation had much bigger things in mind.

First, vast portions of the National Park System were designated as wilderness, thus effectively placing huge chunks of the nation's parks off limits to visitors and to the concessioners who served them.[5] Second, a series of studies was initiated by the Forest Service to determine which of the lands it managed were suitable for wilderness designation, a process that went on interminably.[6] Predictably, listing areas as "suitable" for wilderness gave impetus to a national campaign to legislate them as such. Third, the Federal Land Policy and Management Act of 1976 (FLPMA) (or the Bureau of Land Management Organic Act), which mandated a study of "roadless areas of 5,000 acres or more," was adopted,[7] dramatically increasing the area to be studied for possible wilderness designation.

Today, as a result of that three-pronged process, there are more than 33.2 million acres of federally declared wilderness areas in the eleven Western states. Vast amounts of the West—and even greater portions of the rural counties in which these lands lie—have been set aside forever. Washington State leads with 10 percent of the state in wilderness; Idaho is in second place with 7.5 percent.[8] More than

6 percent of Arizona, nearly 6 percent of California, nearly 5 percent of Wyoming, and nearly 4 percent of Colorado, Montana, and Oregon have been designated as wilderness.[9] California's 5.9 million acres of wilderness cover a larger area than either New Hampshire or Massachusetts. Washington's 4.2 million acres and Wyoming's 4.2 million acres of wilderness cover an area nearly as large as New Jersey and larger than Delaware and Connecticut combined.[10]

Today, most wilderness areas in the West are on lands managed by the Forest Service. Of the 8.7 million acres the Forest Service manages in Wyoming, 35 percent or 3.1 million acres are designated wilderness. In Washington, 29 percent of Forest Service–managed lands are designated wilderness. The percentages are similarly high elsewhere in the West: Montana, 21 percent; Idaho, 20 percent; California, 19 percent; Colorado, 18 percent; and New Mexico, 15 percent.[11]   Even the two states with the least wilderness have sizable portions of Forest Service lands set aside: Utáh, 774,000 acres (10 percent), and Nevada, 798,000 acres (14 percent).[12]

Two of the three Western states with the most national parklands have the most National Park Service wilderness. In California, 43 percent of national parklands have been designated wilderness, and in Washington 92 percent.[13] Likewise, the Western state with the most lands managed by the Fish and Wildlife Service—Arizona—also has the greatest amount of them designated as wilderness: 85 percent.[14] Arizona is also the only state that has had wilderness legislation adopted for the state's Bureau of Land Management (BLM) acreage: nearly 10 percent has been set aside as a result.[15]

Most Westerners believe that far too much land has been swallowed up by wilderness. They would like the wilderness battle to be over. They would like to be able to say that they fought hard to ensure that only those areas truly deserving of wilderness designation were listed, that they won some and lost some, but that they will be allowed to go forward and to work out the appropriate multiple-use activities for the federal lands not designated as wilderness. Unfortunately, the battle is not over.

Westerners hoped that once Congress decided which areas should be designated as wilderness, the lands not included would be the subject of "hard release." Simply put, that would mean that lands not designated as wilderness would immediately return to being managed in accordance with multiple-use principles. But that is not what happened. Lands surveyed for wilderness potential but not designated as wilderness continue to be at risk.[16] At present, these lands sit in a management netherworld that allows environmental groups to appeal and to sue whenever something they regard as "unsuitable" is proposed for the area.[17]

Moreover, yet another wave of wilderness designation is about to take place, various lands having been found "suitable" by the Bureau of Land Management. Unlike much of the lands managed by the Forest Service—high alpine and remote timber lands—lands managed by the BLM are mainly low-lying, wide-open, treeless prairies. And unlike the high alpine lands, these low lands are often used by Westerners for grazing. In addition, Western water rights would be trod upon by new federal demands for water to sustain the wilderness. That is, upstream water users might be told that they could not use their water rights because the wilderness areas needed the water.

The Bureau of Land Management wilderness study included some 612 wilderness study areas in eight Western states and 41 instant study areas in nine states, totalling more than 25 million acres designated as "Wilderness Study Areas" (WSAs).[18] The survey, various hearings, and congressional and administration review dragged on for years. In the end, more than a third of the 25 million acres were deemed "suitable"[19] for wilderness designation, the rest "unsuitable."[20]

Utah's experience—with 22 million acres of federal land managed by the Bureau of Land Management—illustrates the entire process. In the beginning, the BLM placed 3.2 million acres of Utah land in Wilderness Study Areas.[21] After years of hearings and public controversy, and after a change in administrations, 2 million acres were recommended to Congress as "suitable" for wilderness designation.

The response of environmental extremists was predictable: nothing less than 5.1 million acres—23 percent of all Utah's BLM lands, and nearly 10 percent of the entire state—should be declared wilderness and placed off limits to mankind. Isolating 10 percent of the land of a state will inevitably bruise its economy. According to a report prepared for the Utah Association of Counties, designating 5.1 million acres as wilderness would cost the people of Utah $13.2 billion annually and 133,000 jobs.[22] Nor would the blow fall only on such rural counties as Kane, Garfield, and Wayne. Salt Lake City would also suffer, with a loss of as many as 25,000 jobs.[23]

In most Western states, including Utah, local opposition to excessive wilderness land lockup, and the rigid unwillingness of environmental extremists to accept anything less than total victory, have made it impossible for Congress to move any proposals. In some cases an agreement has been made within a state's delegation, but environmental extremists from outside the state have stood in the way of final settlement.[24] This is not necessarily a blessing, for endless stalemate hampers the ability of Westerners to engage in economic activity. In Millard County, Utah, for example, one mining company is interested in developing a gold mine in the Confusion Range some 50 miles southwest of the rural town of Delta. The site of the potential mine was placed in a WSA, although the area is honeycombed with roads, which runs afoul of the requirement that a WSA be "roadless." The Carter administration, however, overcame that obstacle by simply calling the roads in the area "ways."

Although the area was eventually found to be "unsuitable" (twelve years after first being declared a WSA in 1979), the WSA must continue to be managed in such a way as not to "impair" its potential future designation, however unlikely such a designation would be given the opposition of Utah's congressional delegation. In other words, because of a political decision made fifteen years ago by the Carter administration, the area will remain in property purgatory until a wilderness act for Utah—including "release language"—is signed by the president.

Senators and members of Congress from outside the West, seeking to please their environmental constituency, do their best to turn virtually all of the West into a vast wilderness. A classic example is Congresswoman Carolyn Maloney (D-NY) of Manhattan's "Silk Stocking District" in Manhattan. Congresswoman Maloney represents one of the smallest districts in the country, smaller in size than the city of Cheyenne, but with more people than all of Wyoming.[25] Congresswoman Maloney has proposed the creation of what she calls the "Northern Rockies Ecosystem Protection Act," a massive proposal to designate as wilderness—biological connecting corridors, national parks and preserves, and wild and scenic rivers—some 21 million acres in five states.[26] Such a proposal would be devastating, not just to those who live in the rural communities, but to the states themselves.

The danger is not so much that the Maloney bill will become law. That is highly unlikely given the almost universal opposition of Western legislators, governors, and other leaders.[27] The real threat of such a bill is that it sets the outer limits of the debate. That is, it creates an artificial middle ground. "Compromise" between a far-out proposal like Maloney's bill and something proponents from a district or state may propose is hardly compromise. It is more like capitulation or surrender. As matters stand, for those unfamiliar with the facts of a particular wilderness debate, and most are, the position taken by local residents appears obstinate and obstructionistic.

Designation of an area as a wilderness is only the beginning—the nose of the camel in the tent. Designation is then used by environmental extremists to restrict the use of other lands and resources through the administrative process, appeals, litigation, and legislation. Two examples spring immediately to mind: wilderness water "rights" and wilderness "buffer zones."[28]

If an area has been designated as wilderness, environmental groups assert that Congress intended that the wilderness have a certain, as yet undetermined, amount of water. Such "reserved" water rights did not impinge on the water rights of Westerners when the wildernesses were high alpine areas where the water flow begins. They do pose a danger when the wildernesses are on low-lying lands, lands that lie below those with water rights vital to ranching or other economic activity. In other words, if low-lying wilderness areas have water rights that are senior to those of upstream appropriators, the federal government can demand that water from upstream enter the wilderness area. In the arid West, the ability to limit the availability of water translates into the ability to prevent the use of land.

An entire state's water rights can be put at risk this way. Were a wilderness area to be established in southern Utah where waters leave the state, Utah could be compelled to permit waters, to which it has a right under an interstate water compact, to leave the state.

A second issue regarding wilderness areas is "buffer zones." For years Westerners have opposed wilderness designation for fear that the mere presence of such areas would generate restrictions on surrounding, nonwilderness, multiple-use lands. Westerners have seen how park purists and environmental extremists have manipulated national parks to prevent the use of nearby nonpark federal or even private lands.[29] Precisely because Westerners worry about this tactic, nearly every wilderness bill has included a provision prohibiting buffer zones around wilderness areas.[30] True to form, however, the buffer zone language has been ignored. In Washington's Wenatchee National Forest, for example, the Forest Service closed a number of high alpine trails to off-highway vehicles because of the proximity of the Glacier Peak Wilderness Area. When challenged, the Forest Service asserted, "There is nothing contained within the State Wilderness Act which prohibits the Forest Service from creating a 'buffer zone'...."[31] Remarkably, a federal district court upheld the Forest Service.[32]

Another example of the executive branch's defiance of the law concerns "valid existing rights." Every wilderness bill includes language declaring that wilderness classification shall not abrogate "valid existing rights," to ensure that Congress not "take" private property. Thus, for instance, mining claimants with "valid existing rights" in wilderness areas have a constitutionally and statutorily protected right to use their property. But though the Forest Service pays lip service to "valid existing rights," it often effectively negates them by placing such stringent requirements on access to mining claims that it is virtually impossible for the miners to work their claims. One miner, for example, was told that the equipment he wanted to use would have to be "transported to the site using packhorses [since it] is customary to deny motorized access in operations of this type in National Forest wilderness areas."[33]

In Utah, in a quiet title action filed by Millard County under R.S. 2477, which allows local government to declare roads across federal lands to be public roads, the federal government filed a motion to dismiss. Government lawyers argued that when the area was declared a WSA, the federal government exercised a claim to the land that destroyed the county's rights under R.S. 2477. When the county responded that its rights were preserved by the "valid existing rights" language, the government argued that those rights had been waived. Fortunately, the federal district court sided with the county.[34]

In another situation involving wilderness lands—albeit in the Midwest—the Forest Service argued that the phrase "valid existing rights" had virtually no meaning. Owners of property bordering the Sylvania Wilderness in Michigan sought to protect their water rights as guaranteed by state law, arguing that those rights were protected by the phrase "subject to valid existing rights" as included in the Michigan Wilderness Act. The Forest Service argued that the phrase applied only to mining claims. The court rejected the Forest Service's motion.

It is for such reasons that Westerners fight wilderness designation with a passion that few outside the West understand.[35] Unfortunately, actual wilderness designation is not the only "no use" land classification that threatens Westerners.

The National Wild and Scenic Rivers System—a part of the National Park Service—is another device used to restrict, condemn, or seize private property. There are thousands of miles of wild and scenic rivers in the eleven Western states.[36] Currently, the law provides that the U.S. government can restrict all activities on or near such rivers.[37] Like wilderness designations, wild and scenic river designations are often made with total disregard of the rights and wishes of the local citizens.

In Nebraska, before portions of the Niobrara and the Missouri rivers were designated wild and scenic,[38] there was loud outcry from the citizens of rural Nebraska, and public opinion polls showed that the residents of Nebraska opposed the designation. Nevertheless, President Bush signed the bill into law, giving the National Park Service the authority to restrict activity along the river, to "establish detailed boundaries" encompassing up to half of the land alongside it, and to acquire a sizable portion of the lands within those boundaries.[39] With one thoughtless stroke of President Bush's pen, miles and miles of rural farmland were placed under federal control for no reason other than that it made people in America's big cities feel that they had "saved" a portion of "wild" America.

While wilderness and wild and scenic river designations can be made only by Congress, other restrictive land classifications can be imposed by administrative action that is virtually unseen. The Bureau of Land Management publication *Public Land Statistics 1992* lists a number of other restrictive land classifications that the agency can and does apply with great abandon.

"Areas of critical environmental concern" (ACECs) are those areas which, as a result of BLM's land-use planning process, require "special management attention... to protect and prevent irreparable damage to an identified value or to protect life and safety from natural hazards." ACECs are creatures of a little-noted provision of the Federal Land Policy and Management Act (FLPMA) that, like other such provisions, has been expanded beyond recognition. Under the FLPMA, "values" such as historic, cultural, or scenic areas, fish and wildlife resources, or other natural systems or processes may be designated as ACECs.[40] Note that the "historical" values are not historical enough to qualify under the federal protective legislation provided for such things[41]; the "scenic" values are not scenic enough to qualify as parks; and the fish and wildlife resources are not threatened or endangered enough to qualify for listing under the Endangered Species Act. Notwithstanding, the BLM has designated 4.5 million acres of ACECs in ten Western states,[42] restricting human activities within them.

The BLM also designates National Conservation Areas (NCAs), lands having "certain resource values identified in Public Law Statutes."[43] Such values can include "historic, scenic, archaeological, environmental, biological, cultural, educational, recreational, economic, geological, ecological, scientific, or paleontological values; aquatic and wildlife resources; and other wilderness resources." Under that list it is hard to think of an acre of land the BLM could not lock up. Today, nearly 14 million acres of BLM land have been designated as NCAs, 88 percent of which lie in California.[44]

Another designation program of the Bureau of Land Management can be applied to private lands as well as federal lands.[45] National Natural Landmarks (NNLs), are areas that are deemed "nationally significant representative[s] of the nation's natural [ecological and geological] heritage." The Bureau of Land Management has designated forty-three areas, encompassing more than half a million acres in ten Western states, as NNLs.[46]

The Forest Service also has so-called land management tools, such as so-called Research Natural Areas (RNAs), that it can use to place land off limits to multiple-use activities. In Colorado, for example, the Forest Service announced plans to establish a 695-acre RNA, called the Hoosier Ridge RNA, in Park County, Colorado, allegedly to protect the *E. penlandii*, an obscure alpine plant.[47]

Another example is the use by the Forest Service of what it calls "indicator species." In Arizona, for example, the Forest Service asserted that the goshawk (neither threatened nor endangered under the Endangered Species Act) is an "indicator species" that deserves special protection, such as placing its "habitat" off limits to multiple-use activity. In Nevada, a similar gambit was attempted, again regarding the goshawk, until a number of Nevada counties threatened a lawsuit for failure to adhere to proper administrative procedures.[48]

Yet another means by which the Forest Service seeks to lock up vast areas previously accessible to Westerners is what it euphemistically calls "de-roading." Jim Petersen, the editor of *Evergreen*, explains:

> "De-roading" is code for tearing up existing roads. It has been going on in grizzly bear habitat on Montana's Kootenai National Forest for more than two years. There, the U.S. Fish & Wildlife Service has resorted to locked gates to keep hunters, fishermen, berry pickers, and others out of the forest.[49]

Thus the wilderness battle wages on, seemingly endlessly. It goes on not just legislatively, as environmental extremists attempt to lock up the land in the West by congressional designation, not just administratively, as the bureaucrats seek to place more and more lands in restrictive land management classifications, but also before the courts of the land, as environmental groups try to throw yet another monkey wrench into the administrative process.

CHAPTER 8

ENERGY TO BURN

PRIOR TO JOINING THE REAGAN ADMINISTRATION in early 1981, I was
an attorney for the House of Representatives' Committee on Interi-
or and Insular Affairs and its Subcommittee on Mines and Mining.
During 1979 and 1980, the chairman of the Mines and Mining Subcommittee was Congressman Jim Santini (D-NV), a strong supporter of the wise use of the natural resources of the West.

One piece of legislation in need of revision and updating was the
Geothermal Steam Act of 1970. Several provisions of the act were
keeping geothermal power from becoming a significant source of
electricity. A few minor amendments of the 1970 act would permit
geothermal power to grow as an energy source. Chairman Santini set
about to offer those amendments. But before he could move the
amendments out of his subcommittee, we were informed that the
Subcommittee on Parks and Public Lands wanted minor protective

language for three national parks: Yellowstone, Volcanoes, and Lassen. That was acceptable to everyone.

The next time the subcommittee staffs met, the list of three parks had ballooned to twenty-five, and the minor statutory language had become much more complex and burdensome. With each succeeding meeting, the list of parklands and "geothermal features" that needed to be protected got longer and longer and the protective language broader and more ambiguous. In the end, the park protection language killed the legislation—which may have been the intent all along.

Today, twenty-five years after the Geothermal Steam Act was passed and fifteen years after it was decided that it ought to be revised, the act has yet to be amended. Paradoxically, all of this is happening with regard to an energy resource—clean, efficient, renewable, nonpolluting geothermal power—that the environmentalists assert they support.[1] (Since geothermal power uses heat from the earth's interior to generate electricity, it requires no fossil fuels to be burned.)

If that is what environmentalists do to an energy resource they say they like, what will they do to an energy resource they vehemently dislike—energy from hydrocarbon resources?[2] They have nearly killed it.[3]

It comes as no surprise therefore, according to the latest information from the Department of Energy, that America's dependence on foreign oil remained above 45 percent during 1994.[4] The reason is obvious. In late 1991, the *New York Times* reported that exploration for oil in the United States was at a fifty-year low. Not since Japan attacked Pearl Harbor has America done a poorer job of exploring for what is perhaps the single most essential element of our industrial society.

The failure is on the production side as well. In January 1994, the *Oil and Gas Journal* reported that U.S. oil production had fallen to its lowest level since 1958, less than 6.9 million barrels per day.[5] In less than a decade America has lost 2.27 billion barrels a day, which, based upon an average of $16 per barrel of oil, means a loss of $105 billion in production.[6]

Dependence on foreign oil and decreased production have devastating consequences. For example, recently I gave a breakfast address before the Kansas Independent Oil and Gas Association. During her introduction, then-Kansas Governor Joan Finney said that over the past decade 500,000 Americans had lost their jobs in the oil patch. Half a million high-paying jobs, which created wealth through the discovery and development of hydrocarbon resources, had disappeared in just ten years.[7]

The Rocky Mountain West has great oil and gas potential. According to the U.S. Geological Survey, the Rocky Mountain Region—which includes the Colorado Plateau and the Northern Plains—contains 80 percent of the undiscovered recoverable reserves of conventional onshore oil, that is, 2.92 billion barrels, and 82 percent of natural gas underlying federal lands in the lower forty-eight states.[8]

The twists and tucks, bends and folds that have created the scenic tableau of the West have also created the structural traps for the oil and gas that lie far underground. Since at least the early 1970s, geologists have believed that what they refer to as the Overthrust Belt—which runs the length of the Rocky Mountains from New Mexico, through Colorado, Wyoming, and into Montana—has enormous potential for the discovery of vast supplies of oil and gas.

As of the late 1970s, experts judged that the Idaho-Wyoming-Utah portion of the Overthrust Belt had as much as 15 billion barrels of oil and 75 trillion cubic feet of natural gas.[9] The hydrocarbon potential for the northern extension of the Overthrust Belt through western Montana was as high as 10 billion barrels of oil and 100 trillion cubic feet of natural gas.

The search for oil and gas is never easy. Those who search for new sources are called "wildcatters," the best of whom are that rare combination—hard-working scientist and creative artist. One look at the seismic maps used by petroleum engineers to determine where the deposits lie and where to drill shows the complexity and difficulty entailed.[10] Nor do all experts read those charts the same way, which is why some strike dry holes and some strike oil.

The best among them start with a theory, a speculation about how the land forms were created—land forms that they can see and read as easily as some might read a road map—and what took place below ground. Supplementing what they can see with what others have discovered through seismic lines and exploratory holes, they augment or alter their original theory. They then run their own seismic lines and drill their own holes to fill in the gaps in their theory. Even at this relatively early stage, such decisions—on running seismic lines and drilling holes—are made with great care. Those activities are expensive, and choosing the right spot is important.

After the lines are run and the holes drilled, either the theory is confirmed, askew in some way, or utterly wrong. If the theory is correct, the company must put together a "lease play" large enough to cover the size of the potential reserve and to finance all the expenses incurred not just on that play, but on all those that were "dry."

In the late 1970s, oil and gas operators sought to determine the full potential of the Overthrust Belt. They had their theories about where the oil and gas were, but they needed to run the seismic lines and drill the holes to confirm them. The exercise was highly speculative; less than 10 percent of "wildcat" wells yield an oil strike and less than 2 percent of them lead to actual development.[11]

One area on which the oil and gas industry focused attention was the Lewis and Clark National Forest in Lewis and Clark County in west central Montana. But the wildcatters needed complete seismic maps of the area. While much seismic work had been conducted in the region, there was one blank spot, the Bob Marshall Wilderness Area.

The geologists proposed to enter the area during the winter, so as to leave no trace of their having been there. On cross-country skies, they would set and later detonate their charges, take their readings, and be gone. Like hikers, they would have left only footprints, to be erased with the next snow or the melting in the summer, and taken only pictures, albeit of a slightly different subject—what lay beneath the ground. Neither the wilderness, nor those who care for it, would ever know that they had been there.

The environmental groups went nuts. They complained—and complained loudly. In the end, the Forest Service denied the permit, not only locking out those who wanted to enter the Bob Marshall Wilderness Area, but locking in knowledge that would have guided the nation's search for energy.

Nor was the lockout limited to specific, allegedly sensitive areas, such as the Bob Marshall Wilderness Area. It was regionwide, stretching up and down the Rocky Mountains, encompassing virtually the entire Overthrust Belt—because of delays, it was said, associated with a wilderness review process initiated during the early days of the Carter administration.[12] In Wyoming, Idaho, and Utah, as well as Montana, federal officials simply refused to issue oil and gas leases. Over a million acres of potential oil and gas lands were off limits to oil and gas exploration.[13] When Western oil and gas interests sued to remove the administrative roadblocks to leasing, the Wyoming federal district court ruled that the Carter administration's actions were "an unauthorized *de facto* withdrawal."[14] Less than a month later, Ronald Reagan was elected president.

In early 1981, Reagan administration officials began to process the oil and gas lease applications that had been pending for years. At last the potential of the Overthrust Belt as a new source of energy and of economic activity could be realized—or could it?

Using the National Environmental Policy Act (NEPA), various environmental groups filed lawsuits.[15] One challenged seven hundred leases covering 1.3 million acres in the Flathead National Forest in northwestern Montana and the Gallatin National Forest in southcentral Montana.[16] Another challenged a decision to permit exploratory drilling in the Shoshone National Forest in northwestern Wyoming.[17] The issue in both cases was whether the federal government had violated the NEPA and the Endangered Species Act (ESA) when it issued the leases. These cases are so basic to the whole issue of oil and gas development in the West that they bear some explanation.

In the case involving the Flathead and the Gallatin, the Forest Service had encumbered some leases with no surface occupancy (NSO) stipulations—that is, lessees could not occupy or use the surface of the leased land without further approval from the federal government.[18]

The leases also contained a threatened and endangered species stipulation that guaranteed compliance with the Endangered Species Act, even to the point of "disallow[ing] use and occupation" of the lease.[19] During the course of an environmental assessment (EA),[20] the government had concluded that no environmental impact statements (EISs) needed to be prepared since no proposal had been made to drill for oil and gas.

Environmental groups disagreed, asserting that a full-blown EIS, as well as a complete study under the Endangered Species Act, had to be prepared on the entire 1.3 million-acre area. Both the federal district court in Montana and the U.S. Court of Appeals for the Ninth Circuit agreed.[21] Although no one knew what oil and gas activity would take place, let alone where—in the unlikely event that oil or gas would be discovered and in the even more unlikely event that it would be developed—a study of the impacts had to be prepared.[22]

Furthermore, the court ruled that a full-blown study regarding the potential risk to threatened and endangered species had to be completed even in the face of what the court acknowledged was "incomplete information."[23] The court determined the federal agencies had violated the law by issuing leases without preparing an EIS and without obtaining a "biological opinion" to consider the effects of oil and gas activities on endangered species.[24] As a result, the court prohibited the federal agencies "from allowing any surface-disturbing activity on the lands already leased and from selling any more leases in the Flathead and Gallatin National Forests until they comply with NEPA and the ESA."[25]

The court's decision not only devastated those seeking to discover and develop oil and gas resources in the Overthrust Belt, it also was in direct conflict with an earlier decision of the U.S. Court of Appeals for the Tenth Circuit.

The Bureau of Land Management (BLM) had issued an oil and gas lease on 10,174 acres of nonwilderness, multiple-use land in the Shoshone National Forest in Wyoming.[26] Subsequently, the BLM approved an application for a permit to drill (APD) upon the leased acreage. Prior to issuing the lease, federal agencies prepared an EA, concluding that oil and gas lease issuance created no environmental impact.[27]

Furthermore, before approving the APD the federal agencies prepared a full-blown EIS that studied not just the 2.5-acre well area and the 10,000-acre lease, but some 39,000 acres around the proposed well. In the end, the agencies recommended that the application be approved, but they limited access to the site to helicopters alone. Yet even that access was too much for environmental groups. They sued.

When the district court ruled against the environmental groups on all counts, they appealed to the U.S. Court of Appeals in Denver. That court ruled against them as well, concluding that "NEPA is in essence a *procedural* statute," and that "the hybrid goal for this nation is to encourage the development of domestic oil and gas production while at the same time ensuring that such development is undertaken with an eye toward environmental concerns."[28]

Thus, two circuit courts of appeals, whose decisions define federal law in vast areas of the West, disagreed on the precise requirements of the NEPA regarding the issuance of oil and gas leases. In Wyoming, Utah, Colorado, New Mexico, Kansas, and Oklahoma, the NEPA did not require a full-blown EIS when oil and gas leases were issued on federal lands. In Montana, Idaho, Washington, Oregon, Nevada, Arizona, and California, the NEPA mandated a complete EIS on such leases.[29]

Conflicts such as these—between and among various federal courts of appeals—are resolved by rulings of the Supreme Court, sought by filing a petition for *writ of certiorari*.[30] The disappointed parties in *Conner v. Burford*, the Ninth Circuit case, asked the Supreme Court to hear their case.[31]

Although the impact of the *Conner* decision upon the various oil and gas lessees might interest the Supreme Court, the more serious effect was upon the federal government. After all, the burden imposed by *Conner* fell almost exclusively upon the federal land managing agencies. Those agencies would be required to complete years of environmental studies not just upon the 1.3 million acres of land involved in the *Conner* case, but upon millions of acres throughout the West. Had the federal government joined in asking for Supreme Court review of *Conner v. Burford*, the Court would almost assuredly have heard the case.

Unbelievably, given the significance of the *Conner* decision, the multimillion-dollar burden it would impose upon the federal government, and the manner in which it would frustrate the discovery and development of vital energy supplies, the solicitor general declined to join in the call for Supreme Court review. The Supreme Court, without comment, denied the petition filed by the lessees.[32] Federal oil and gas leasing activities were put on hold while the federal agencies spent years preparing the documents required under *Conner v. Burford*. Had the Supreme Court granted review and ruled that the Tenth Circuit's approach was the proper one, oil and gas leasing would have gone forward.[33]

Nor is it just lawsuits that have frustrated the ability to search for oil and gas in the Rocky Mountain West. The agencies responsible for managing federal lands under multiple-use requirements—the Forest Service and the Bureau of Land Management—have cut back on the amount of land made available to oil and gas leasing.[34] For example, in 1983, 134,000 leases (on 163 million acres) were on lands under the control of the Bureau of Land Management. By 1992, that number had been cut in half to 69,177 leases (on 51 million acres). On lands managed by the Forest Service, the amount of acres under leases fell from 32 million in 1985 to 6 million in 1993, a drop of more than 80 percent.[35]

As a result, Westerners involved in the search for oil and gas on federal lands find themselves embroiled in battles over what remains of federal lands after parks, wilderness areas, wilderness study areas, and national wildlife refuges have been subtracted—areas where oil and gas activity is not permitted. Today nearly half, well over 300 million acres, of the 660 million acres of federally controlled land is off limits to oil and gas leasing.[36] Yet, as is the case with Western loggers, that is only half the story; the half that remains, if not off limits, is so severely restricted as to make oil and gas activities difficult if not impossible. For example, "outstanding natural areas," "areas of critical environmental concern," "primitive non-motorized recreation areas," and many wildlife areas are all but closed.

In the past decade, under unrelenting pressure from environmental extremists, the Forest Service and the Bureau of Land Management have cut back dramatically on the ability of Westerners to search for and discover oil and gas. Even those federal lands ostensibly available to oil and gas leasing—not subject to special, sensitive controls—are being restricted.

For example, there has been a 300 percent increase in the use of no surface occupancy stipulations as well as a 50 percent increase in the use of seasonal stipulations in the Bureau of Land Management's San Juan Resource Area in Utah. In Wyoming, the Bridger-Teton National Forest has implemented a 400 percent increase in new no-lease areas, and the BLM's Green River Resource Area proposes to increase no-surface occupancy stipulations by nearly 50 percent and seasonal stipulations by 11 percent.[37]

The situation now taking place in Wyoming bears special mention for two reasons. First, it is worth exploring because, as will be explained below, the economic impact has been so serious. Second, the Wyoming energy experience is important because Wyoming has had a long tradition of exploring for and producing energy while preserving the unique quality of the human environment. As Rick Robitaille, executive director of the Petroleum Association of Wyoming, puts it, "We've been developing oil and gas here for more than one hundred ten years, and Wyoming still is what everyone else wants. We must have been doing something right if this state is still beautiful and worth protecting. But that doesn't matter to those who want to put oil and gas operators out of business."[38]

Wyoming oil and gas operations, in particular, have suffered from the paralysis of federal bureaucrats, who operate in part from fear of lawsuits by environmental groups and in part under orders from the Clinton/Gore administration.[39] New environmental studies on 95 percent of the national forests in the northern Rocky Mountain and intermountain regions have slowed leasing to a standstill. While some have been completed, leasing on Wyoming's Shoshone National Forest and the Beartooth Unit of the Custer National Forest, just across the Wyoming border into Montana, have been awaiting resolution for more than a year, with none likely in the foreseeable future. These decisions, it is said, are being held up because the areas fall within the Greater Yellowstone Area and thus merit further study, ignoring the fact that voluminous supplemental studies had already been completed.[40]

South of the Shoshone National Forest lies the Bridger-Teton National Forest, where, in the mid-1980s, the Forest Service's oil and gas leasing decisions awaited the completion of a forest land and resource management plan. After ten years and a federal expenditure of $4 million—as well as the hundreds of thousands of dollars expended by interested parties—leases were finally issued.[41] Then the Clinton administration stepped in, responding to the demands of environmental extremists. An order from Secretary Babbitt suspended leasing on the Bridger-Teton National Forest in order to "review" leasing policies.[42] Although the review was to take two months, it may never be done.[43] The Clinton administration's plans to implement "ecosystem management" portend more study, more delays, and more land off limits to oil and gas leasing.[44]

The numbers illustrate the point. In 1985, Wyoming received $189 billion in royalty revenue from oil and gas production. By 1993, royalty revenue had fallen by nearly a third to $136 million. Worse yet, production taxes have been cut in half, from $575 million in 1985 to $287 million in 1993. Accordingly, in the past decade, direct employment in the Wyoming oil and gas industry has fallen from 32,000 to 17,000 jobs.[45]

More than just federal land management agencies are involved in energy development in the West. Officials in the Environmental Protection Agency (EPA) launched a highly publicized assault upon oil and gas operators in southeastern New Mexico by alleging that every operator in the region had violated the Clean Water Act. The EPA, however, had long since agreed that the "sinkholes" dotting the land in the region were not "waters of the United States" and therefore not under federal jurisdiction. Water produced from oil and gas activities was therefore disposed of in these sinkholes. Despite the testimony of scientists that the water being disposed of was of a higher quality than the waters that, on occasion, would pool there, the EPA changed its mind and brought action against the various operators and others.

One of those others was Dr. Larry Squires, a man who, under contract, disposed of the produced waters upon land he owned as well as land he leased from the Bureau of Land Management. He not only had a lease from the BLM to engage in such activities, he had a letter from the EPA stating that the agency did not consider the "sinkholes" to be waters of the United States. Nevertheless, he was forced out of business when the EPA changed its position and issued a cease-and-desist order.[46]

Yet one more illustration of environmental regulation gone wild is Dr. Squires' attempt to challenge the federal government's jurisdiction over his private property.[47] The government has argued that the landowner could not challenge the federal government's cease-and-desist order until he had violated it and exposed himself to a $25,000-a-day fine and possible jail time.[48] If this is upheld, the government will be able to stop almost any activity in the West.

The Endangered Species Act poses still more problems for the men and women of the oil patch. One minor, relatively innocuous example demonstrates the level to which some federal officials will descend in order to use the Endangered Species Act to prevent the use of Western lands.

An oil and gas operator with a lease issued by the Bureau of Land Management for property in western Colorado was working out the details of the operating permit under which he would drill his exploratory well. The BLM advised him that, should he discover oil or gas, he would be required to take steps to ensure "the capacity of [the] area to serve in national efforts for the reestablishment and recovery of black-footed ferret populations."[49]

The BLM's action was not part of an approved habitat plan. No notice had been published in the *Federal Register* that the area that included the leasehold was to become critical habitat. The county had not been advised that the federal government was embarking upon a program to return this endangered species to the area. In essence, the BLM was taking a stand that, if successful, would lock up or greatly restrict yet one more parcel of land.

Environmental regulations have also limited the ability to refine and process oil and gas products.

In Casper, Wyoming, the Amoco Oil Refinery closed in December 1991 because of the high cost of retrofitting to comply with the expanded requirements of the Clean Air Act of 1990. More than 220 people were suddenly out of work—some took early retirement but nearly 200 left Casper—sending shock waves through an economy still suffering from previous cutbacks in oil and gas exploration. In addition, the ability of the residents of northern Colorado, including Denver, to obtain gasoline supplies was impaired, which in turn drove the prices of gasoline and other petroleum products higher yet.[50]

Not all of the problems stem from actions by the federal government. Some are self-inflicted, particularly by the state wildlife agencies.[51] In some cases, these entities act like outside interests because the federal government funds them liberally and because the agencies are often far removed from the economic needs of the citizenry.

In Wyoming, for example, the Wyoming Game and Fish Commission is often crosswise with the economic activity of its citizens. Since the commission receives a significant amount of funding from the Fish and Wildlife Service, it has little interest in the economic matters of the state.[52] In consequence, the Game and Fish Commission acts as an arm of the federal government in opposing multiple-use activities on federal lands. The commission has become the most obstructionist agency in Wyoming when property owners or others propose any economic activity on the land, particularly in cases regarding oil and gas activities. It is not unusual, for example, for the Wyoming Game and Fish Commission to demand that the Bureau of Land Management adopt leasing stipulations making oil and gas activities more costly or even prohibitively expensive. More disturbing still is an increasing tendency, on the part of the BLM, to accede to demands of the Game and Fish Commission to withhold entire areas from oil and gas leasing. Such a narrow focus on wildlife, to the exclusion of all else, ignores the fact that oil and gas reserves are "resources" as well, and more important, resources that help in large measure to support the people of Wyoming.[53]

Unfortunately, the government's intrusion—doling out federal dollars—into the life of Westerners is taking place not only in Wyoming, but throughout the West, and causing grave problems wherever it appears.

Like every other economic undertaking in the rural West, oil and gas activity faces a long and growing list of threats from federal environmental statutes, the restrictions they impose, and the enforcement actions they engender—laws such as the Clean Water Act, the Clean Air Act, the Endangered Species Act, and others too numerous to mention. The bottom line of so much environmental "policy" is not so much to ensure environmental protection as to prevent some activities from going forward at all. The great irony of this assault on the economy of the West, especially when directed against oil and gas activity, is that America needs more energy. Even the Clinton/Gore administration claims it supports the increased use of natural gas, a resource the West has in abundance.

During debate on the floor of the House of Representatives with regard to oil and gas leasing on Western federal lands, the director of the Bureau of Mines reported:

> Faced with this growing need for petroleum, we have to consider seriously the means whereby an adequate supply for the future can be obtained. We know that the domestic output does not meet the present consumption.... A diminishing output, with increased consumption, will make the United States more dependent upon foreign oil fields.[54]

This statement could have been made in 1969, prior to the adoption of the Mining and Mineral Policy Act of 1970, when Congress was considering United States dependence on foreign sources for vital mineral supplies. It could have been made in 1979, when a federal court was hearing arguments regarding the millions of acres of federal lands, rich in oil and gas potential, that had been illegally withdrawn. It could have been made in 1989, after a federal appeals court ruling that oil and gas leases on millions of acres of federal land had to be redone to meet procedural requirements.

Incredibly, it was made in 1919, when Congress debated the Mineral Leasing Act of 1920, which provided for oil and gas leasing on the federal lands of the West.

IF IT CAN'T BE GROWN,
IT HAS TO BE MINED

THE YEAR 1872 WAS AN IMPORTANT ONE in the history of the West. That was the year Congress adopted legislation to create America's first national park—Yellowstone National Park. In that year too Congress adopted a unified mining law to permit the development of some of the natural resources of the West—the General Mining Law (GML).[1] The federal law permits the discovery, delineation, and development of world-class mineral deposits beneath federal lands, in accord with current environmental statutes.

Now environmental extremists and Eastern liberals want to "reform" the law. In reality they would destroy it, an action that would be devastating to Westerners since mining is crucial to the Western economy.[2]

Nevada provides an excellent example. While using only one-tenth of 1 percent of the total land area of Nevada, mining generates

47,100 direct and indirect jobs, $1.37 billion in personal income, $81,170,000 in state and local taxes, and $4.7 billion in increased state output.[3]

As in most issues affecting the West, it is important to understand what this battle is *not* about. It is not about money. While leading proponents of "reform" decry the "rip-off," the "give away," and what they call the "great terrain robbery," their objective is not to secure money—a "fair return"—for the federal Treasury.[4] Rather, it is to stop mining activity altogether on federal lands. That was evidenced in this exchange between Senator Frank Murkowski (R-AK) and Philip M. Hocker of the Mineral Policy Center, an antimining advocacy group:

> Senator Murkowski: "If the mine is marginally profitable and if the 12.5 percent royalty on gross would put that mine out of business, would you support the 12.5 percent royalty, yes or no?"
>
> Mr. Hocker: "Yes."[5]

The money, like the northern spotted owl in the battle over the forests of the Pacific Northwest, is simply camouflage for the real issue. Money is the vehicle used by environmental extremists to convince the American public—a public that does not share their disdain for private property rights and economic activity—that they are pursuing a broader public interest objective, like getting a "fair" return.

The attack on mining in the West is not about royalties, but about whether mining is going to be permitted at all. Whether as a result of the destructive net royalty requirement, or the withdrawal of available mining lands, or the exclusive power of the secretary of the interior to mandate operating methods, or the activity-stopping, lawyer-boosting citizen suit proviso, mining on federal lands in the West is doomed if environmental extremists get control of the GML.

Unlike other federal laws relating to the extraction of natural resources, the GML places the initiative solely in the hands of private *individuals.* That is as it should be given the nature of hard rock minerals—their rarity, their relative obscurity, and the unique and even bizarre clues that reveal their location.

The U.S. government, however, is the worst possible entity to assess the mineral potential of federal lands. For example, in the early 1900s, the U.S. Geological Survey (USGS) declared that the area south of Tucson, Arizona, was "devoid of mineral characteristics."[6] Today, that same region produces a substantial portion of the nation's copper.[7]

The authors of the GML recognized that private property rights provide the incentive for people to struggle mightily, and often interminably, to discover something that will benefit society. As a result, the concept of "self-initiation" is the cornerstone of the GML; it permits private citizens, on their own, to search out and, upon discovery, to lay claim to valuable mineral deposits.

With "self-initiation" there is no need to spend time, energy, and money persuading federal bureaucrats that an area has mineral potential, let alone persuade them to permit private individuals to explore the area. If an area is not otherwise closed to the operation of the GML, then it may be explored for possible mineral deposits.

Having established a claim, the claimant is required to pay $100 per claim to the federal government each year. At that point, he or she has the right to develop the ore, but most claimants do not do so until they have obtained full title to the property itself, since full title is usually necessary to procure the necessary financing.[8] The document that conveys the title is called a patent.[9]

When a patent is issued, the miner must pay $2.50 an acre.[10] For a 20-acre claim, this translates to a cost of $50.[11] Needless to say, environmental extremists have stamped this small sum a colossal "rip-off." But the $2.50 an acre is only a tiny part of the cost of acquiring a patent. According to the Nevada state office of the Bureau of Land Management, the real cost—to the claimant—of acquiring a patent is nearly $40,000 per claim.[12] When Crown Butte Mines sought to obtain a patent on five partial claims (fractions of full 20-acre claims) totalling 43.9 acres, it spent more than $1.7 million on drilling-, assay-, and geology-related charges alone to prove discovery and to test the economic viability of the mining claims.[13]

Once patenting has been completed, theoretically the mine may begin to operate. That, at least, would have been the case if the General Mining Law had not been "amended" over the years by a profusion of federal environmental laws. Contrary to the charges of environmental extremists, the GML is merely a land tenure statute that sets out the manner in which discoveries may be made, claims held, and patents obtained. The GML does not address how the ore body may be developed to ensure compliance with modern environmental statutes and to prevent damage to other lands and resources. Those objectives are ensured by a long list of environmental statutes, including the Clean Air Act, the Clean Water Act, and the Endangered Species Act.[14]

In 1984, Viceroy Resource Corporation discovered a gold deposit in the Mojave Desert of California, some 100 miles east of Barstow, California, and 70 miles south of Las Vegas, Nevada.[15] Explorations throughout 1986 convinced the company that the site contained a deposit that could be mined commercially over a nine-year period. Following a positive feasibility study in July 1987, the company filed the required environmental documents (an environmental assessment) with the Bureau of Land Management. In November 1987, the BLM approved Viceroy's production permit.

At this point, two environmental groups challenged the BLM's decision, and Viceroy was asked to file a new plan of operation and to complete a full-blown environmental impact statement (EIS). By now, Viceroy had spent more than $23.5 million "to acquire, consolidate, explore and develop the property," but had yet to begin production.

As part of the EIS process, the BLM conducted a series of "public scoping" meetings in San Bernardino and Barstow, California, as well as in Las Vegas, Nevada—just a few of the more than sixty-three meetings conducted during the permitting phase of the project. What the BLM discovered was that the local residents overwhelmingly supported the new mine. Public opinion polls revealed that 71 percent of those in Searchlight, Nevada, and 83 percent of those in Baker, California, favored the project. Not surprisingly, opposition came from Los Angeles (200 miles away) and San Francisco (400 miles away).

In March 1989, the EIS was approved. Permitting seemed imminent—that is, just as soon as the sixty-day comment period was completed in mid-May 1989. But at this point the Fish and Wildlife Service listed the desert tortoise as endangered. The company contended that the mine site was west of the tortoise population and that during its five years at the site only one tortoise had been sighted on the far edge of its mining claims. Nonetheless, a $250,000 biological survey and assessment of the area was required. It found only three tortoises (actually one, sighted three times), which in any case did not inhabit a burrow on the mine site. Nevertheless, tortoise mitigation was demanded. Viceroy therefore purchased the 150,000-acre Walking Box Ranch for $635,000, retired the ranch's cattle-grazing permits, and sold the ranch, for half the purchase price, to the Nature Conservancy for use as a desert tortoise habitat. Viceroy also erected a tortoise-proof fence at the mine site at a cost of $100,000.

In the fall of 1990, following yet another EIS, this one addressing the tortoise issue, the BLM and San Bernardino County approved the project.[16] Finally, on October 31, 1990, four years and $30 million after the company first sought a permit, the BLM issued a Record of Decision giving Viceroy final approval.

Construction on the site began on April 15, 1991, and, after the expenditure of an additional $49 million, the first gold was poured on February 17, 1992. According to the Bureau of Mines, the mine has created 180 well-paying jobs in an area of high unemployment in eastern San Bernardino County. The mine has an annual payroll of $7.2 million, averaging $40,000 per employee per year, will generate $60 million in local, state, and federal tax revenues, and will purchase $145 million in goods and services over its initial ten-year life.

Another company, Crown Butte Corporation and its New World Mine in southwestern Montana, has just begun this long process. Whether it will survive remains to be seen.

The New World Mine, like the Castle Mountain Mine, is in an area that has seen great mining activity ever since the white man first came West.[17] Unfortunately, it is located near Cooke City, Montana, just outside Yellowstone National Park, and hence is part of what single-minded National Park Service employees and their environmental allies call the Greater Yellowstone Ecosystem.

When in 1978 Congress created the Absaroka-Beartooth Wilderness Area some 2 miles to the north and east of the New World Mining District, it specifically excluded the mining area as a result of a U.S. Geological Survey recommendation based on the mineral history of the area and its potential for future mineral development. The USGS was right. Today, the New World Mining District is the site of two underground gold-copper-silver–bearing, massive sulfide replacement deposits, which will support a ten- to twelve-year mine with year-around employment of 175 people with an average annual wage of $35,000 (as compared with the current average of $16,000) plus benefits. The annual payroll will exceed $7 million, with an additional $7 million expended on goods and services in the local economy. Eighty secondary jobs will also be created. Annual taxes will exceed $2.33 million.

According to plans, the total maximum area to be disturbed will be about 185 acres on which neither surface mining nor heap leaching—through the use of cyanide—will take place. Crown Butte Mines, Inc., plans an aggressive voluntary reclamation program, including the reclamation of past mining activity as well as 38,000 feet of roads, 20,000 of which were associated with mining activity long since abandoned.

Despite its relative proximity to Yellowstone National Park, the New World Mine will not be visible from any part of the park. The proposed mine falls under the jurisdiction of a number of federal and state agencies—primarily the Forest Service (the Gallatin National Forest is lead forest) and the Montana Department of State Lands—which will produce the Environmental Impact Statement. Meanwhile, environmental extremists, unfazed by the long history of this mining district and unimpressed by the significant contribution mining will make to the local, state, and national economy, have put the New World Mine in their crosshairs. These opponents have gone national already with their opposition in strident stories in the *New York Times* and elsewhere. Brushing aside the fact that mining has always been an integral part of the area, environmental extremists assert, "This is an inappropriate place to put a mine."[18]

Crown Butte Mines, Inc., has started down a long and very expensive road. Eight years have passed since it began its active exploration of the New World District in June 1987, during which the company has expended more than $35 million, and it anticipates capital construction costs of about $107 million.

Obviously, the GML does not allow or encourage environmental depredations; it allows lands to be explored only for mineral potential and, assuming all the various environmental requirements are met, to become important contributors to the economies of Western communities. How important, in just one state and for one mineral, is instructive.

In 1992, the copper industry had a combined (direct and indirect) impact on the economy of Arizona of $6.5 billion, which included $1.7 billion in personal income—that is, 69,400 jobs, $4.3 billion in business income, and $396.4 million in state and local government revenues. More than seven thousand government workers throughout Arizona received their salaries from taxes paid by the Arizona copper industry; of these, more than four thousand were involved in public education. The copper industry's $1.7 billion contribution included direct payments of $117.5 million to state and local governments in taxes and fees; $1.1 billion to other Arizona businesses for products and services; and $450.3 million in wages and salaries for more than twelve thousand copper industry employees.[19]

As a result of the multiplier effect, the total direct and indirect impact of the Arizona copper industry on the national economy was almost $28 billion in 1992—including $8.6 billion in personal income, over $14 billion in sales by businesses in other industries, and $1.8 billion in state and local government revenues. The Arizona copper industry generated, directly and indirectly, more than $3.5 billion in federal government revenue. The Arizona copper industry also lowered the nation's trade deficit in 1992 by selling $454 million worth of copper and copper concentrates to overseas customers.[20]

Amazingly enough, the copper industry produced this wide array of benefits from 174,900 acres—less than 0.3 percent of the land in Arizona.[21] No other sector of the economy uses such a relatively small amount of land to make such a large contribution to the nation's well-being.[22]

How much land is involved? Once again, given the contribution made and compared with other land uses, the land used for mining is almost insignificant. Today, metal mining—that is, mining permitted under the much-maligned 1872 General Mining Law—involves only 508,000 acres, a mere .022 percent of the nation's land area.[23] Today, nearly 32 million acres are used for roads. Moreover, the nation has more than 18,000 airports whose land area far exceeds that used for mining.[24] (Incidentally, the average commercial airliner uses 10,000 pounds of copper.[25])

Or just look around any room. Everything you see was either grown or mined. As a congressional committee noted nearly fifteen years ago: "It comes as a surprise to most that each American man, woman and child requires the annual mining of about 21,000 pounds of nonfuel minerals. Few realize that their colored television set contains about 35 mineral commodities and that a telephone contains about 40."[26]

Although the United States will always depend upon other countries for many of the building blocks of our modern society, the West possesses enormously important mineral resources. Copper is only one example. Molybdenum was discovered in Colorado in an area where none was thought to exist.[27] A major copper-silver province was discovered in northwestern Montana after many futile searches.[28] A major deposit of platinum was located in southwestern Montana in an area in which most geologists and other "experts" had long since given up looking for major ore bodies.[29]

With the United States as part of a worldwide economy and with prices determined, not in this country, but on the London Metal Exchange, mineralization does not become a discovery, let alone a developable ore body unless the deposit can compete with similar deposits in South Africa or Brazil or Gabon or the former Soviet Union. Yet in the United States, even with the highest wages in the world and upward spiraling costs for environmental protection, there are deposits—some as yet undiscovered—that can compete internationally, in part because of American technology, in part because of the high productivity of American workers.

But to find such deposits, miners must be permitted to search.[30] This is not as easy as it sounds. As of 1977, the Department of the Interior under President Jimmy Carter concluded that 42 percent of federal lands had been closed to hard rock mineral activity, 16 percent had been severely restricted, and another 10 percent moderately restricted.[31] Only three years later, the House of Representatives' Interior and Insular Affairs Committee, examining the Carter study, found that "[a]lthough no update has been made, it can only be assumed that lands now closed or restricted have increased by 10–15 percent."[32] With a prophetic look down the road, the committee worried:

> [I]t is impossible to predict the total acreage that will be severely restricted, or effectively withdrawn under the National Wilderness Preservation System—both BLM and Forest Service-administered lands—under the BLM's new "Areas of Critical Environmental Concern," and under other restrictions, withdrawals, classifications, and designations yet to be developed.[33]

The committee was right. Land lockup followed land lockup. Each Congress saw—and passed, in short-sighted succession—new proposals by environmental groups to lock up more land in wilderness areas and other single-use land classifications. Administrative appeals were followed by lawsuits and challenges by environmental groups. Today, an estimated 62 percent of federally owned and managed lands in the West are unavailable for mineral exploration under the GML.[34]

Now environmental extremists are directing a frontal assault on the law itself. Longtime opponents of Western mining, like Senator Dale Bumpers (D-AR) and Congressman Nick Joe Rahall (D-WV), have sought to replace the GML with an unworkable federal law that will not only destroy Western mining jobs, but cost the federal government hundreds of millions of dollars and years of costly litigation.

Like many matters of public policy, the GML of 1872 is not easily understood and is therefore easily misconstrued. It lends itself to the visual media—abandoned mine sites, tailing ponds, and other alleged horribles. "See," reporters cry out. "Isn't this awful! It's all because of a federal law that is still on the books, a law signed by President Ulysses S. Grant, of all things."

As for the print media, opponents of Western mining have filled national newspapers and magazines with articles decrying the "environmental atrocities" being perpetrated under "this outdated federal law," demanding an end to such "abuses." The articles run the gamut from the error-filled "The Great Terrain Robbery," as carried by the *Reader's Digest,* to Hollywood star Robert Redford's latest in the *New York Times,* "The Gold in Our Hills."[35]

This may make for great theater but certainly not for good public policy. Unfortunately, it can no longer be dealt with in an informed fashion. In today's climate, in large part as a result of what *Washington Post* editorial page editor Meg Greenfield calls the "melodramatic, wildly overstated end-of-the-world bulletins [from environmentalists] every hour on the hour for the last 20 years," it is almost impossible to discuss issues like mining sensibly[36]—certainly not in Congress, a pushover for the sky-is-falling rhetoric of environmental extremists.

Everyone who knows anything about the GML acknowledges that there have been some abuses in the past.[37] Nearly everyone associated with mining in the West wishes to remedy such deficiencies—but without gutting the mining law or destroying a major segment of the economy of the West.[38]

But for environmental extremists nothing short of a total rewrite of the federal law will do. While it is beyond the scope of this book to examine the various bills on the subject, the three fatal flaws of some are worth noting: (1) royalty payments; (2) a leasing and land-use planning system; and (3) citizen lawsuits, "unsuitability" designations, and operating standards that are impossible to meet.

Let's look at the first of these, royalties. Like the United States, other large countries on whose federal lands significant hard rock mining takes place do not exact a royalty for the production of mineral resources—not Australia, not Canada, not South Africa.[39] Those governments recognize the truth as declared by one commentator on the subject:

> The lack of rental or royalty does not mean that the federal government receives no return on its minerals. The various tax consequences of mining are too complicated to deal with here, but hard rock mineral development under the Mining Law, like any income-producing business, eventually produces some direct or indirect payment to Uncle Sam. The argument for greater revenue return is thus not an overwhelming argument for reform of the Mining Law.[40]

Ironically, the author of this rather thoughtful and thoroughly correct statement is John Leshy, solicitor of the Department of the Interior under Secretary Babbitt.

The Department of the Interior has concluded that an 8 percent royalty would cost 1,100 jobs in the first year of enactment alone and rob the federal Treasury of $11 million in tax revenues annually.[41] A study by Cooper & Lybrand disclosed that, over a ten-year period, 44,000 jobs would be lost as well as $422 million in tax revenues.[42]

The reason is simple. Ore is recovered only insofar as technology, economics, and operating conditions will permit. To determine whether the ore is worth recovering, one must, as always, calculate the cost of recovery and the price of the ore at the mine mouth, and, these days, such added factors as the cost of delay in moving forward with a project, the cost of environmental compliance, and the cost of taxes and royalties, if any. As royalties rise, more ore becomes uneconomic and must be left in the ground. Make the royalty high enough and some mines will never open.[43] With the tens of millions of dollars required to open a mine, there will just not be enough economically recoverable ore to recoup the investment.

A good example is the Stillwater Complex in southeastern Montana. The mining company has spent about $110 million in capital expenditures to develop America's only platinum and palladium mine. The company employs 300 people with an annual payroll exceeding $16 million in an economically depressed area, pays $2 million in state and local taxes, and purchases $21 million of goods and services each year, but it has still to turn a profit. Yet it is the only such mine in the country, or even in the Western world. The only other sources of these metals, which are used in automobile catalytic converters, are South Africa and the former Soviet Union.[44]

Unfortunately, the royalty provision is not the only aspect of the new legislation that will help to kill the mining industry in the West. The second is the leasing and land-use planning system requirements in various bills, such as designating federal lands as unsuitable for mining, that will put an end to the concept of self-initiation—and hence kill mineral exploration on federal lands in the West.

Mineral deposits of sufficient quality and quantity to justify the investment necessary to mine, mill, and otherwise process them are truly small, isolated, geologic quirks of nature. Only a tiny fraction of mineral prospects are ever turned into producing mines. Exploring as many as ten thousand mineral prospects may yield only a single mine. This reveals two basic truths about mineral exploration. First, a broad-based search, over as large an area as possible, dramatically increases the likelihood of discovering recoverable ore bodies. Second, commercial ore bodies can only be developed where they are found.

All of this sounds rather fundamental, even simplistic. Yet it seems to have slipped by those in Congress who would transfer the search from the hands of geologists and prospectors to the hands of federal bureaucrats, all the while removing vast amounts of federal land from the search. In doing so, they are helping to create a self-fulfilling prophesy—that America has run out of world-class mineral deposits. It has not. But if these antimining measures are pushed through, America will have lost both the will and the ability to search.

To convert the current mining law, which permits the self-initiated search for minerals upon federal lands not otherwise closed to mining, into one in which the prospector must first obtain permission to conduct a search, is just another way of saying "no." A look at any current federal mineral program demonstrates that anyone in Washington, D.C., can say "no," and no one can say, unequivocally, "yes." For this very reason, America's search for oil and gas in the Outer Continental Shelf (OCS) is in shambles today—petroleum companies having been driven to search in other countries.[45]

The third destructive aspect of current mining reform proposals is the dramatic, unprecedented enhancement of the ability of private citizens, at any stage in the process, to sue to stop permitting, to stop mining, or to declare an area off limits to mining as "unsuitable."[46] In other words, after the expenditure of tens of millions of dollars, after adopting mitigation measure after mitigation measure, and the very day before the ground breaking ceremony, environmental extremists could sue to stop the project. What responsible corporate entity would risk such a possibility?

This matter of citizen lawsuits, now an almost accepted part of every environmental statute, bears special mention. For nearly two hundred years, only the U.S. government could sue on behalf of the American people. Since the power to sue and to impose federal fines and sanctions is awesome, various restrictions have hitherto been imposed: regulators empowered to file lawsuits are answerable to and supervised by federal officials appointed by the president, with the advice and consent of the Senate; they perform their duties via a carefully constructed chain of command and control; and, finally, their conduct is constrained and subject to censure through a myriad of laws to ensure that they behave legally, ethically, and responsibly.

Over the past two decades, however, in numerous environmental laws, the power to sue has been delegated to private citizens. Unlike their colleagues in the federal government, those who bring citizen suits— mostly powerful environmental groups—are supervised by and answerable to no one. Only they decide whom they will sue, why, and how.[47]

Such lawsuits are undertaken by environmental groups not simply to ensure that the law is enforced but to change the law. Legislative defeat can be transformed over time, and before a variety of federal courts, into a judicially created victory and expanded legal authority.

The use of citizen suits to create new law is a well-known tactic in the regulatory community. Many federal bureaucrats look to citizen lawsuits to extend their authority. For example, the Environmental Protection Agency (EPA), commenting on a new regulation, noted that "[t]he final rule establishes... requirements that are easy for... citizens to enforce through citizen suits."[48]

That is exactly what legal scholars such as Bruce Fein fear. "The inescapable result [of citizen suits]," Fein writes, "is a costly and unrestrained growth in litigation against federal agencies," the consequence of which is "to shift policy making from the legislative and executive branches of government to the unelected and politically unaccountable judicial branch."[49]

The presence within the Clinton/Gore administration of many former top environmental leaders adds a new dimension to those fears. The Clinton/Gore administration welcomes "sweetheart lawsuits" and settles them quickly under terms advantageous to the environmental group bringing the suit. In October 1993, the Justice Department and the EPA even sponsored a meeting with environmental groups to discuss how the Clinton/Gore administration and environmental groups could cooperate on citizen suits.[50]

For a very different reason, businesses are similarly anxious to settle citizen lawsuits. Corporations, fearing years of costly litigation, want to know what it would cost to get on with the business of doing business. These settlements do more than enrich the environmental groups bringing the suits. Often they expand the reach of federal regulations, implementing policies and procedures that may not be justified, either environmentally or economically.[51]

Unfortunately, the war against mining in the West is not confined to the battle being waged on Capitol Hill over the future of the GML.[52] Nor is the battle only before regulatory agencies through whose hoops and over whose hurdles mining operations are forced to jump. Today, a frontal attack on the mining law is being waged by Secretary of the Interior Bruce Babbitt. Despite the federal law stating that the secretary must issue patents to those claimants who meet the requirements of the GML, Secretary Babbitt refused to comply until ordered to do so by a federal court.

The precedent was set by his predecessor, former Secretary Manuel Lujan. In 1991, Lujan placed a moratorium on issuing patents. He was overruled by a federal court in Colorado and again by the U.S. Court of Appeals for the Tenth Circuit.[53]

Secretary Babbitt's approach is more sophisticated. Instead of declaring a moratorium, he created a *de facto* moratorium by withdrawing the authority of other officials to issue patents, taking that authority solely upon himself.[54] Most suspected it was a clever ruse for further delay, most especially after Babbitt, during testimony on Capitol Hill and again before the National Press Club, brought up the patent application by Barrick Goldstrike Mines, called the GML "ludicrous," and urged Congress to change the law before he "complied with it."[55] Barrick Goldstrike was forced to take Babbitt to court.

The federal magistrate found that Secretary Babbitt had indeed effected a *de facto* moratorium and in so doing had engaged in a "shameful" refusal to adhere to the letter and the spirit of the law. Finally, concluded the magistrate:

> This labyrinthine process is not the only evidence of Secretary Babbitt's intent to delay patent issuance.... This willful

delay by the Secretary... is inexcusable [for] he has disman-
tled an efficient system and replaced it with a system *intended* to delay. He publicly opposes both the Mining Act as it
stands, and Barrick's efforts to use the law to its advantage
(emphasis in original).[56]

When Secretary Babbitt next testified on Capitol Hill, he stated
that he had "a handful of pre-1990 first-half certificates and patents
[that] have either been signed or will be signed this week [and that]
[t]here are no old ones in [our] office at this point."[57] Four senators
found differently. A very strongly worded letter to Secretary Babbitt
said, "Your Department's own data reveals a different story [from the
one you presented to the committee]... [Y]ou have no discretion to
delay processing patent applications for the purpose of awaiting proposed changes in the law.... You have a congressional obligation and
duty to fulfill and we expect you to carry it out immediately."[58]

Finally, on May 17, 1994, Secretary Babbitt signed the patents
over but bemoaned the alleged loss to the taxpayer. Although Babbitt
asserted that he was handing over $10 billion, what he was actually
handing over was the right to spend billions in order to recover ore
and in the process provide jobs, pay taxes, support communities, and
expand the economy.[59]

How surreal it all is! A secretary of the interior who decries the
outrageous behavior of Westerners seeking to eke out an existence to
provide for family and community, while he himself ignores the
requirements of the federal law.

What Babbitt and his allies are doing is trying to stop mining altogether in the West. It is a purposeful, planned, and carefully orchestrated assault that puts at risk a significant portion of the economy of
the West.

CHAPTER 10

THE FALSE HOPE
OF TOURISM

LIBBY, MONTANA, A TINY LOGGING TOWN surrounded by other tiny logging towns and by a once abundant and thriving forest, is scrambling. The surrounding forests have been virtually shut down to logging, and an attempt by a major mining company to develop a world-class deposit is being stymied by environmental extremists as well as the Fish and Wildlife Service. Libby would like to develop a ski hill for alpine and cross-country skiing, but fears what the Fish and Wildlife Service would demand as "mitigation" for disturbing grizzly bear habitat. Other development is also on hold because of the demand of the Environmental Protection Agency that Libby improve its air quality. Libby's air quality suffers from its inversion layer and the burning of wood for heat, the only fuel many Libby residents can afford. It's a "Catch 22" situation. They cannot afford cleaner burning fuel without better jobs; they cannot have better jobs without cleaner air.

Moreover, the recreational pursuits of the people of Libby are being limited because the national forests that surround them are restricted by the same approach to grizzly bear management that is taking away their jobs. The U.S. government asserts that grizzly bear habitat can only have .75 miles of road for every square mile of forestland, so Forest Service roads are being gated and closed.

As if that weren't enough, the largest nearby body of water, Lake Koocanusa—a 90-mile-long reservoir that has been a magnet for fishermen and campers—is now being used to provide water to "save" the salmon downstream. The 300-yard barrier of knee-deep mud surrounding the receding lake has caused the locals to refer to their lake as "Whocanuseit."

Today, Libby residents are searching desperately for new jobs so that the men and women who love the isolation of their remote and beautiful community can continue to live there. One solution, they are told by the environmental groups and their allies from academe, who are responsible for closing the forest to logging, is tourism. It is an answer Westerners repeatedly hear when they ask how they are to survive once their industries are destroyed. It is a lie.

A recent study conducted in connection with the University of Montana School of Economic Research reveals that, in order to replace the timber jobs already lost, 675,000 visitors to Libby would have to spend more than $100 each on their way through town.[1] This has led one resident to jest, "We're planning to set up roadblocks to make sure we get that amount from everybody passing through."

Tourism is an important part of the economy of the West. But it is not now and will never be the complete answer.

For one thing, many Westerners like what they do for a living and have no desire to change. Thus, when environmental activists like Oregon's Andy Kerr come into ranching towns like Lakeview, Oregon, and say that "more espresso [will be] sold than barbed wire [in the future in Lakeview]," it sounds more like a taunt than sound advice.[2]

For another thing, portions of every Western state will never be year-round, or temporary, tourist attractions, even if they wanted to be.

The *Denver Post* reported that for every Aspen, Vail, or Telluride, there is a Lake City that, while conducting a reasonably good tourist business in the summer, all but rolls up its sidewalks during the winter.[3]

My own hometown of Cheyenne, Wyoming, features the world famous "Cheyenne Frontier Days—The Daddy of 'Em All" during the last ten days in July. With daily rodeo events for big prize money, night shows with famous country and western singers, parades, and a host of other events, Cheyenne does a thriving business in July. But once it's over, Cheyenne reverts to being just one more town on the way to Yellowstone National Park. Growing up there, we used to joke that there were two seasons, Cheyenne Frontier Days and winter.

Of course, Cheyenne is Wyoming's largest city at 50,008 and the state capital, so there is something else to do there. The Western communities that depend solely on tourism are not so fortunate.

Several years ago an attorney from Connecticut told me what happened after her family fell in love with the West and, in particular, New Mexico. Her father left his corporate job in the East and hung out his shingle in Angel Fire, a beautiful little town within sight of New Mexico's highest mountain—Wheeler Peak.

Her family has gone back to Connecticut. As the lawyer told me, "There were two seasons outside of the tourist season, the mud season and the dead season. There just wasn't enough economic activity to support one more family."

Ironically, some of the environmentalists who agitate for a "New West" totally dependent upon tourism will often turn around and condemn some of the results. In a *New York Times* commentary, Hollywood's vocal environmentalist Robert Redford attacked "mining, logging, grazing and the newest shovel on the block, real estate development."[4]

Redford should know. Towns like Aspen and now Telluride, Colorado, have become "in spots" for the nation and Hollywood's elite, places where they can jet in to ski, sun, and savor the jazz. But as such communities become increasingly monied, the question stands out: where will the less affluent live?[5]

Nonetheless, environmental extremists and their allies in Congress and in the various federal agencies continue to claim that, as Bruce Vincent of Libby says with bitter irony, "tourism is our future."[6] However, there is a great difference between what those inside the Washington, D.C., beltway promise and what they deliver. Perhaps the best example is the promise made to the people of northern California about the creation and expansion of the Redwood National Park astride Highway 101 north of Arcata, California.

What is now known as Redwood National Park was created in two segments: the first in 1968, the second ten years later. In 1968, Congress created a 58,000-acre park over the objections of the Sierra Club, which demanded a 90,000-acre park in the Redwood Creek drainage. Since 27,500 acres of the 58,000 total had been preserved in three California state parks, the net expansion was 30,000 acres with 2 billion board feet of redwood and Douglas fir timber.[7] At the time, Congress estimated that the cost of acquiring 30,000 acres would be $92 million.[8]

Environmental groups asserted that the federal acquisition of 30,000 acres would not result in job loss, claiming that increases in tourism and higher allowable timber harvest levels on the Six Rivers National Forest would make up for any park-related unemployment.[9] Two high-ranking officials, one of them Secretary of the Interior Udall, testified that there would be a net employment gain. Their testimony was incorporated in a written report:

> After its first year of operation, the Redwood National Park will create more jobs than it will eliminate in Del Norte County. During the first year, however, there will be a net loss of 25 jobs. By five years after Park Service acquisition of the redwood lands, direct employment associated with the Park will have created 95 more jobs than would have been provided by the displaced lumber industry.
>
> We estimate that such acquisition will result in an immediate

loss of $252,000 in real estate taxes to Del Norte County, and an immediate loss of 235 jobs in the timber industry. After five years, however, we expect the stimulating effect of expanding tourist businesses to eliminate the loss of county revenues and to result in a net gain of 273 jobs in the area. By that time we estimate that there will be increased visitation of 950,000 visitor-days per year over the present visitation to the two State parks within the proposed Redwood National Park boundary....[10]

The environmental groups that advocated the acquisition of private land for the park were bullish on tourism, as was the National Park Service: "After establishment of such a park, assuming adequate development, total attendance is estimated at 1.2 million visitor days by the fifth year of operation, and 2.5 million by the fifteenth year...."[11]

Every prediction was false.

To begin with, the total cost to the taxpayers of the 1968 taking was over $306 million—two and a half to three and a half times greater than the U.S. government estimated and six to ten times greater than the various estimates of the Sierra Club.[12] Actual job losses due to a decline in timber industry employment were 718 local and 2,039 regional jobs.[13] Between 1980 and 1986, jobs with the National Park Service fell, from a high of 100 full-time and 232 part-time to 73 full-time and 139 part-time jobs.[14]

The greatest difference between the abstract and the actual was what happened regarding tourism. Ten years after the park was created, visitor days reached slightly more than 39,000—less than 4 percent of what the National Park Service had predicted.[15] More telling, the National Park Service numbers revealed that the vast majority of those counted as visitors to the Redwood National Park came to visit areas that were attractions before the park was formed. In 1975, for example, almost half the total visits were made to one of two locations, the Crescent Beach area—an oceanfront setting with camping facilities—or the Lagoon Creek picnic area—an attractive setting featuring picnic tables and other amenities beside U.S. Highway 101. Only 4 percent of the park visitors stopped at the Lyndon B. Johnson grove located in the heart of the 1968 acquisition.[16]

The best statement of the failure of tourism was given by Gloria Zuber, president of the Orick Chamber of Commerce. Orick, the city closest to the Redwood Creek portion of the Redwood National Park, should have benefited from increased tourism at the park. Ms. Zuber testified in 1977, nine years after the park was created:

> There has been a drastic and severe decline in the number of businesses operating in Orick since the creation of the Redwood National Park (RNP) in 1968. In 1968 we were informed that the next 10 years, 1968–1978, were to be a period of transition to tourism. Tourism was to be the major base of Orick's economy. However, RNP is one of the least visited National Parks in the country. Unemployment in our area is twice the national average—14.6 percent—and the RNP has helped relieve our high rate of unemployment by hiring ONE local resident. Any expansion whatsoever to Redwood National Park would be highly detrimental to Orick and its surrounding communities.[17]

Ms. Zuber's warnings notwithstanding, the Sierra Club and others demanded that the park be expanded.[18] The lessons of the recent past were totally ignored.

Sierra Club and Secretary of the Interior Cecil Andrus' estimates of the final cost of the new expansion varied from $150 million to as much as $359 million. Timber industry representatives placed the cost at between $600 million and $750 million.[19] The congressman from the district predicted that land acquisition would cost "one-half billion dollars."[20]

As to jobs, the Sierra Club testified that any jobs lost due to park expansion would be lost anyway, so it didn't matter; the U.S. government testified that the number of lost jobs would be between 921 and 1,268.[21] By contrast, economists for landowners foresaw a loss of between 2,230 and 2,700 jobs; the local congressman cited the work of another economist who projected that the destruction of the tax base of the area would be an annual loss of $9.6 million.[22]

Once again, the Sierra Club and others predicted that the new park would "enhance the future economic prospects of tourism in the two county park regions. The diversity of redwood recreational experiences will be substantially increased."[23] Interestingly, this time around no firm job numbers were offered. Landowners, however, could see no reason to be optimistic about the future of tourism: "Actual visitor days to Redwood National Park are running at less than 5 percent of the projections made to Congress a decade ago. Adding acres will not increase the number of visitors."[24]

The inevitable happened. As of March 1981, the National Park Service estimated that the total cost for the 1978 expansion would likely exceed $1 billion—two to three times the National Park Service's original estimate. In addition, by January 1981, the U.S. government had paid out nearly $33 million in job entitlements to over 2,500 recipients and had cut allowable timber harvest in the Six Rivers National Forest by nearly 50 percent compared to 1971 harvests, causing the loss of 870 direct jobs and nearly 2,500 regional jobs.[25]

As for tourism, the National Park Service "experts" were wrong once again. Instead of the predicted 1.6 million visitor days by 1983, the number was 42,464 or 2.7 percent of the estimate.[26] Visitor hours are up about 1 percent while the length of stay is still less than one hour.[27] One reason the park has so few visitors is that, contrary to their public pronouncements regarding tourism, environmental groups and the government moved to limit and discourage use of the park. Superintendent Robert Barbee, for instance, apparently believing that two thousand annual visitors to the Tall Tree grove area of the park were "too many," curtailed access to the area to a day's hike along a footpath. (When the area was private property, people could drive right up to the Tall Tree Grove.[28])

The Redwood National Park experience—like that of the creation and expansion of other federal restricted lands (parks, wilderness areas, and others)—suggests that the old phrase, "one hand giveth, while the other hand taketh away," should be "one hand taketh away, while the other hand taketh away as well." In 1968, there may have been novelty in the representation that federal parklands would attract tourists sufficiently to replace the jobs lost by taking over private property. No one should have been fooled ten years later when the park was expanded to include the lands environmental elitists had demanded all along. No one should be fooled today.

There are other ways to prevent people from using parks. The Fish and Wildlife Service has placed the wolf in Yellowstone National Park. Over the opposition of thousands of rural Westerners, Secretary of the Interior Bruce Babbitt is taking steps to ensure that eventually one hundred wolves will roam throughout Yellowstone, with two hundred more in both Idaho and Montana.[29] Perhaps realizing that most Americans are not in touch with the thrill of returning the "wild" to Yellowstone, the federal government is now asserting that introducing the wolf will increase tourism.[30] Oh? The wolf is known to be a reclusive, nomadic creature of the night. How can such a creature be seen by tourists in a 2.2 million-acre national park, only a small portion of which is accessible by roads? It can't. This assertion, like the promised jobs in the Redwood National Park area, is the bait before the switch.[31] The switch in this case will be to close portions of the park to protect the wolf's habitat from being disturbed by humans.[32]

To put it bluntly, environmental extremists don't want tourists to see the wolf. At least one of them has even admitted that part of the reason for placing the wolf in Yellowstone is to frighten away tourists. Mark Obmascik, environmental columnist for the *Denver Post*, wrote

> [T]he plan also will bring back another ingredient that has been vanishing from the western back country. The ingredi-

ent is fear. Wolves are killers. They run in packs and rip the guts out of their live prey. They don't think fawns are cute and cuddly; wolves look at Bambi and see fresh meat. Sometimes wolves look at humans the same way.

Although wolves usually try to avoid people, they have been known to order up an occasional course of homo sapiens, especially foolish specimens of the species.... [This] could serve as a rude awakening for hordes of recent western visitors who now view the back country as an adventure theme park.... People will think twice before traipsing into the back country.[33]

If wolves don't attract tourists, maybe snails can be used as inducement. In Kane County, near the small (population 3,289) southern Utah town of Kanab, endangered snails have been discovered upon the property of Brandt Child. Mr. Child, who bought 400 acres of land and its accompanying precious water rights—several ponds are upon his land—for commercial purposes, has been told he can't use his property because of the presence of the Kanab ambersnail. "Listing the half-inch-long snail may prompt Child to sell the land to the government," one federal official said.[34]

What does the U.S. government intend to do with the land? According to Mr. Child, Fish and Wildlife officials told him they intend to build a visitor center on a portion of the property and flood the rest of the land so that people will be able to come from all across the country and watch the snails grow.[35]

For a number of years, environmental extremists have been asserting that designating wilderness areas created jobs in local communities and that there was a net economic gain to such land lockup. That was until grassroots activists as well as county leaders attempted to quantify the impact of wilderness designation. A remarkable work in this area, performed for the Utah Association of Counties by Dr. George F. Leaming of the Western Economic Analysis Center, analyzed the cost of wilderness designation to Utah and Utahans. Dr. Leaming's conclusion: a 5-million-acre wilderness proposal pushed by environmental groups would cost Utah $13.2 billion a year and 133,000 jobs.[36] Other studies, moreover, including one performed by Utah State University, demonstrate that the majority of visitors to wilderness areas tend to be from the local area and at most account for "less than .5 percent of the total taxable sales... [to] slightly over 1 percent of the total sales in the [c]ounty."[37]

As a result of these revealing studies, wilderness proponents—even the economists among them—today rarely justify wilderness designation on the basis of the likely economic benefits to the local community. Tom Power of the University of Montana, for example, now speaks of an "intrinsic value" of wilderness, a power that mysteriously "draw[s] people to... communities and hold[s] them there."[38]

A primary reason for the limited economic value of wilderness is the nature of the activity and of the people who visit. As the Utah State University study shows, wilderness visitors "are dominated by high income, relatively young white visitors."[39] According to this study, visitors "stay one night in a motel or hotel, eat one or two meals, and purchase food and gas in the local area." The major purchases, especially the high-priced items, occurred long before leaving home: the backpacks, hiking gear and boots, lightweight camping gear, and other expensive paraphernalia. Furthermore, the impact of even the relatively small expenditures made in the local area may be diminished somewhat by the nature of the industries involved—mostly service industries with their lower wages—and the absence, in Montana and Oregon, of a sales tax.[40]

Recounting the history of the creation of Redwood National Park and similar episodes at other national parks might suggest that only the National Park Service is busying itself making lands inhospitable. Unfortunately, that is not the case. So too are the other federal land managers, including the Forest Service.

Colorado's Mount Evans was immortalized by the famous painter Albert Bierstadt, who in 1863 journeyed some 35 miles west of Denver and found himself gazing up at a peak that, at 14,264 feet, towered above all around it. He called his painting of that mountain "A

Storm in the Rockies—Mount Rosalie," naming the mountain after his future wife. His painting became famous, but in 1895, the Colorado General Assembly changed the name to Mount Evans, in honor of Colorado's second territorial governor.

Since others wanted to see the view that inspired Bierstadt, roads were already making their way there when construction of a highway to the summit began in 1922. In 1930, the Mount Evans Highway was completed—the highest road for motorized travel in North America, the third highest in the world.

In the late 1930s, three Colorado civic leaders decided that the visitors to the peak needed a structure from which to enjoy more fully all that Mount Evans offered. For Mount Evans—the fifteenth highest peak in the lower forty-eight—can be brutally cold, even on summer days, and the weather can change quickly and dramatically. These men also reasoned that the view was so spectacular that it warranted a stay long enough to take refreshment. Thus, in 1940 construction began on what became known as the Crest House. Famed Colorado architect Edwin A. Francis thought it his best work, noting that he had been inspired by "the moon, stars and heavens." In 1941, the Crest House was completed. Built of native boulders and stone, the building was later deemed eligible for historic landmark status.

On September 1, 1979, an accidental propane fire destroyed the Crest House. The Forest Service, which by then owned the Crest House, received more than $500,000 in damages and insurance that it could have use to rebuild the structure. But after years of study, the Forest Service decided not to rebuild the Crest House, ignoring the pleas of Clear Creek County, of nearby Idaho Springs, of the Alpine Rescue Team, which had performed many daring rescues using the Crest House as a much needed base of operations, and of thousands of visitors to Mount Evans.[41] Most incredible of all was the Forest Service's response to those who thought the Crest House met a safety need: "There is no requirement or obligation for the Forest Service to ensure the presence of people on a relatively continuous basis at the summit of Mt. Evans for safety-related purposes."[42]

What a far cry from the day in 1941 when the local forest ranger wrote to the original operator of the Crest House: "The Summit House meets a very outstanding public need, and the Forest Service is anxious to cooperate with you in any particulars that may serve to meet this need more fully."[43]

With the decision of the Forest Service not to rebuild the Crest House, recently upheld by the U.S. Court of Appeals for the Tenth Circuit, one more tourist attraction was removed from the rural West. Not surprisingly, visits to the peak plummeted. The nation—not to mention Clear Creek County, which shared the revenues generated at the Crest House—is the poorer for it.

Yet places like Mount Evans—unique and unusual and therefore highly susceptible to attack—are not the only ones in the crosshairs of those who seek to halt all activity on federal lands. Even the highly lucrative ski industry, which brings millions of visitors and tens of millions of dollars to a virtual handful of Western counties each winter, is under attack. Recently, a congressional report targeted the fees paid by those operating ski resorts on federal lands.[44] Stand by for the kind of attack currently being waged against the operators of concessions in the nation's parks.

Recent studies have indicated that the time of the long, two-week, drive-across-the-country-and-see-the-sights vacation may be a thing of the past, becoming more and more rare.[45] The more likely vacation is the long weekend holiday at a nearby spot. Lately, for many Westerners, tourists have been their neighbors. All this makes the definition Dave Rovig of Billings, Montana, gives for "tourist" highly relevant: "someone with a job." No matter how attractive we may make our Western towns to visiting tourists, no matter how willing federal officials are to cooperate in providing the types and kinds of facilities that will attract tourists, we who live here and are the most likely visitors won't be making the trip, unless we too have jobs. As the old saying goes, "We can't all be pressing each others' pants."

"TAKINGS" TIME:
"PRIVATE PROPERTY" FOR
"PUBLIC USE"

OF ALL THE WORDS IN THE UNITED STATES CONSTITUTION, perhaps the clearest are those found in the "Takings Clause" of the Fifth Amendment. In straightforward and simple fashion, the Founding Fathers stated: "nor shall *private property* be taken for *public use*, without *just compensation*" (emphasis added). They could not have chosen more basic words nor put them together in plainer fashion.[1] Although the Constitution, as interpreted over the years by the Supreme Court, is filled with perplexities, the average layman has always been able to understand what the property owners who wrote the Bill of Rights wanted to protect. In short, the Takings Clause dictates that if the government decides it needs someone's property for a public purpose, the owner of the land has to be compensated.

Professor Richard A. Epstein, in his exceptional book, *Takings, Private Property and the Power of Eminent Domain*, stated: "The

Lockean system was dominant at the time when the Constitution was adopted... and the protection of property against its enemies was a central and recurrent feature of the political thought of the day."[2]

For the first 131 years of the Republic, the Supreme Court held that the Takings Clause applied only to the "direct appropriation" of property,[3] or the functional equivalent of a "practical ouster of the owner's possession."[4] In 1922, all that changed.

In what Epstein and most others regard as "one of the most important takings cases in the Supreme Court literature," *Pennsylvania Coal Company v. Mahon*, the Court found that the state of Pennsylvania effected a "taking" when it enforced a statute that prohibited coal mining on private property.[5] In that case, the owner of land with coal deposits sold the surface to others, but expressly reserved the right to mine the coal beneath the surface. In addition, the buyers of the surface waived all rights regarding any possible damage caused by the mining of the coal beneath their land. Subsequently, the state of Pennsylvania enacted a statute that forbade any mining that could cause damage to surface owners.[6]

Justice Oliver Wendell Holmes, writing for the Court, held that the Pennsylvania statute constituted a "taking." "While property may be regulated to a certain extent," Holmes wrote, "if regulation goes too far it will be recognized as a taking... [Otherwise] the natural tendency of human nature [would be] to extend the qualification more and more until at last private property disappear[ed]."[7] Perhaps Justice Holmes' most enduring statement, one that resonates with meaning even more powerfully today than when it was first written, was that "a strong public desire to improve the public condition is not enough to warrant achieving the desire by a shorter cut than the constitutional way of paying for the change."[8]

Some seventy years after the Supreme Court's landmark decision in *Pennsylvania Coal*, the Court was asked to rule in another case— *Lucas v. South Carolina Coastal Council*—a significant case well worth somewhat lengthy treatment here.[9] The 1992 case involved David H. Lucas, who in 1986 purchased two residential lots on the Isle of

Palms in Charleston County, South Carolina, upon which he intended to build single family homes.[10]

Unfortunately for David Lucas, on July 1, 1988 (after he purchased his property but prior to submitting proposals to build), the South Carolina legislature enacted the Beach Front Management Act. Having decided that the beach/dune system along the South Carolina coast was important as "the basis for a tourist industry," "as a storm barrier," and as "a natural healthy environment for the citizens of South Carolina to spend leisure time which serves their physical and mental well-being," the legislature sought to "discourag[e] new construction in close proximity to the beach/dune system...."[11] Thus the South Carolina Coastal Council began the process of saving South Carolina's portion of the planet from David Lucas.

In accordance with the act, the South Carolina Coastal Council drew a "baseline" along the beach that passed landward of David Lucas' lots. Since under the act, constructing homes seaward of the "baseline" was flatly prohibited, this put an end to David Lucas' plans for a dream home.[12]

Denied the use of his property, Lucas brought a lawsuit in the South Carolina Court of Common Pleas asserting that the Beach Front Management Act effected a "taking" of his property without just compensation. The trial court held that Lucas's property had been "taken" by South Carolina and ordered "just compensation" in the amount of $1.23 million.[13]

South Carolina appealed to the South Carolina Supreme Court. In a 3-2 decision, the South Carolina Supreme Court reversed. Finding that "the Beach Front Management Act [was] properly and validly designed to preserve... South Carolina's beaches," the court held that when a regulation concerning property was designed "to prevent serious public harm," no compensation was owed regardless of the effect on the value of the property.[14]

Lucas was left with one last recourse. He asked the Supreme Court to hear the case and thereby "to revisit regulatory takings law."[15] Remarkably—the Supreme Court hears less than 3 percent of the cases it is asked to review—the Court agreed to hear the Lucas case; that is, the issue at stake seemed to strike the Court as being eminently important.

The defining moment occurred when Justice Sandra Day O'Conner asked, "What is the great threat to life or property?"[16] The question went straight to the heart of the case. South Carolina argued that the Beach Front Act sought to prevent "great public risk of harm"—that is, a nuisance.[17] Since under numerous decisions of the Supreme Court, preventing a nuisance is not a "taking," Lucas would not be entitled to "just compensation."[18]

The attorney representing South Carolina responded, "It is well recognized that portions of homes, even homes themselves during times of great storm events, will be blown or washed into houses behind them." Justice O'Conner asked her follow-up question:

> Well, [counsel], with reference to the adjacent homes, the homes that have been built on adjacent property, I guess under your theory South Carolina could require those homes to be removed because it still is the same threat to public safety that exists with respect to allowing new construction on these lots.

Several uncomfortable moments elapsed until the attorney for South Carolina finally admitted that Justice O'Connor was right since "[t]he houses that have already been built there will be removed over time...."[19]

On June 29, 1992, Justice Antonin Scalia wrote the Court's ruling in *Lucas v. South Carolina Coastal Council.* It was a victory for Lucas and property owners throughout the country and a strong revival of Justice Holmes' ruling in *Pennsylvania Coal.*[20] In fact, Justice Scalia began by crediting Justice Holmes for recognizing:

> that if the protection against physical appropriations of private property was to be meaningfully enforced, the government's power to redefine the range of interest included in the

ownership of property was necessarily constrained by constitutional limits. [21]

After reviewing the evolution of "takings" law since 1922 and noting
that the Supreme Court had declined to give any "set formula" for
finding a "taking," Justice Scalia set forth two "categories of regulatory actions" wherein compensation would be required without any
"*ad hoc,* factual inquiry."[22] Under Scalia's analysis, a "taking" occurs
(1) when the property owner "suffer[s] a physical 'invasion' of his
property," or (2) when "regulation denies all economically beneficial
or productive use of land."[23]

Since Lucas' property had "been rendered valueless" by the construction ban, Justice Scalia found that the case was premised upon the
Court's "no economically viable use" language.[24] Thus, Justice Scalia
concluded, South Carolina could avoid compensating Lucas only if an
examination of "the nature of the [Lucas] estate" demonstrated that
the prohibited use "[was] not part of his title to begin with."[25]

The Supreme Court thus reversed the decision and remanded the
case for an inquiry into whether "common-law principles [which]
would have prevented the erection of any habitable or productive
improvements on [Lucas'] land" existed in South Carolina.[26] While
Justice Scalia noted that the issue was "one of state law," he thought
it "unlikely" that such principles would "support prohibition of the
'essential use' of land."[27] Nonetheless, Justice Scalia was unwilling to
leave anything to chance:

> We emphasize that to win its case South Carolina must do
> more than proffer the legislature's declaration that the uses
> Lucas desires are inconsistent with the public interest, or the
> conclusory assertion that they violate a common-law maxim
> such as *sic utere tuo ut alienum non laedas*.[28] As we have said, a
> "State, by *ipse dixit*, may not transform private property into
> public property without compensation." Instead, as it would
> be required to do if it sought to restrain Lucas in a common-

law action for public nuisance, South Carolina must identify background principles of nuisance and property law that prohibit the uses he now intends in the circumstances in which the property is presently found. Only on this showing can the State fairly claim that, in proscribing all such beneficial uses, the Beach Front Management Act is taking nothing.[29]

On remand, the South Carolina Supreme Court found a "taking" and ordered that David Lucas be compensated for his property.

In an interesting postscript to this case, one of the most famous and closely watched property rights cases of our day, South Carolina, after paying Lucas and acquiring his property, offered it to the highest bidder for development purposes. South Carolina's attorney said, supposedly with a straight face, "[W]ith a house to either side and in between the lots, it is reasonable and prudent to allow houses to be built."[30]

Regrettably, the history of "takings" cases between 1922—when Justice Holmes wrote *Pennsylvania Coal*—and 1992—when Justice Scalia wrote *Lucas*—is pitted with cases in which the Court all but ignored Holmes' decision. The Court rarely reverses itself. Instead, by distinguishing a new case from earlier decisions, which would otherwise be controlling, it effectively ignores them.

Thus it was that the Supreme Court began to dig away at Justice Holmes' holding in *Pennsylvania Coal*. Over the years the Court found a variety of reasons why an unconstitutional "takings" had not occurred, while preserving the facade that government regulations could go "too far." What constituted "too far" depended solely on which justice was writing at the time. For example, in 1962, forty years after Holmes' opinion, the Court, in *Goldblatt v. Hempstead*, while affirming that government regulation could "be so onerous as to constitute a taking which requires compensation," held that in the case before it—an attempt to prohibit the mining of sand and gravel—the regulatory body had not stepped over the line; therefore, the prohibition stood.[31] Sixteen years later, in *Penn Central Transportation v. City of New York*, the Court again embraced the language of

Justice Holmes but again ruled for the regulatory body against the property owner.[32]

Finally, sixty-five years after Justice Holmes' decision in *Pennsylvania Coal Company*, the Court, in a return to Pennsylvania coal country, came full circle. In *Keystone Bituminous Coal Association v. DeBenedictis*, the result could not have been more different.[33] For despite Justice William Rehnquist's observation that the two cases were "strikingly similar," the Court upheld the constitutionality of Pennsylvania's limitations on bituminous coal mining.[34]

As if these distinctions were not impediment enough, the Supreme Court began erecting yet another hurdle for property owners seeking relief from regulatory "takings," something called "ripeness." Since courts, especially the Supreme Court, do not wish to make declarative judgments, they demand that cases be "ripe for judgment," that is, possessed of "finality."[35] In other words, the Court wants to ensure that none of the factual underpinnings of a case are subject to change.

Over a decade, from 1978 to 1987, the Supreme Court decided five cases in which property owners maintained that their property had been "taken" by a regulation, in violation of the Constitution. All five cases were decided against the landowners, three on ripeness grounds. Concerning the other two, the Court later cited those cases as prime examples of its unwillingness to review premature cases.[36] As the Court noted in *McDonald, Sommer & Frates v. Yolo County:*

> It follows from the nature of a regulatory takings claim that an essential prerequisite to its assertion is a final and authoritative determination of the type and intensity of development legally permitted on the subject property. A court cannot determine whether a regulation has gone "too far" unless it knows how far the regulation goes.[37]

No wonder some experts opined that "[t]he ripeness barrier… offered little hope to future litigants claiming regulatory takings. While the

Court repeated… that regulations are invalid if they 'go too far,' it was apparent… that the Justices had little eagerness to make those determinations. Landowners' hopes springing from the clear adoption of Holmes' test proved to be more ephemeral than substantial."[38]

However, in 1987, the Court once again embraced the rationale of *Pennsylvania Coal* as Holmes intended it—in favor of landowners.[39] In *First English Evangelical Lutheran Church v. County of Los Angeles*, an ordinance adopted by Los Angeles County prevented a church from rebuilding a retreat center and recreational facility for handicapped children because the facilities would be in an area designated by the county as a "flood protection area." In its ruling, the Court for the first time answered the question of whether the Fifth Amendment required compensation for a temporary "taking."[40] Remarkably, it answered "yes:"

> [W]here the government's activities have already worked a taking of all use of property, no subsequent action by the government can relieve it of the duty to provide compensation for the period during which the taking was effective…. [W]e hold that invalidation of the ordinance without payment of fair value for the use of the property during this period of time would be a constitutionally insufficient remedy.[41]

As can be seen from the above, while the Court may find it difficult to discern what is going "too far," there is one area in which it sees the "takings" issue clearly. The physical invasion of property is a "taking" per se—that is, on its face.[42]

It was on this basis—physical invasion—that the Court ruled in favor of property owners in *Nollan v. California Coastal Commission*.[43] The Nollans rented California beach front property, with an option to purchase. Over the years the property fell into disrepair, and they executed their option to purchase. Yet when they sought a permit to raze the building to construct a home, the California Coastal Commission demanded that they cede access across their property to the public. They refused. Alleging an unconstitutional "taking" of their property, they sued.

Justice Scalia, writing for the Court in favor of the Nollans, found a "taking." Scalia held that an impermissible permanent physical occupation, and hence "taking," occurs:

> where individuals are given a permanent and continuous right to pass to and fro, so that the real property may continuously be traversed, even though no particular individual is permitted to station himself permanently upon the premises.[44]

Justice Scalia also disputed California's assertion that the easement was simply a condition imposed in exchange for a land-use permit. As far as Justice Scalia was concerned, to support such a claim California would have to show that the regulation "substantially advance[d] legitimate state interests" and did not "den[y] an owner economically viable use of his land." On this point, Justice Scalia found that California fell far short: "Whatever may be the outer limits of 'legitimate state interests' in the takings and land-use context, this is not one of them." In fact, the California restriction was "not a valid regulation of land-use but 'an out-and-out plan of extortion.'"[45]

In *Nollan*, Justice Scalia found a "taking" even though the property owners had suffered no economic impact. There was a "taking," he wrote for the majority, not because the regulation had gone "too far," but because there was no relationship between the end desired by California and the means it selected to accomplish that end. For Justice Scalia, that relationship had to be "substantial," not just "rational," as some governmental entities would have it, for it is "more than an exercise in cleverness and imagination."[46]

One area in which the state has a legitimate interest, one that is clearly substantial, involves nuisances:

> The most distinctive aspect of the police power under the eminent domain clause has been its antinuisance component.

Supreme Court cases have repeatedly referred to control of nuisances as a proper end of the state, and there is no doubt today, as in times past, that this proposition is sound in principle.[47]

This does not mean that the nuisance issue should be invoked merely to reflect some social consensus about how property should be used. Then Justice Rehnquist correctly expounded the legal theory regarding "takings" and nuisance: "the government can prevent a property owner from using his property to injure others without having to compensate the owner for the value of the forbidden use."[48] Later, in *Keystone*, the majority appeared to have accepted Rehnquist's approach:

> [T]he special status of this type of state action can also be understood on the simple theory that since no individual has a right to use his property so as to create a nuisance or otherwise harm others, the state has not "taken" anything when it asserts its power to enjoin the nuisance-like activity.[49]

Of course, defining what "use" amounts to a nuisance could become as difficult as describing when regulation goes "too far." Justice Scalia attempted mightily, in his opinion in *Lucas*, to prevent just such confusion, demanding that South Carolina "identify background principles of nuisance and property law that prohibit the use [Lucas] now intends in the circumstances in which the property is presently found." In addition, Justice Scalia noted that South Carolina must analyze "the degree of harm to public lands and resources, or adjacent private property, posed by [Lucas'] proposed activities."[50]

While trying to clarify what constitutes a real nuisance, Justice Scalia seemed to move away from the "harmful or noxious uses" construct. After noting that "the distinction between 'harm-preventing' and 'benefit-conferring' regulation is often in the eye of the beholder," Justice Scalia concluded that "noxious-use logic cannot serve as a touchstone to distinguish regulatory 'takings'—which require compensation—from regulatory deprivations that do not require compensation." Thus, in Justice Scalia's view, the Court has made a "transition" from its "early focus on control of 'noxious' uses to its more contemporary statements that 'land-use regulation does not effect a taking if it [']substantially advances[s] legitimate state interests[']....'"[51]

Clearly, Justice Scalia seeks to replace the focus upon what a regulatory body (and environmental extremists) might call a nuisance—at a time when building a home on a beach is labeled as such—with whether the regulation substantially advances a legitimate state interest.[52]

Such heightened scrutiny by the Court is in sharp contrast with the approach espoused by the Clinton/Gore administration, its regulators, and friendly environmental groups. For them, all that a regulatory body needs is a "rational basis" for its decision to deny the use of property. Since the "rational basis" test almost always favors the regulatory body, adopting such an approach in "takings" cases is tantamount to eviscerating the Fifth Amendment.

The Clinton/Gore administration has gone even further, advocating that the only time a property owner should win a "takings" action is when he or she can demonstrate that the regulatory body's action is merely a "pretext" to achieve control over the land. The administration took that position in the most recent "takings" case considered by the Supreme Court, *Dolan v. City of Tigard*.[53]

Mr. and Mrs. Dolan wanted to double the square footage of their electrical supply store in downtown Tigard, a suburb of Portland, Oregon. The Dolans hoped to pave some 20,000 of their property's 71,000 square feet.[54]

The city of Tigard, according to a state land-use statute, put conditions on approving the Dolans' permit. The Dolans had to (1) cede the 10 percent of the property that lay within the one-hundred year flood plain; (2) cede an additional 15-foot-wide strip of property for a bike path; and (3) build the 8-foot-wide bike path. The reason for the city's actions was obvious: it wanted the Dolans' property for its open space system and for its bike path.

The Dolan case was appealed to the Oregon Supreme Court, which held that the city's action did not constitute a "taking" since "[the Dolans] may avoid physical occupation of their land by withdrawing their application for a development permit."[55] In other words, there could never be a taking since a property owner could always avoid the taking by withdrawing the application to use his or her land. Florence Dolan (her husband had since died) petitioned the Supreme Court for review, which was granted on November 29, 1993.

The decision by the Supreme Court to hear the Dolan case unleashed a flurry of activity by the public interest legal bar. When the Court convened on March 23, 1994, there was a stack of *amicus curiae* (friend of the court) briefs before each justice.[56] The "takings" issue has become the front line of the environmental debate. For years environmental groups have been saying that the American people are willing to pay any price and bear any burden to achieve the goals espoused by environmental groups. That assertion has never been put to the test.

With the advent of "takings" decisions with real dollar signs attached, the willingness of the American people to bear burdens and pay costs to achieve various environmental goals is being severely tested. As a result, environmental extremists, who are alert to political realities, have aggressively attempted to thwart recovery under the Takings Clause.[57] For example, in a brief filed in support of the City of Tigard, the Audubon Society asserted that a ruling for Mrs. Dolan would "frustrate the efforts of democratically elected officials to cope with serious environmental... problems."[58] Furthermore, Audubon suggested, "while the Court has recognized that the Constitution protects 'property rights'... the Court has never recognized a general 'right to use property.'" (Such a statement is of course in direct conflict with Justice Scalia's majority opinion in *Nollan*, see above.[59])

On June 24, 1994, the Supreme Court, in a 5-4 opinion by Chief Justice Rehnquist, held that the demands by the city of Tigard constituted an uncompensated taking of the Widow Dolan's property.[60] The Court held that an "essential nexus" must exist between a "legitimate state interest" and any permit conditions imposed upon a landowner by local government.[61] As to what a government must do to demonstrate that "nexus," the Court held that there must be "rough proportionality" between the goal sought and the means utilized to achieve it.[62] Applying these Fifth Amendment requirements, the Court held that the city of Tigard had failed to meets it burden.[63]

As important as the holding of the Court was the language it used. To those who asserted that property rights are inferior to other rights, Chief Justice Rehnquist answered, "We see no reason why the Takings Clause of the Fifth Amendment, as much a part of the Bill of Rights as the First Amendment or Fourth Amendment, should be relegated to the status of a poor relation in these comparable circumstances."[64] To those who argued that application of the Takings Clause would impose new costs on local government, the Court quoted its earlier holding in *Pennsylvania Coal:* "A strong public desire to improve the public condition [will not] warrant achieving the desire by a shorter cut than the constitutional way of paying for the change."[65]

Although the Supreme Court interprets the Constitution and its provision for "just compensation," the U.S. Court of Claims is the court that orders the federal government to hand over the compensation. Thus, many of the future battles over "takings" of landowners' property will occur in that court. Some have already been won.

Whitney Benefits, Inc. v. United States dealt with a provision of the Surface Mining Control and Reclamation Act of 1976 that prohibited mining coal beneath alluvial valley floors.[66] Whitney Benefits, prevented from mining a substantial amount of highly prized low sulfur coal beneath alluvial valley floors in Wyoming, sued to obtain "just compensation" under the Fifth Amendment. The federal government argued that no "taking" had occurred since Whitney Benefits could still graze cattle on the surface. The Court of Claims rejected the government's argument and awarded Whitney Benefits more than $60 million, plus interest and attorneys' fees.[67]

This is why environmental extremists fear the Takings Clause. Suddenly, the real costs of "costless" environmental purity must be paid.

In *Florida Rock Industries, Inc. v. United States*, a large-scale miner of limestone claimed a "taking" when "wetlands" policy, allegedly under the Clean Water Act, prevented it from mining limestone on its property in Dade County, Florida.[68] The government claimed it was merely preventing a nuisance and did not need to provide "just compensation." The court disagreed: "Rock mining of the type planned for plaintiff's property never has been considered a nuisance." The court awarded Florida Rock Industries, Inc., $1,029,000 plus interest from October 2, 1980, for the 98-acre parcel on which mining had been denied.[69]

In *Loveladies Harbor, Inc. v. United States*, the purchasers of 250 acres of vacant land in Long Beach Township, Ocean County, New Jersey, developed all but 51 acres of the property. When the landowners' attempt to develop the remaining acreage was frustrated by wetlands policy, they sued for a "taking" of some 11.5 acres. The court dismissed the government's assertion that the land was valuable for hunting, agriculture, as a mitigation site, or as a marina.[70] Instead, the court held that:

> the value of the property virtually has been eradicated as a result of government action.... As a result of government action, there is no market; the only potential buyer is a governmental unit, and the only remaining value is a nominal one.... [T]he denial of plaintiff's permit application effected a taking of 12.5 acres of plaintiff's property as of May 5, 1982. To fulfill the mandate of the Fifth Amendment, the court awards plaintiff the amount of $2,658,000 plus interest from the date of taking....[71]

Another area almost ripe for "takings" litigation is the Endangered Species Act and other statutes involving wildlife. Recently, a court in Florida held that prohibiting a landowner from using a portion of his property because it held bald eagle nests was a "taking" of his property.[72]

The Endangered Species Act—when applied to private property

owners—requires that private property be used as habitat, that is, as the source of food or shelter for protected animals. The inequity of such a requirement was obvious to then-Supreme Court Justice Byron White:

> There can be little doubt that if a federal statute authorized park rangers to come around at night and take petitioner's livestock to feed the bears, such a governmental action would constitute a "taking".... Thus, if the Government decided (in lieu of the food stamp program) to enact a law barring grocery store owners from "harassing, harming, or pursuing" people who wish to take food off grocery shelves without paying for it, such a law might well be suspect under the Fifth Amendment.[73]

The use of private lands by wildlife—whether endangered or not—is a problem afflicting a multitude of Westerners. State fish and game agencies benefit greatly—to the tune of tens of millions of dollars—from selling licenses to hunt such animals, but when those same animals cause damage or destruction, the agencies turn around and assert that they have no control over them. Such a case recently occurred in California.

In 1978, the California Department of Fish and Game (DF&G) began to relocate from forty to sixty tule elk to Pillsbury Lake in Mendocino County, though roughly 90 percent of the property in the area was privately owned and the elk would compete with the private livestock for food and drink.

Since 1976, Robin R. Moerman has owned a 200-acre ranch in Potter Valley, Mendocino County, where he raises sheep and cattle; these animals depend on Moerman's well-irrigated pastures for grazing. In the winter of 1984, tule elk began to invade Moerman's ranch. While their numbers were initially upward of fifty, there are now as many as one hundred of the animals on Moerman's ranch. Moerman complained to the DF&G. When the DF&G refused to alleviate the situation, Moerman, assisted by Pacific Legal Foundation, brought suit alleging that DF&G's actions in bringing in the elk had resulted in a "taking." In a remarkable twist of logic, the California courts held that the tule elk were not instruments of the state nor controlled by the state. Therefore, held the courts, there had been no physical taking of Moerman's property. Moerman's request for review by the Supreme Court was denied.[74]

The use of private land as habitat for species listed under the Endangered Species Act or for wildlife in general seems to strike at the heart of the Takings Clause of the Fifth Amendment; that is, "to bar Government from forcing some people to bear public burdens alone which, in all fairness and justice, should be borne by the public as a whole."[75] Until then-Justice White's view is embraced by others on the Supreme Court, and until other courts admit the obvious—that wildlife are used by and are instruments of the state—injustices will occur.

There appears to be no shortage of property owners willing to do battle with the federal government by using the Fifth Amendment, not just as a shield, but as a sword. Nevada rancher Wayne Hage has sued the Forest Service in a U.S. Claims Court asserting that the federal government's seizure of his cattle and grazing rights has denied him property rights—including water rights.[76] Texas property owner B.H. McDaniels has also sued the Forest Service, alleging that its mismanagement of a federal wilderness area in eastern Texas permitted the southern pine beetle to infest and destroy his private forestland.[77] Two Colorado ranchers, Dennis and Nile Gerbaz, who are being sued by the Environmental Protection Agency for an alleged wetlands violation, have countersued the federal government for permitting their property to be flooded by a government-approved water project, causing both a temporary and a permanent taking.[78]

Another front in the battle over "takings" occurred administratively in the federal bureaucracy and more recently in the states.[79] Following the decision of the Supreme Court in *Nollan v. California*

Coastal Commission, President Reagan's Justice Department recognized that federal bureaucrats needed to act with an eye to the potential cost of their actions—estimated as in excess of $1 billion—on the U.S. Treasury. As a result, in 1988 President Reagan signed Executive Order (E.O.) 12630, the Takings Implication Assessment (TIA) order. Under E.O. 12630, federal agencies are required to determine whether proposed regulations will result in an unconstitutional taking of property and, if so, to determine the cost to the Treasury.

Arizona was the first to adopt a state version of the Reagan executive order. Efforts to enact what became known as the Private Property Protection Act were launched when a handful of angry farmers drove into Phoenix to meet with the then-president of the Arizona Farm Bureau, Cecil Miller. In short order, the act received vigorous support from an unusually broad and diverse constituency.

The legislation was good government at its best. It simply required Arizona officials to inform the people of the state of the potential cost of a proposed action. The outcry from environmental groups was deafening. They labeled the legislation the "Polluters' Protection Act," among other wild accusations, and said it would end all state health and safety regulation. The bill passed.

For a brief period, Governor Fife Symington threatened a veto. Then he heard from the people of Arizona. In the end the bill was signed into law with a powerful message from the governor.

> [Does] environmentalism require its adherents to denigrate the principle of private property as it has been known in America from the very dawn of our national existence? If so, then they have embraced an environmentalism which is foreign to me.... The right to property is a civil right, no less than the rights to freedom of speech and worship, and the rights to due process and equal protection under the law.[80]

The ground-breaking victory achieved by the people of Arizona caught on throughout the West. As of April 1994, private property protection acts have been adopted in Arizona, Utah, and Idaho, and introduced in Washington, California, and Colorado.[81]

For the past twenty and more years, environmental extremists have used the courts of the land—particularly in the West—to clutch courtroom victories from the jaws of congressional defeat, to expand statutes and regulations beyond recognition, and to apply laws in seemingly impossible situations. In the process, property rights have been spurned and the efforts of landowners to seek constitutional redress have been thwarted.

More recently, courts, in particular the Supreme Court and the Court of Claims, have read the Fifth Amendment as our Founding Fathers intended and our liberty demands. This has afforded landowners a means of fighting back, of ensuring that a sense of balance and justice will be returned to environmental policy.

The Supreme Court has taken important steps in the right direction, but those steps have occurred relatively recently in a journey that began back in 1922. Much remains to be done.

Nothing will be done unless property owners are willing to do everything in their power to ensure that the Fifth Amendment remains strong. Nothing will be done if Westerners stay afraid—afraid that they will lose their liberties and their rights. Nothing will be done unless Westerners remain angry—angry that there are those who would take away their liberties and rights.

FIGHTING BACK: THE
GROWTH OF GRASSROOTS
OPPOSITION

IN 1993, THE FIRM OF MACWILLIAMS COSGROVE SNIDER, "a media, strategy and political communications consulting firm,"[1] researched and wrote a "Report on the Wise Use Movement," that "was prepared under the direction of the Wilderness Society and its president George Frampton."[2] "Wise Use" has become a catch-all term for the Western grassroots opposition to attempts by environmental extremists and government bureaucrats to drive Westerners off the land. "Wise Use" is the classic American conservationist ideal of balancing a love and respect for nature with a commitment to living and working on the land productively, using its wealth without destroying its richness.

The "Report on the Wise Use Movement" is the culmination of what its authors call a "lengthy, state-by-state review of Wise Use activities."[3] For all of its analysis, it is little more than a campaign manual for attacking Wise Use, primarily its "leadership," so as to "isolate them and cut off some of their funding."[4]

The report's authors state:

> We believe environmentalists can no longer afford to ignore the popular appeal of the Wise Use *mainstream message*. The *mainstream message* of the Wise Use Movement is often the most prominent communication in a given community of a can-do, entrepreneurial philosophy that promotes stewardship and husbandry and reaffirms the morality of rural life. The core arguments of the positive message are:
>
> 1. **Balance:** Man and nature can exist in productive harmony. Nature can be properly protected by the wise management of economic activity.
>
> 2. **People Come First:** Man is the preeminent species. Nature exists for man. Man's needs come first.
>
> 3. **Can-Do Attitude:** Science, technology, and our own ingenuity can solve our environmental problems.
>
> 4. **Freedom of Choice Is Our Individual Right:** The best government is the government that governs least. Individual freedom, individual choice must be predominant[5]

According to the report, these precepts "tap into basic American values." The report adds that the movement's leaders hope "to strike a rich vein of popular support for their agenda" and concludes, "There is evidence they may be on to something." The reason? There is broad public support for each of the "core arguments of the [movement's] positive message":

♦ **Balance:** "virtually everyone in America (92 percent) agrees that a good balance can be established between economic progress and the environment."

- **People:** "in [a] 1991... Roper Organization [poll]... 'Americans voted in favor of... loggers [over owls], by a margin of 45 percent to 35 percent.'"

- **Can Do:** "[i]n Roper's 1992 study almost 6 in 10 agreed with the statement that 'technology will find a way of solving our environmental problems.'"

- **Freedom:** "[w]hile Americans generally support more environmental regulations, they are leery about the government's ability, especially the federal government's ability to regulate efficiently."[6]

The bottom line, according to the report's authors:

> From balance to freedom of choice, we believe the national leaders of the Wise Use Movement have constructed a moderate message that consolidates their base and reaches out to the 50 percent of Americans who are weak environmentalists. What we are left with after rereading this analysis is regret for the great unrealized potential of the environmental movement and fear of the great potential of Wise Use's message.[7]

The report continues: "Many environmentalists we spoke to during the past several months believe the Wise Use message is neither finely honed nor persuasive. We disagree." Those who find no threat in the movement, the report goes on, fail to realize that the movement "paints a convincing portrait of *environmentalists* as the extremists in the debate over striking a balance between man and nature," and that its leaders have had remarkable success "in popularizing their message." "We must take them seriously or suffer the consequences [since the "anti-environmental movement"] has a strong message that is targeted at our Achilles Heel."[8] (emphasis in original)

As to the likely impact of the movement:

> Journalists and investigators who have spent time with Wise
> Use activists… come away believing there is a strong grass
> roots component to this movement waiting to be tapped
> across the country.
>
> In other words, in community after community, hard eco-
> nomic times, government regulations, and radical-sounding
> proposals to restrict commercial use of public land, create
> compelling vignettes of the little guy versus the powers of
> government/environmentalism.[9]

Thus far, the report notes, most activities by the anti-environmental
movement have been highly localized, with its forces battling local,
not national issues. But the report detects a troubling trend:

> [A]cross the country, groups initially organized to fight the
> resource battle on one front have a stake in connecting these
> fights. And there are several important links already estab-
> lished in the growing chain of Wise Use organizations at
> work in the grass roots.[10]

Quite right. For years environmental activists have been doing just
that—urging their followers to "think globally, act locally." Now, the
"anti-environmental" movement has followed suit.

The first battle in what appears to be a full-scale war against the
"anti-environmental" movement took place during a gathering of the
environmental elite in October 1992 at the San Juan Islands' Rosario
Resort off the coast of Washington State. There, the Environmental
Grantmakers Association held its fall retreat. During its two-day
conclave, the program that generated the most interest was Session
26: "The Wise Use Movement: Threats and Opportunities."

Presented by Debra Callahan of the W. Alton Jones Foundation
of Charlottesville, Virginia, "Threats and Opportunities" was the

first public release of what would become the "Report on the Wise Use Movement."[11] Culminating months of research, the conclusion reached after "a fifty-state fairly comprehensive survey" was simple:

A fast-growing movement opposed to environmentalism has seized the moral and rhetorical high ground. This is a threat, Callhan said, that environmentalists can't ignore.[12]

"[T]he minute the Wise Use people capture that high ground, we almost have not got a winning message left in, in our quiver."[13]

But an empty rhetorical quiver does not mean that environmental extremists don't still wield extraordinary power.

The vice president of the United States—titular head of the environmental movement, with an annual budget approaching a billion dollars—calls ABC's Ted Koppel and asks for a program to impugn the motives of a handful of dedicated and highly regarded scientists and grassroots leaders.[14] The Wilderness Society, with an annual budget of $17.9 million and a third of a million members nationwide, prepares a campaign manual on how to conduct war against those grassroots leaders.[15] While the report is being prepared, a media strategy and political communications consulting firm is hired to do the research and writing. The W. Alton Jones Foundation, with assets exceeding $173 million and which, in 1990, made nearly 100 grants totalling more than $7 million to environmental groups, assists in the preparation of that report.[16] The Environmental Grantmakers Association, an adjunct of the Rockefeller Family Fund, Inc., and a virtual Who's Who of environmental grantmakers (more than 130 are listed as members, including the John D. and Catherine T. MacArthur Foundation, the Pew Charitable Trusts, and the Rockefeller Foundation), devotes substantial time discussing the results of the report.[17] Finally, a Clearinghouse on Environmental Advocacy and Research (CLEAR) is established in Washington, D.C., to provide information regarding "Wise Use and the anti-environmental backlash."[18]

KEEP ON TREKKIN'

Just who are the men and women of whom these very powerful people and organizations are so afraid? One of them is Bruce Vincent of Libby, Montana. Bruce, a logger, whose father and grandfather were also loggers, was in Libby the day the federal bureaucrats came to town. The bureaucrats said they had come to create a grizzly bear habitat out of the woods surrounding Libby. They had decided that northwestern Montana should be designated as the "Grizzly Bear Habitat One" area, meaning that some 120 grizzly bears would be relocated there.

"What does that mean for us?" asked someone.

"Minor behavioral changes," the bureaucrats said. "You'll have to do what the natives on Alaska's Kodiak Island do: their children wear bells to ward off the grizzly bears. Of course, if we ever hear of a 'bad' bear, we'll come and remove it."[19]

The bureaucrats had not come to town to get permission; they had come to tell the people of Libby the way things were going to be. This realization ignited the community and led to the formation of the Coalition for Balanced Environmental Planning, created specifically to address problems regarding the grizzly bear.

The people's response to the grizzly bear question would have remained highly localized, and Bruce Vincent would have been strictly a local hero, had it not been for another event that took place a short time later in Missoula.[20]

An environmental organization, the Montana Wilderness Association (MWA), hosted a seminar attended by some sixty people from western Montana. According to materials distributed during the two-day meeting, the MWA taught attendees how to challenge unfavorable Forest Service decisions by appealing every activity that took place in every national forest in Montana. They were told to be "exhaustive, imaginative, nit-picky, philosophical in coming up with arguments; the goods ones will score, the bad ones will just get shot down."[21] As one speaker said, the only important thing was delay; the mills couldn't last for three years without timber. (The Missoula meeting and others like it in the main achieved their objective. Then-chief of the Forest Service Dale Robertson presented Congress with a seven-foot stack of appeals on Montana's Flathead National Forest, making it the most appealed forest in the country.)

Bruce Vincent found out about the meeting from his friend, Bill Crapser, then a forester for Darby Lumber, who had managed to attend. Bill's presence went undetected until the end of the first day, when each attendee stood up, spoke his or her name, and then proudly announced, "I've appealed [some number of] timber sales." The audience fell into stunned silence when Bill stood up, spoke his name, and said, "I've murdered 15 million trees in the Bitterroot National Forest."

Bill's report convinced Bruce that the environmental movement was at war with the people of the timber-producing communities. He began to move on various fronts.

Bruce discovered that a meeting with Forest Service officials had been scheduled to address a technical issue regarding the proper measurement of logs. Bruce called the Forest Service to ask that the topic be changed to access. "If we don't do something about access," Bruce said, "we won't have any logs to measure." That meeting drew more than 275 people from throughout northwestern Montana and resulted in the formation of twelve separate grassroots organizations. "I told everyone there to start his or her own group," Bruce said, "since all politics is local."

A short time later environmental extremists succeeded in tying up timber sale after timber sale, cutting the timber supply to the Darby Lumber Mill that was situated in the Bitterroot National Forest. When the mill announced that, as a result, it would be forced to shut down, Bruce Vincent and others swung into action and organized the Great Northwest Log Haul to save the small, threatened mill.

On May 13, 1988, logging trucks came from five states and from as far as 350 miles away. In tiny community after tiny community, men, women, and children pitched in to help. In Colville, Washington, stores opened early to make sandwiches for the participants. In many other small towns, the high school band played as the trucks roared out of town. Not just logging trucks but cars, pickups, school buses, every type of rig, converged on Missoula, where they lined up for the final trek to Darby.

In the end, the incredible convoy was 26 miles long, with 303 fully loaded logging trucks carrying 1.5 million board feet of timber. Bruce Vincent, waiting in Darby, could hear the roar of the diesel engines and the blare of the horns from miles away. Overhead helicopters monitored the convoy over the airwaves the local radio stations kept playing the Nitty Gritty Dirt Band's "The Working Man."[22] People stood on the street, on housetops, on the roofs of cars, waving the American flag, singing and cheering.

"We changed a whole bunch of people's lives that day," says Bruce. "I knew how important what we did was, but I don't think it really hit me until the next day. I was gassing up my rig when an old, beat-up station wagon pulled in. The lady driving got out and came over to me. She had two kids in the back of the wagon and one on her hip. She asked if I was who she thought I was. When I told her yes, she started sobbing. Her husband had been laid off for three weeks and had just gotten the call to report for work Monday morning. The look on that woman's face made it all worthwhile."[23]

Bruce Vincent had thought what was happening to Montana loggers was an isolated problem. But when he returned home the phone started ringing. One call was from Jim Petersen of Grants Pass, Oregon, who had seen the NBC report on the truck haul and had driven over 750 miles to Libby, Montana, to meet Bruce.

Jim Petersen was also fighting against the lockup of federal timber resources—this time efforts by environmental extremists to halt a proposal to salvage 200 million board feet of lumber burned in the Silver Fire Complex near Grants Pass, Oregon. Jim Petersen's tale wasn't the only one Bruce heard in the following weeks. There were dozens of others, from all over the country, as far east as Indiana. In Bruce's words, "If there was a national forest in the area, we got a call from the people living there. I was amazed. For the first time we all realized we weren't alone."

Bruce and others created Communities for a Great Northwest (CGNW) to fight for a balanced approach in using Western forests. The group focused on the five states that had participated in the log haul to Darby: Washington, Oregon, Idaho, Montana, and Wyoming.

On August 19, 1988, Bruce Vincent helped organize the Solidarity Celebration in Rathdrum, Idaho. Later, Bruce and Jim Petersen organized the Silver Fire Roundup, a show of support for local loggers that drew more than 1,200 logging trucks from all over the Pacific Northwest. The following year the Solidarity Celebration was held in Missoula, Montana, and it drew more than 5,500 people. Soon other rallies sprang up throughout the Pacific Northwest—in Eugene, Salem, and Roseburg, Oregon; in Yreka and Ukiah, California; in Forks, Puyallup, and Chehalis, Washington; and on and on.

At first the rallies were just for loggers. "Then people," says Bruce Vincent, "began to realize that we were all in this together." The first multiple-use rally—a tactical watershed—took place in Omak, Washington, in May 1989, and it brought loggers, ranchers, miners, and orchardmen together for the first time.

"We held a cowboy logger celebration in Missoula, Montana, in May 1990," says Bruce. "We did it up right. We had a rodeo and a carnival, logging trucks from all over, and more than five thousand folks. We started making the connection among all the groups, not just the loggers in other states, but every other natural resources industry in all the Western states. We had a pretty broad cross-section of rural America."

VOICES IN THE WILDERNESS

Back home in Libby, the onslaught against natural resources activities continued. It wasn't just the grizzly bear recovery plan or the endless procession of forest service litigation—some brought by people from as far away as Brooklyn, New York. It was the demand by environmental extremists for more and more wilderness designation, although vast tracts of Montana had already been designated under the Wilderness Act of 1964.

In the fall of 1989, Libby resident Ed Eggelston, thinking he was at a meeting of the Libby Rod and Gun Club, happened into a gathering of the Kootenai Wildlands Alliance (KWA). He decided to stay. A local schoolteacher and leader of the KWA, Dave Erickson, announced that Senator Max Baucus' staff had met with a handful of environmental leaders and announced that if the KWA would pick the roadless areas they wanted set aside, Senator Baucus would have them designated as wilderness.[24]

The KWA drew up a proposal to designate 500,000 acres of roadless areas as wilderness in the Kootenai National Forest and the Lolo National Forest. Although the KWA asserted that it was willing to negotiate with other groups, when Bruce's CGNW asked which points were negotiable, the KWA responded, "None."

CGNW nevertheless persisted, and the KWA agreed to meet with CGNW on June 7, 1990, at 6:00 P.M. to try for a local resolution of the wilderness issue. At 10:00 A.M. Bruce Vincent was notified that the KWA was holding a press conference at 11:00 at Union Hall. Bruce was stunned when the KWA announced that the Montana Wilderness Association and the Montana AFL-CIO had reached an agreement on 400,000 acres of new wilderness, an agreement they called "The Kootenai Accords." The next week, Senator Baucus introduced a bill to put the "Accords" into law. Compelled to hold hearings in Libby, hearings Bruce Vincent said "were not pretty," the legislation died. But Senator Baucus introduced the same bill in the new Congress.

Coincidentally, the people of Libby discovered that a county ordinance permits county commissioners to poll their constituents. Bruce Vincent and CGNW led the way in demanding that such a nonbinding poll be conducted.

On May 19, 1991, when polling officials announced, "The polls are open," more than one hundred people were already in line. During the day, the wait was as long as two hours, but still the people came. When the wilderness votes were tallied, 86 percent had voted against the "Accords."

Bruce Vincent and CGNW countered the expensive television and radio blitz waged by environmental groups with fliers and a door-to-door campaign that explained the meaning of the vote and what the "Accords" would do to jobs and to recreational opportunities.[25] Finally, days before the vote, 421 of the 450 workers at the mill signed a newspaper advertisement in the *Western News*, breaking ranks with their union's endorsement of the "Accords." "We won," says Bruce, "for two reasons: first, since all politics is local our neighbors listened to us; second, they could never live down all the lies they had told—Washington, D.C., tactics didn't go over well here."

A few weeks later, when a Senate committee came to Missoula for a hearing on Baucus' wilderness proposal, 3,500 northwestern Montana residents were there in force, protesting the wilderness proposal and carrying a casket labeled, "The Kootenai Accords." A few months later, the Baucus wilderness proposal was lying in the same casket.

Shortly after the Darby log haul, an Oregon logger named Tom Hirons asked Bruce to meet with him and John Kunzman, who owned a chain saw store in Sweet Home, Oregon. The three created the protimber grassroots organization, Communities for Great Oregon, as well as its Sweet Home and Mill City chapters.[26]

Meanwhile, in Portland, Oregon, Valerie Johnson, daughter of a timber mill builder and owner, was working for Stimson Lumber Company. In the winter of 1988–1989, Valerie's fellow employees asked her to look into what was happening to the timber industry.

At Valerie Johnson's request, the company's timber manager spoke to the assembly about the seriousness of the environmental battle. Valerie Johnson and the others decided to do something about it. In May 1989, they sponsored a gathering of their colleagues at the World Forestry Center in Portland.

Valerie Johnson learned of others who were actively involved in Oregon's tiny timber-producing communities, those who had been hardest hit by the environmental extremists' battle to shut down the timber industry. She learned of Rita Kaley and Dixie Reisch, of their truck rallies and gatherings and grassroots groups; of Charlie Jantz's Yellow Ribbon Coalition; of Bill and Barbara Grannell's Oregon Project; and of Bruce Vincent and Tom Hiron's Communities for Great Oregon in Sweet Home and Mill City.

At the time, the summer of 1989, Senator Hatfield was pushing compromise legislation—what became known as the Northwest Timber Compromise, or Section 318—to balance even more protection for the owl with mandated timber harvests. Around that issue, the various timber groups coalesced. On August 31, 1989, Valerie's group met to select a name that not only reflected timber issues, but would serve as a rallying point for all Oregonians threatened by environmental policy gone wild. The organization was named the Oregon Lands Coalition (OLC) and voted Valerie Johnson and John Kunzman as its cochairs.

Within two weeks, timber advocates from throughout the Pacific Northwest were desperately needed in Washington, D.C., to support Section 318. It was the beginning of what became the annual "Fly in for Freedom."[27]

Three weeks later, the Oregon Lands Coalition helped coordinate its first major public relations event—a truck caravan to Joanne Etienne's mill and a massive timber rally in St. Croix, Indiana. The event was another watershed for Valerie Johnson and the Oregon Lands Coalition. "For the first time we realized we were not alone. For the first time we realized that this was not just an Oregon, or even a Pacific Northwest issue, but a national issue, involving truckers, mill workers, lumber dealers, and millions of others."[28]

That fall, Hurricane Hugo swept ashore in South Carolina, devastating the countryside and rendering hundreds of South Carolinians homeless. The people of South Carolina needed lumber. The people of the Pacific Northwest had it. All that separated the two were 3,000 miles. With the help of the Oregon Lands Coalition, tens of thousands of dollars in lumber and freight were donated and railed cross-country to the victims of the natural disaster.

"The convoy to South Carolina taught us something else—the difficulty of getting media attention if you're on the wrong side of the dominant media culture," says Valerie Johnson. "The media barely gave us a glance for what we did. If we had been some bleeding-heart liberal group, we probably would have been on all three networks. We were learning huge lessons every day."

It wasn't long, though, before Valerie Johnson and the Oregon Lands Coalition were in the national spotlight. Thanks in large part to the hard work of OLC's indefatigable Jackie Lang, the *Christian Science Monitor* began to cover OLC's work. Then, in June 1990, Valerie Johnson appeared on CNN's "Crossfire" with Pat Buchanan, opposite Oregon environmentalist Andy Kerr.

At the first meeting of what became the Oregon Lands Coalition, eleven organizations met at the table, all involved in timber harvesting, with a total membership of between four thousand and five thousand people. Today, the Oregon Lands Coalition has sixty-two organizations with a total membership of 81,000 Oregonians, representing a varied mixture of natural resource-related activities.

The impact in the timber debate of the Oregon Lands Coalition and its allied grassroots groups cannot be underestimated. Almost daily, these grassroots groups were showing Oregonians in full and dreadful detail how Oregon's economic lifeblood was being drained away.

All across the state, "Timber Dollars" signs sprouted up and thousands of Oregonians stuffed "This bill paid with timber dollars" slips into the envelopes of their monthly bills. In a little more than two years, the number of Oregonians who opposed job loss to protect the northern spotted owl shot up from 48 percent to 64 percent.

In January 1992, what became known as the "God Squad Hearings" were convened to consider a request by the Bureau of Land Management to conduct forty-four timber sales in Oregon notwithstanding the northern spotted owl. As explained in an earlier chapter, relief from the Endangered Species Act's draconian requirements may be granted only by a cabinet-level entity called the Endangered Species Committee. Since it appears to have the power of life and death over species, it is often called "the God Squad."

Immediately, a number of environmental groups sought to intervene in the process, as did a regional timber association and the affected counties. This time, the Oregon Lands Coalition, represented by Mountain States Legal Foundation, also demanded a place at the table.

"Until the God Squad convened, there was no role for the people," says Valerie Johnson. "The rallies we held in Portland during the hearings made national news and helped people to understand that the battle did not just involve environmental organizations and the timber industry, but also the men, women, and children of tiny communities all over Oregon."

"Today, more than ever before, industry knows how important the grassroots is to its eventual success," Valerie Johnson adds. "Industry understands that it cannot win this battle alone. This is not just a battle that is being fought on Capitol Hill with legislation, or within the federal bureaucracy on regulation, or before the courts with litigation. It is a battle for the hearts and minds of the American people. Industry cannot win that battle alone, but with the grassroots we will. We intend to win."

PEOPLE FOR THE WEST

In 1990, Bill (a former state legislator) and Barbara Grannell, fresh from their successful grassroots campaign to organize the timber-producing communities in Oregon, turned their attention to yet another major crisis facing Westerners: the assault on the 1872 General Mining Law.

The Western States Public Lands Coalition, a nonprofit and non-partisan organization, was formed by the Grannells in 1988 to advocate continued multiple use of the nation's federal lands. Their goal was to ensure a balanced approach to the use of federal land, a balance that recognized the importance of a variety of activities—mining, livestock grazing, recreation, water development, and timber harvesting.

In 1990, faced with the increasingly militant calls of the national environmental organizations for more land closures, the Grannells knew that an effective counterforce was essential. "We knew that if we were to keep multiple use alive," said Bill, "federal lands users would need to unite as never before for greater strength in numbers."[29]

When environmental extremists demanded the end of all mining in the West, the Grannells set about organizing grassroots support for mining workers and their communities. People for the West, as their campaign is called, set up chapters throughout the West. As of this writing there are more than one hundred chapters. Today, it is impossible to go to almost any small town in the West or attend any rally or county fair or meeting without seeing "People for the West" buttons, banners, and bumper stickers. Bill and Barbara Grannell's articles appear in newspapers and magazines throughout the country, advocating a sensible approach to Western economic issues. By means of a monthly newsletter, *People for the West*, which reaches ten thousand, the Grannells continue to spread the word, attracting new members and chapters almost daily.

People for the West was well in place when Congress held hearings in Nevada and Colorado to take testimony on "reform" of the 1872 General Mining Law. At the hearings, the congressional committees were surprised to see hundreds of local citizens protesting the attempt to destroy the federal law that had created tens of thousands of high-paying jobs and hundreds of millions of dollars of revenue for the states and local communities. Thousands turned out in Reno, Nevada, filled the hearing room to overflowing, and lined the hallways and streets outside with placard-carrying miners and their families, friends, and neighbors.

VISION IMPAIRED

Perhaps one of the great grassroots successes of the Wise Use Movement took place with regard to the Yellowstone Vision Document.

Yellowstone National Park (YNP)—the nation's first and largest national park—sits at the junction of three states. Although most of the YNP lies in the northwest corner of Wyoming, a narrow strip of its northern and western boundary extends into neighboring Montana and Idaho, respectively. Situated up the spine of the Rocky Mountains and its abundant forests, the YNP is surrounded by lands owned by the federal government and managed by the Forest Service.[30] In all, some 13.5 million acres of land are included in the seven national forests that surround the Yellowstone National Park.[31]

Not all of this land is federally owned. Thousands of people live on privately owned "inholdings." For the most part, these landowners consider the YNP and its managers to be good neighbors, though there have of course been exceptions.[32] Generally, however, unlike the YNP, the people of the region engage in economic activities, such as ranching, farming, forestry, mining, and oil and gas exploration.

Thus the neighbors of the YNP were taken aback when the National Park Service (NPS) began to circulate a proposal to restrict sharply the manner in which the lands surrounding the YNP—public *and* private—could be used. The vehicle for this dramatic switch came in a document entitled "Vision for the Future: A Framework for Coordination in the Greater Yellowstone Area (Draft)," which became known as the "Yellowstone Vision Document" or the "Vision Document."

Ostensibly, the NPS proposed to protect not just Yellowstone National Park but millions of acres surrounding YNP from what it called, with typical hyperbole, "threats to the park." The roundabout language of the proposals lacked almost all real substance. But it didn't take the Western neighbors of the YNP long to realize that it was they who were being threatened. Natural resources groups and others throughout the tri-state region also began to worry about what the NPS was trying to do under the trendy umbrella of "protecting an ecosystem."

Peggy Olson Trenk of the Western Environmental Trade Association hosted a meeting in Bozeman, Montana, at which Carolyn Paseneaux of the Wyoming Public Lands Council informed the group of what she had discovered regarding the Vision Document and at which Chuck Cushman of the National Inholders Association and Multiple Use Land Alliance discussed what could be done at the grassroots level. When the meeting was over, the forty grassroots leaders in attendance had decided to mobilize the region behind a variety of groups. And mobilize they did.

In Wyoming, Carolyn Paseneaux volunteered to take the lead in mobilizing groups and individuals against the NPS's proposals.[33] In Idaho, Adena Cook of the Blue Ribbon Coalition took the issue to those in that state who wished to do battle against the NPS.[34] In Montana, Peggy Olson Trenk took the lead coordinating with People for the West and a variety of user groups, including Montana Snowmobilers, Communities for a Great Northwest, Montana Logging Association, and the Water Resource Association, all of which were charged with mobilizing the local citizenry.[35]

What happened in Montana illustrates what happens when Westerners mobilize against a common threat. At every public meeting, hundreds of farmers, ranchers, miners, loggers, and other citizens marched in protest, demonstrating that they were "mad as hell" and weren't "going to take it anymore."

Gatherings like those in Cody, Riverton, Jackson, and Cheyenne, Wyoming; Billings, Ennis, and Bozeman, Montana; and Idaho Falls, Idaho had an impact far beyond the region. The demonstrations conducted at those meetings carried a message to National Park Service regional headquarters in Denver, and to Washington, D.C., that the NPS was going to pay a very high price for moving forward with the "Vision Document," if it could move at all. And elected leaders were made to realize exactly how the politically active citizens in their constituencies felt about it. Before long, all three governors cosigned a letter to President Bush objecting to the heavy-handed tactics and insatiable demands of the NPS.

In the end, the National Park Service abandoned the "Vision Document." In addition, the two high-level federal officials most responsible for the "Vision" were reassigned out of the West.

The grassroots had won, but the work entailed in the winning was formidable.

Chuck Cushman of the National Inholders Association and Multiple Use Land Alliance (now the American Land Rights Association) was himself alerted to the fray when the National Park Service threatened to destroy his cabin in the village of Wawona inside Yosemite National Park. He organized his fellow property owners and together they forced the NPS to back down. Other communities suffering the same governmental oppression learned about the victory in Wawona and asked Cushman for help.

Today, from his old farmhouse in Battleground, Washington, Chuck Cushman uses every modern tool at hand—computers, modems, fax machines, and more—to inundate Congress with letters and phone calls. His mastery of the imaginative nonviolent protest demonstration led *Time* magazine to recognize him as "the tank commander of the Wise Use Movement."

Chuck Cushman attributes much of his success to a series of conferences held in the late 1980s that drew public attention to Western problems. Chuck noted that community after community was being assailed, but there was little coordination amongst them. "They were being picked off one at a time," he said. "We needed to get it together."

A short time later, Chuck teamed up with Ron Arnold of the Center for the Defense of Free Enterprise in Bellevue, Washington, who was planning a Multiple Use Strategy Conference in Reno, Nevada. "That," said Chuck Cushman, "was the real beginning of what some call the Wise Use Movement."

Yet another early grassroots leader was Grant Gerber, an Elko attorney, who started the Wilderness Impact Research Foundation to fight excessive wilderness legislation in Nevada and to expose the real cost of wilderness designation. The results of one of the most comprehensive studies on the cost of wilderness designation were announced at one of Grant Gerber's conferences. According to the study, a 5.1 million-acre wilderness bill sought by environmental extremists would cost Utah $13.2 billion and 133,000 jobs.[36]

Ruth Kaiser, a frequent participant at Gerber's conferences, was born in Oklahoma, the granddaughter of sharecroppers who had suffered through the Great Depression.

She understands how much dedication and hard work is needed to make a living raising animals and crops.

When Ruth Kaiser was approached by several Western cattlemen for advice concerning the problems they faced from the heavy hand of government and the special interest environmental groups, she took the job of executive director of the National Federal Lands Conference (NFLC).

"We needed to educate people on how to protect their rights. We needed to offer solutions," said Ruth Kaiser.[37] The organization distributed information and began holding seminars. Under the leadership of Wayne Hage, a Nevada rancher and avid student of constitutional law, the NFLC began to spread the word throughout the rural West.

When the National Federal Lands Conference met in Boise, Idaho, in April 1989 for one of its first meetings, cowboys filled the room. They came from all over Idaho, from Oregon, from Nevada, from Utah, and from Washington too. In shiny boots and pressed levis, spotless white shirts and huge hats, they sat at the tables, notebooks out, pencils poised. They took copious notes as they listened intently to some of the West's top lawyers and rangeland experts. They mastered all the legal and technical issues involved. They learned what they needed to know to win the fight against the environmental machine that spelled their doom.

The NFLC held meetings in Las Vegas, Nevada; Denver, Colorado; Albuquerque, New Mexico; Pocatello, Idaho; Bend, Oregon; Chico, California; Kalispell, Montana; Salt Lake City, Utah; Reno, Nevada;

Grand Junction, Colorado; Tucson, Arizona; Casper and Rock Springs, Wyoming; Hibbing, Minnesota; and Ocala, Florida, to name but a few. Wayne Hage, Ruth Kaiser, Dick Manning, and the other leaders of the NFLC weren't satisfied to carry their message only to the hardy men and women who worked the range. They reached for a larger audience, realizing the vital role played by the local government, particularly the county government—the place where "the rubber hits the road."

As a result, the National Federal Lands Conference began holding sessions for local government leaders and citizens. These sessions prepared them to address the myriad legal challenges to Western economic activity such as the Endangered Species Act and the National Environmental Policy Act. Noting that almost every federal statute required that the local government be consulted, and aware of the deference Congress paid to local culture and heritage, the NFLC offered a series of ordinances for county commissioners to consider, ordinances that, if adopted, could effectively challenge federal control of local activities. Often referred to as the Catron County Ordinances, after the New Mexico county that first adopted them, they have been put on the agenda of county after county across the West.[38]

At about that time, Western county commissioners began taking their complaints regarding the attacks on the Western economy to their national organization, the National Association of Counties (NACo). In 1990, for example, the Western Interstate Region (WIR) of NACo turned the tables on environmental extremists by designating ten Western communities as "endangered."[39] Due to the efforts of intrepid Western county commissioners like Louise Liston of Garfield County, Utah, Western economic issues found a national forum and Westerners won the support of an important national entity, the NACo.

Western officials were also organizing. Louise Liston's good friend, fellow rancher, and "neighbor" Met Johnson, along with Speaker of the Arizona House Mark Killian, founded the Western States Coalition, which met for the first time in Denver, Colorado, in 1993. Today, the coalition, whose membership includes hundreds of state legislators, county commissioners, and city officials, as well as stakeholder groups, represents 23 million people throughout the West.

Something else was changing. Yet another arrow from the environmental quiver was taken over by the aroused Westerners. As Bruce Vincent put it: "We used to think that suing was a radical notion. We now know that what is radical is for us to sit back while the other side destroys us." That realization caused Lincoln County, Montana, and Boundary County, its Idaho neighbor, to bring a lawsuit against the Forest Service for cutting back allowable timber harvest on a particular sale area by 43 percent to achieve a 1 percent increase in grizzly bear habitat.[40] Lincoln and Boundary counties were not alone.

In Oregon, Douglas County brought a lawsuit against the U.S. Fish and Wildlife Service (FWS).[41] In Utah, Millard County sued the Bureau of Land Management (BLM) in order to gain local control of a thoroughfare that the BLM had designated as part of a "wilderness study area" and thus off limits to economic activity.[42]

Remarkably enough, the federal government contended—in the Lincoln County and Douglas County lawsuits—that counties do not have legal standing, that they have no legal right to sue the federal government over land policy decisions. The court in the Lincoln County case agreed, but the court in the Douglas County case disagreed. Both cases remain in litigation.

THE GREAT SNAIL RACE

Perhaps the best example of local government fighting back, and of a perfectly orchestrated campaign, involved the Bruneau hot springsnail (*Pyrgulopsis bruneauensis*).

The Bruneau hot springsnail—slightly larger than the letter "B" in the word "LIBERTY" on a dime—was designated "endangered" by the U.S. Fish and Wildlife Service on January 25, 1992, nearly seven

years after the creature was first proposed for listing in Idaho. Despite
the opposition of the local citizenry, despite the scanty evidence upon
which the federal government relied, and despite the evidence from
Idaho officials that the snail was not endangered, the FWS marched
on, pressed by the demands of environmental extremists.

Shortly after the listing, the Fish and Wildlife Service wrote to the
Farmers Home Administration (FmHA) stating that no FmHA operating loans could be granted in Owyhee County, Idaho, in 1994. In
addition, the Fish and Wildlife Service started action to deprive fifty-
nine farm and ranch units involving nearly one thousand people of
their right to use water on 21,206 acres of irrigated farmland, causing the loss of $1.3 million in net family farm income annually—that
is, half the economic activity of Owyhee County.[43]

Faced with such a crisis, the Owyhee County Farm Bureau, the
Owyhee Cattlemen's Association, the Idaho Farm Bureau, the Idaho
Cattle Association, and the Owyhee County Commissioners mobi-
lized to fight back. Together they created the Bruneau Valley Coalition and dedicated themselves to raising $100,000 to carry the fight
to the government and "to teach the federal bureaucrats that they
must follow the law like everybody else... [and] use good science and
common sense and implement the laws correctly."[44]

Teach them a lesson they did. On May 7, 1993, the Bruneau Valley Coalition filed a complaint in federal district court in Boise.[45] As
the case progressed, the Bruneau Valley Coalition made sure that
Idaho, the West, and indeed the nation learned about their plight.
"Wanted!" posters in living color were circulated to search for other
habitats for the snail; a "Contribution Thermometer" was set up in
Bruneau and the Great Bruneau Snail Race was held on September
25, 1993, to raise money for the lawsuit and publicity; and a billboard
posted just outside Bruneau read: "Would the Last Person to Leave
Bruneau Please Feed and Water the Endangered Snail?" The tactics
piqued the curiosity of national commentators Rush Limbaugh and
Paul Harvey, both of whom responded in good fashion.[46]

The best news of all came when the federal judge declared that the listing by the Fish and Wildlife Service was "arbitrary and capricious" and ordered it stricken.[47] It was the first time in the history of the Endangered Species Act that a listing of a species under the act had been declared unlawful.

As important as the victory of the people of rural Owyhee County over the all-powerful Fish and Wildlife Service was the manner in which it was won. It was a team effort by a variety of groups and organizations—some of which have been around for more than one hundred years, some little more than one hundred weeks. It also demonstrated that even a tiny community like Bruneau in a tiny rural county like Owyhee could fight back and win.

The victory in Owyhee County and the growing grassroots battle against environmental oppression reveals something else that is important about what is happening in the West. The Wilderness Society's report on the Wise Use Movement said, in conclusion:

> [A]cross the country, groups initially organized to fight the resource battle on one front have a stake in connecting these fights. And there are several important links already established in the growing chain of Wise Use organizations at work in the grass roots.[48]

WHAT CAN YOU DO?

WHAT CAN YOU DO? A great deal!

For starters, you can decide to do something, anything. Make that decision and then do it today. Mail the letter. Make the phone call. Get in touch with the group. Sign and mail the check. Gather the information. Write the letter or article.

Where to start? Here's my list.

FIRST: SAVE THE CHILDREN

When my son Perry was in the third grade, I made an Earth Day presentation to his class. Most were stunned to learn, for example, that a Montana rock I showed the class contains the ore used to remove pollutants from automobile exhaust; that another Montana rock is the original state of talcum powder; that the brownish block from

Wyoming is used to make glass or clothes detergent; that the equivalent of a 100-foot tree is cut down every year for each and every one of them. Afterward, when the teacher asked what each child had learned, one little boy said, "I learned that a lot of stuff comes from stuff that you don't think comes from stuff."

As important as it is for children to learn about the "stuff stuff," an equally important issue has to be confronted. Running through much of the information our children are exposed to is a very dangerous antihuman, antimankind thread. Little wonder children swallow animal "rights," dislike business, believe we are running out of trees and every other resource, and are absolutely convinced that pollution will doom the planet.

Several months ago, when my son Luke and I were at a toy store, I discovered a new series of G.I. Joe toys: the Eco-Warriors series—a classic good guy–bad guy battle between those who seek to save the planet and those committed to destroying it. According to the packaging, one nefarious villain, code-named "CEO Cesspool," was "the Chief Executive Officer of a huge multi-national corporation with vast holdings in oil refineries, chemical plants and mills.... Armed with an acid assisting chain saw, [he] is determined to make the world as ugly and nasty as he is." This particular toy is for five-year-olds. No wonder environmental extremists have captured the children.

Yet I believe children can be saved from all this nonsense, for two very simple reasons.

First, children are incredible optimists. Though environmental groups fill them full of gloomy stories—the only cure for which is a generous contribution to an environmental organization—children naturally rebel against such dreary predictions.

Second, unlike the more radical in the environmental movement, children believe in technology. Although Vice President Al Gore opined in *Earth in the Balance* that "we are not that clever, we never have been," children know intuitively that we are "that clever." Only environmental extremists believe that technology is the problem and not the solution.

It is up to us to give children the facts and to restore their hope, not just in the future, but in humankind. The process of doing that begins at home and then must continue in our schools.

SECOND: COMMUNICATE WITH OUR COMMUNITIES

Too few people know how important the economic activities in which we engage are to the well-being of their community. In the Pacific Northwest, millions have learned that lesson from the hundreds of "timber dollars" signs posted on lawns and in homes and businesses and the thousands of "timber dollars" slips included with checks.

Our first step in any grassroots campaign is to educate the local community, whether with lawn signs or lectures to societies and groups. The victories our side has had, and there are a wealth of such, are stories of local activism. That's where it all starts.

THIRD: MAKE EMPLOYEES PART OF THE SOLUTION, NOT PART OF THE PROBLEM

Something heard increasingly from working men and women involved in the grassroots battle against environmental oppression is, "If you are unwilling to fight to save your job, you don't deserve to work for the company." Yet many of these same men and women complain that industry has not been forthright about the impact of environmental policies. One grassroots leader, on her first visit to Washington, D.C., was shocked by the profusion of proposals that could affect her job. "Why isn't the company telling us about these things so we can fight back?" she asked.

For too long American industry, bending backward to be a good corporate citizen, has given the impression that it can pay any price, bear any burden. Forgotten in such feel-good rhetoric are the men and women who suddenly find their jobs sacrificed on the altar of politically correct environmentalism. These people have the right to

know about all relevant public policy issues. They have the right to
fight for their jobs.

FOURTH: COMMUNICATE WITH THE
AMERICAN PEOPLE THROUGH THE MEDIA

We all love to hate the media, and often with good reason. But like
it or not, it is the only game in town. If the media don't report it, it
hasn't happened. The key to media exposure is your knowledge and
expertise combined with a desire to be heard.

Become a source of information for the media. If they don't get the
facts from you, where will they get them? Talk to reporters, editors,
and editorial boards. Write articles and letters to the editors. Volunteer as a guest on talk shows and call in to express your point of view.

FIFTH: THE WORLD IS RUN BY
THOSE WHO SHOW UP—SHOW UP!

In the early years of the environmental movement, environmental
activists filled meeting halls and protested loudly outside government
and corporate offices. Over the years, they have been doing less and
less of that since they are now running those government agencies
from the inside and, through litigation and congressional oversight,
from the outside.

It is our turn, as Bruce Vincent says, "to show up." I am convinced
that Westerners have altered public policy by the manner in which
they have shown up over the past two years. The fact that Secretary
Babbitt was not appointed to the Supreme Court, even though he
was clearly President Clinton's first choice, demonstrates the impact
of grassroots activism and showing up.

SIXTH: HELP YOUR FRIENDS

Perhaps the most important undertaking is to join and support those
who share your views. There are hundreds of organizations out there

fighting for your point of view, your rights, your liberties. All of them desperately need one thing: more members. They also need what I call the five "p's" of any successful organization: presence, participation, passion, prayers, and pocketbook.

John Stuart Mill stated that one person with "beliefs" is more powerful than ninety-nine people with "interests." Ralph Waldo Emerson opined that what matters is not what's behind us or what's ahead of us, but what's inside of us. And from some anonymous source comes this:

> Count that day lost whose low descending sun
> Views from thy hand no worthy action done.

WHAT YOU NEED TO KNOW

TIMBER [1]

♦ Trees grow old, become diseased—and die—like every other living thing.

♦ A "wild" forest may begin with 15,000 small seedlings per acre, but over the average 60- to 100-year cycle, at least 14,700 of those seedlings will die as growing trees compete for space.

♦ One-third of the country (731 million acres) is forested with 230 billion trees; that's nearly 1,000 trees for every man, woman, and child in America.

♦ America's forested land totals two-thirds of the forested

land present when Columbus sailed in 1492; there are more trees today than just 70 years ago.

♦ Two-thirds of that forested land (518 million acres) is "timberland," that is, it is capable of growing 20 cubic feet per acre per year of commercial wood.

♦ Sixty percent of our national forests are managed in a way that prevents timber harvesting, including set-asides for national parks, wilderness areas, and other "noncommercial" areas.

♦ The amount of the nation's forests that is off limits to timber harvesting is larger than Norway, Sweden, Denmark, Austria, Holland, Switzerland, Belgium, and Israel combined.

♦ America has more than 13 million acres of old-growth trees (200 years or older), more than half of which (8 million acres) are protected in national parks, wilderness areas, and other legislative and administrative set-asides.

♦ If America's protected old-growth trees were arranged in a band 5 miles wide, they would stretch from coast to coast.

♦ Insects and disease destroy about 4.5 billion cubic feet of timber each year, that is, a quarter of what America consumes for wood and paper products each year.

♦ Annually, more than 1.7 billion seedlings are planted by the forestry community; an average of 4 million trees a day; and six new trees for every man, woman, and child in the country.

♦ America grows more wood than it harvests, with tree growth three and one-half times what it was in 1920.

♦ Every year, each man, woman, and child in America uses

wood and paper products equal to what can be furnished from one 100-foot tree.

♦ America's need for paper and wood products will increase 50 percent by the year 2040, in order, for example, to publish books (more than 2 billion a year); magazines (more than 350 million a year); and newspapers (more than 24 billion a year).

♦ Trees are a renewable resource and more energy efficient than other materials: wood studs are 9 times more energy efficient than steel; wood siding is 22 times more energy efficient than a brick veneer wall and 4 times more energy efficient than aluminum siding; and a wood floor is 21 times more energy efficient than concrete.

♦ As an acre of trees in a young, healthy forest grows 4,000 pounds of wood a year, it consumes 5,880 pounds of carbon dioxide while discharging 4,280 pounds of oxygen. When the forest ages, more wood is decaying than growing; as a result, for every pound of wood decaying, a pound of oxygen is used and a pound and one-half of carbon dioxide is released into the atmosphere.

♦ As many as ten people are involved in the harvesting and milling of each tree.

♦ Twenty-five percent of the gross revenues generated by Forest Service sales of timber are returned to the county where the harvest occurred for use for roads and schools.

RANCHING [2]

♦ America's cattle industry is run mostly—more than 97 percent—by small- and mid-sized single families.

♦ Forty-two percent of America's cattle operations with

more than one hundred head have been in the same family for over fifty years; 21 percent have been in the same family for more than seventy-five years; and 12 percent for more than one hundred years.

♦ The West has more than 140,000 cattle and calves operations, which generate more than $8.5 billion in cash receipts.

♦ Cattle perform a key role in the chain of sun-to-grass-to-human food; 85 percent of the nutrients cattle consume comes from grasses and other roughages inedible to humans. Cattle also consume 25 percent of the by-products generated from food processing.

♦ By-products from cattle include edible fats, leather, pharmaceuticals, synthetic rubber, abrasives, shaving creams, soups, paint, printing inks, steel-rolling solutions, and thousands more. Leather for sports equipment alone uses the hides of more than 100,000 cattle each year.

♦ One-third of the sheep and lamb in the country graze on federal lands and one-half of the pasture grazed by the sheep industry in the eleven Western states is federal and state-owned lands. More than 71 percent of the country's sheep industry is located in the eleven Western states.

♦ More than 90 percent of the land classified by the U.S. government as grazing land is not suitable for farming or growing crops; it's too high, too rough, or too dry.

♦ Federal grazing lands are in the best condition of this century. Wildlife numbers—elk, bighorn sheep, moose, deer, antelope, and more—are at an all time high.

♦ Eighty percent or more of wildlife in the continental United States depend on private land for food, water, and shelter.

♦ Western ranchers have contributed a substantial amount of their own funds to improve conditions on federal lands. This includes stock ponds and water troughs for wildlife and livestock, as well as erosion controls. Grazing improves vegetation quality and diversity; it also stimulates forage growth and controls noxious weeds.

♦ Federal grazing fees are set by a market-driven formula, with the understanding that ranchers incur additional costs. These include improvements to land, transportation costs, and losses to predators. Twenty percent of federal grazing land is unused because of its high cost.

♦ Federal grazing lands are the backbone of the rural Western economy, since half the cattle graze part of the year on these lands. In many Western states, the number exceeds 80 percent.

MINING [3]

♦ Minerals are where you find them.

♦ Approximately 1,200 mines supply 90 percent of the free world's mineral requirements.

♦ America's $6.7 trillion economy is built upon the extraction of nonfuel minerals (silver, gold, copper) valued at one-half of 1 percent ($38 billion) of the economy.

♦ Metal mining in America uses only 508,000 acres, a mere .022 percent of the nation's land area—far less than used for roads or even airports.

♦ The average mining company can stay in business if it makes one significant discovery every twenty to thirty years.

♦ Forty thousand pounds of new minerals and metals must be mined every year for every man, woman, and child in America.

♦ Nearly fifty pounds of gold is used every day by dentists— requiring the mining of 18,500 tons of ore each day.

♦ Forty-seven percent of the land mined between 1930 and 1980 has been reclaimed; most of the rest is still producing minerals and metals.

♦ The same geological forces that created the West's mountains also created the ore bodies that supply the building blocks of a modern civilization.

♦ Less than 29 percent of federally owned land is available for mineral exploration and development.

OIL AND GAS [4]

♦ Oil and gas are where you find them; like mineral ore, the more expensive they are to recover, the more of them will be left in the ground.

♦ Seven to nine of every ten wells will be "dry."

♦ The Rocky Mountain West contains 80 percent of the undiscovered recoverable reserves of conventional onshore oil and 82 percent of natural gas underlying federal lands in the lower forty-eight states.

♦ America imports almost 50 percent of the oil it consumes; in 1973, during the nation's first energy "crisis," U.S. dependence on foreign oil was only 34.8 percent.

♦ Total recoverable U.S. oil may exceed 200 billion barrels—about 75 years worth at the current rate of consumption.

♦ In one decade (1980–1990), the men and women employed in the oil and gas industry declined by 30 percent—from 560,000 to 392,000.

♦ In one decade (1982–1992), the number of independent oil and gas companies declined by 67 percent, from 12,955 to 4,244.

APPENDIX C

WHAT NO ONE KNOWS
ABOUT THE WEST

A FEW MONTHS AGO, I was in Oklahoma City, Oklahoma, to attend the Oklahoma Cattlemen's Association Annual Convention. As I waited to check into the motel, I stepped over to a rack of pamphlets promoting local tourist attractions. One caught my eye: the one for the "Arbuckle Wilderness," south of Oklahoma City.

For Westerners the word "wilderness" has a very particular meaning. It is reserved for those areas designated by Congress to be set aside under the Wilderness Act of 1964, as land "where the earth and its community of life are untrammeled by man" and "where man himself is a visitor who does not remain."[1]

Westerners are extremely sensitive about the use of the word "wilderness," since they realize that the senators and members of Congress who vote for wilderness are not from the area being designated or even from the West, but from a district or state far removed.

For these distant supporters of wilderness, a vote for designation is an easy call, since it doesn't affect their constituents economically. Moreover, often their constituents who are aware of the issue have driven through some of those "wilderness" areas "out West" and believe that they should be protected.

I thought about that as I stood there in Oklahoma City reading about the Arbuckle Wilderness, 75 miles south of the Capital, which featured, a massive zoo, a drive-through park with free-roaming animals, a petting zoo, camel and llama rides, go carts, a playground, kiddie and adult bumper boats, and a maze, as well as other attractions. No wonder people from outside the West can't understand why we Westerners don't rush to embrace wilderness designation.[2] No wonder people from outside the West can't understand that those "wide-open spaces" they see when they visit aren't part of a vast "wilderness."

While the federal government owns the majority of the land in the West, not all of it is managed by the National Park Service, or the Forest Service, or even the Bureau of Land Management. Each of those agencies has millions of acres that it manages in accordance with a variety of federal statutes to serve a host of purposes.

When those from elsewhere think of the West, they most often envision its magnificent national parks: Yellowstone, Yosemite, Redwood, Zion, Rocky Mountain, Grand Canyon, and Glacier. They do so with good reason. The largest parks in the country are in the West. Excluding the state of Alaska, whose national parks dwarf the rest of the nation, more than 69 percent of the nation's parklands are in the eleven Western states.[3] Of the Western states with the most parklands, California has 4.6 million acres, Wyoming has 2.3 million acres, Arizona has 1.9 million acres, Washington has 1.8 million acres, and Montana has 1.2 million acres.[4]

Not all lands managed by the National Park Service, however, are national parks—that is lands that meet the criteria for and are restricted in the manner of parklands. Thus, the National Park Service system also includes three broad land categories: natural areas, recreational areas, and historical areas.

Despite their size, and the fact that they most often spring to mind when discussing Western federal lands, National Park Service–managed lands are a relatively minor encroachment upon the model provided by other states, where citizens own most of the land. For example, 95 percent of the state of Texas is owned by private citizens, despite the fact that Texas has more federal park lands than all but seven other states. The reason: national parks are just about the only type of federal land ownership in Texas. That isn't the case with other Western states.

The National Park Service is only one of several federal agencies within the Department of the Interior that manages federal lands in the West. The Bureau of Reclamation manages more than 5 million acres throughout the West, with nearly a million acres each in Wyoming and Arizona, and a half a million or more in Idaho, Nevada, and Utah.[5] Another Interior Department agency, the Fish and Wildlife Service, manages wildlife refuges totalling more than 4 million acres in the eleven Western states, with 1.6 million acres in Arizona and more than a half a million acres each in Nevada, Montana, and Oregon.[6] A number of other federal agencies within the Interior Department manage relatively small holdings throughout the West, including the Bureau of Indian Affairs—not including individual Indian reservations—(170,060 acres), the Geological Survey (247 acres), and the Bureau of Mines (105 acres).

The Interior Department agency with the largest land management responsibility in the West is the Bureau of Land Management (BLM). BLM holdings dwarf every other agency, inside and outside the Department of the Interior, making the BLM, in Western state after Western state, the biggest single landlord. Of the 178,488,065 acres managed by the Bureau of Land Management in the lower forty-eight states, 99.8 percent, or 178,083,728 acres, is in the eleven Western states.[7]

The top three states, in terms of BLM-managed land, are Nevada, with 47.956 million acres, or 68 percent of the state; Utah, with 22.139 million acres, or 42 percent of the state; and Wyoming, with

18.393 million acres, or 30 percent of the state.[8] California has
17.258 million acres of land managed by the BLM, or 17 percent of
the state, while Oregon has 15.783 million acres of BLM land, or 26
percent of the state.[9]

To put the lands managed in the state of Nevada by the BLM in
perspective, imagine an area the size of the state of South Dakota, the
nation's sixteenth largest state, within Nevada, the seventh largest
state. BLM-managed lands in Utah total an area the size of the state
of Indiana, while BLM-managed lands in Wyoming total an area the
size of the states of Connecticut and West Virginia combined.[10]

Little wonder, then, that the secretary of the interior, whose
responsibilities include the National Park Service, the Bureau of
Land Management, the Fish and Wildlife Service, the Bureau of
Reclamation, and the Bureau of Indian Affairs, is one of the most
important officials in the West—certainly as important as governors
and senators and members of Congress.

Another land management agency with substantial holdings in the
West is the U.S. Forest Service (USFS), an agency within the
Department of Agriculture. Of the 162.8 million acres of land managed by the USFS in the lower forty-eight states, 138.8 million acres
or 85 percent are in the eleven Western states.[11] The states with the
most lands managed by the Forest Service include California with
20.5 million acres, or 21 percent of the state; Idaho with 19.9 million
acres, or 38 percent of the state; Montana with 15.8 million acres, or
17 percent of the state; and Oregon with 15.6 million acres, or 25
percent of the state.[12]

For California and Idaho, that means an area within their borders
larger than the state of Maine is managed by the Forest Service. Forest Service-managed lands in Montana, Oregon, and Colorado are
comparable to an area the size of the state of West Virginia within
each of those states.[13]

Unlike the vast majority of the lands managed by the National
Park Service, most of the lands under the management of the Bureau
of Land Management and the Forest Service are to be managed for

multiple use, including recreation (such as skiing, hiking, camping, off-road vehicle use, hunting), mining, oil and gas exploration, grazing, logging, and other activities. While a portion of lands managed by the BLM and a much larger portion of lands managed by the USFS have been set aside for management as wilderness, most lands remain within a multiple-use classification.

Of course, that is not the case with yet another sizable portion of Western lands managed by the federal government: military reservations. Obviously, such lands are set aside for single-purpose military use. The Department of the Army controls nearly 6 million acres of land throughout the West, with its largest holdings of 2.8 million acres in New Mexico and nearly a million acres in both Arizona and Utah. The Department of the Navy lays claim to 216,000 acres, 93 percent of which is in California.[14] The largest amount of Western land devoted to military purposes is that managed by the Air Force— in excess of 7 million acres—most of which is in Nevada (2.99 million acres) and Arizona (2.59 million acres).[15]

The point of all this is that while much Western land looks the same passing through, the fact of the matter is that it is owned and overseen by a variety of federal land managers with differing obligation, objectives, and orientations. It may all look like "wilderness" to folks from somewhere else, but there is a big difference between the statutory basis upon which a BLM district official manages the land under his or her control and the laws that govern an adjacent military reservation, national park, wildlife refuge, wilderness, or national recreation area.

About the Author

WILLIAM PERRY PENDLEY WAS BORN and raised on the western edge of the Great Plains, east of Cheyenne, Wyoming. A graduate of the University of Wyoming College of Law, he first battled on behalf of the West as an attorney to Senator Clifford P. Hansen (R-WY), later as an attorney to the House of Representatives Interior and Insular Affairs Committee, and then as a high-ranking official in the Reagan administration. He has represented hundreds of Westerners in the battle against environmental oppression and has traveled, on business and for pleasure, in every county in the West. He is the author of *It Takes a Hero: The Grassroots Battle Against Environmental Oppression*. He and his wife, Lis, and two sons, Perry and Luke, live in the Rocky Mountains west of Denver, Colorado.

Notes

CHAPTER 1

1. Rand McNally, *1995 Road Atlas*, pp. 108, A18.

   A trip from Washington, D.C., through the South, visiting the state capitals of Virginia, North Carolina, South Carolina, Georgia, and Alabama, is only slightly longer than the trip between the state capitals of two Western neighbors—Wyoming and Idaho. Ibid., p. A18.

2. 1990 Census of Population and Housing, U.S. Department of Commerce, Bureau of the Census, October 1993. The eight states of the Mountain West (Montana, New Mexico, Arizona, Nevada, Colorado, Wyoming, Utah, and Idaho) are ranked 4th, 5th, 6th, 7th, 8th, 9th, 11th, and 13th in land area, but place 48th, 37th, 24th, 39th, 26th, 50th, 35th, and 42nd in population.

   While the other Western states are more densely populated—Nevada has 10.9 people per square mile; Idaho, 12.2; New Mexico, 12.5; Utah, 21; Colorado, 31.8; Arizona, 32.3—they are still the most sparsely settled states in the Union. Ibid., 77–144. In fact, the fourteen most sparsely populated states include the eight states of the Mountain West, plus Alaska, the four Great Plains states (South Dakota, North Dakota, Nebraska, Kansas), and Oregon, p. 131.

3. Western counties, however, are extremely large. Only 21 percent of the nation's counties are larger than the state of Rhode Island, but 48 percent of those counties are in the West. U.S. Census, op. cit., p. 411. Only 9 percent of the nation's counties are larger than the state of Delaware, but 74 percent of those are in the West. Only 2.4 percent of the nation's counties are larger than Connecticut, but 71 percent of those are in the West. Ibid.

   Arizona's Coconino County (18,619 square miles) and Nevada's Nye County (18,147 square miles) and Elko County (17,181 square miles) are each nearly as large as Vermont and Maryland combined. Ibid. pp. 115,

126, 132–133, 144. Arizona's Mohave County (13,312 square miles) is larger than New Jersey and Hawaii combined, while Arizona's Apache County (11,205 square miles) is larger than Maryland and Rhode Island put together. Ibid., pp. 115, 119, 126, 133, 139.

4. Drive north out of Billings, Montana's largest city (population 81,151), and within an hour you're in Musselshell County (2.2 people per square miles), which is 700 percent more populated than its neighbor to the north, Petroleum County (.3 people per square mile) or its eastern neighbor, Garfield County (.3 people per square mile). U.S. Census, op. cit., pp. 131, 502.

    A trip south out of Boise, Idaho's largest city (population 125,738), takes one through Elmore County (6.9 people per square mile) and then, within the hour, into Owyhee County (1.1 people per square mile). Crossing into Nevada, people get a little closer together in Elko County (two people per square mile), but then spread out as one continues west through Eureka County (.4 people per square mile), Lander County (1.1 people per square mile), Humboldt County (1.3 people per square mile), and Pershing County (.7 people per square mile). At this point, it is still a three-hour drive to Reno (population 133,850). Ibid., pp. 120, 132–33, 452, 504.

5. In Utah, the highest reading ever was 117°F in Saint George, with the lowest reading ever of -69 degree at Peter's Sink. *The World Almanac and Book of Facts 1993* (New York, N.Y.: Pharos Books), pp. 188–189.

6. *Goode's World Atlas*, 17th ed. (Chicago, Il.: Rand McNally, 1987), p. 83.

7. Ibid., p. 82. The coastal areas of Washington, Oregon, and California, as well as the northern mountains of the West, receive significantly more rainfall each year than the remainder of the region—anywhere from 40 to over 100 inches.

8. Several months ago, I was in Wolf Point, Montana, in the northeastern corner of the state. When I stopped at a gas station, I was amazed to hear the Colorado Rockies baseball game being broadcast over the station's outdoor speakers. It was like driving from Kansas City to Detroit and being able to listen to the Kansas City Royals play the Los Angeles Dodgers.

9. "Public Land Statistics 1992," U.S. Department of the Interior, Bureau of Land Management, p. 5. This is particularly the case, of course, in those Western counties in which federal land ownership predominates. It is troublesome enough that as much as half of the land area in a state is held and managed by the federal government. It is far worse when the federal government owns 60, 70, 80, and even 90 percent of the land area of a given county. For example, 78 percent of Lincoln County, Montana, is federally owned; 84 percent of Kane County, Utah, and Coconino County, Arizona, are federally owned; and 97 percent of Teton County, Wyoming, is federally owned.

10. See Appendix C, "What No One Knows About the West."

11. As to the use of the word "extremistist" *Field & Stream* conservation editor George Reiger wrote this in a letter to the *New York Times:* "People who believe that no creatures should be killed, that no forests should be cut, that, in fact, the goldfinch that comes to their feeder this winter is the very same bird that visited them a decade ago should be called ultra-preservationists,

radical environmentalists, unrealistic extremists, or residents of the twilight zone, but please, please, don't call them conservationists. They are not."

January 10, 1978, quoted in *Competitive Enterprise Institute Update*, February 1994.

12. Conversation with Ms. Jane Cushman of Clayton Yeutter's office on September 28, 1994.

13. Environmental groups wage war on four fronts: (1) lobbying Congress for legislative change; (2) pressing the executive branch for regulatory change; (3) litigating in the judicial branch, both to change that with which they disagree and to compel that which they support; and (4) building public support through media and cultural outlets.

14. Quoted in Ron Arnold and Alan Gottlieb, *Trashing the Economy: How Runaway Environmentalism Is Wrecking America* (Bellevue, Wash: Free Enterprise Press, 1993), p. 333.

15. The best data-filled analysis of Environment, Inc. can be found in Arnold and Gottlieb, op. cit.

16. Capital Research Foundation's annual Report on Corporate Philanthropy reported in 1993 that "[t]he grades received by this year's sample must discourage any citizen who favors private initiative over collective coercion, individual responsibility over public compulsion, and a free market rather than a regimented social and economic system." Furthermore: "It may come as a surprise to some to learn that Corporate America is NOT inherently conservative and does NOT carry the banner for free markets, private property and private contract. On the contrary, the philanthropy of the largest public corporations is 'politically correct' beyond any doubt."

Stuart Nolan, Gregory P. Conko, Dr. M. Bruce Johnson, "Patterns of Corporate Philanthropy," Capital Research Center, Washington, D.C., 1993, pp. 1–3.

17. Many regard environmentalism, if not as a religion, at least as a belief system with the trappings of religion. Fred Barnes, editor of the *New Republic*, remarked at the National Review Institute Conservative Summit in January 1993 that Gore's approach to environmental policy is similar to that associated with a religion: that is, there are doctrines and dogma; the beliefs are matters of faith, not science, and are therefore not subject to disproof; there are high priests; and finally, those who disagree are little more than heretics. See also Michael S. Coffman, *Saviors of the Earth?* (Chicago, Il.: Northfield Publishing, 1994), and Michael S. Coffman, *Environmentalism! The Dawn of Aquarius or the Twilight of a New Dark Age?* (Bangor, Maine: Environmental Perspectives, 1992).

18. A listing of the music and movie stars who are outspoken supporters of environmental groups looks like the attendance list at the annual Academy Awards.

19. The Fish and Wildlife Service (FWS) insists that when a bear rears up as did this one, it is not the sign of an imminent attack but merely what the government might call a "scoping operation." "[This is t]he worst time to shoot," says the FWS. When the bear comes down on all fours and charges (at 40 m.p.h.) that too is a poor time to shoot, according to the FWS, because it may be a "false charge."

20. *U.S. Fish and Wildlife Service v. John Shuler,* Docket Number Denver 91-2, Slip Op., March 11, 1993, pp. 7, 8.
21. John Shuler is represented by Mountain States Legal Foundation. The decision of the administrative law judge is on appeal to the Interior Board of Land Appeals in the U.S. Department of the Interior.
22. Quoted in the late Dixy Lee Ray's *Environmental Overkill: Whatever Happened to Common Sense* (Washington, D.C.: Regnery Gateway, 1993), p. 204.
23. Al Gore, *Earth in the Balance: Ecology and the Human Spirit* (New York, New York: Houghton Mifflin Company, 1992), pp. 223, 236.
24. For Gore, "saving the planet" means "embarking on an all-out effort to use every policy and program, every law and institution, every treaty and alliance, every tactic and strategy, every plan and course of action… [that will lead to] sacrifice, struggle, and a wrenching transformation of society…." Ibid., p. 274.
25. Quoted in Robert James Bidinotto, "Animal Rights: A New Species of Egalitarianism," *The Intellectual Activist,* September 14, 1983, p. 3. Quoted also in the most definitive and in-depth examination of the animal rights movement, Kathleen Marquardt's, *Animal Scam: The Beastly Abuse of Human Rights* (Washington, D.C.: Regnery Gateway, 1993).
    My son Luke came home from the first grade a few years ago with a book called *The Most Dangerous Animal in the World.* Page after page depicted ferocious and fearsome beasts; the last entry labeled "the most dangerous animal" was of two men in safari gear standing in the jungle. Similarly, a logger sent me a page from a preschooler's workbook asking which of four drawings did not belong. Three drawings were of animals in the woods, the fourth was a logger with a chain saw beside a pile of logs.
26. Quoted in Katie McCabe, "Beyond Cruelty," *Washingtonian,* February 1990, p. 191.
27. Quoted in Chip Brown, "She's a Portrait of Zealotry in Plastic Shoes," *Washington Post,* November 13, 1983, p. B10.
28. Dixy Lee Ray, op. cit., pp. 203–204.
29. David M. Graber, *Los Angeles Times Book Review,* October 22, 1989, p. 9. Manes quotes Dave Foreman, cofounder of Earth First, as saying: "It's time for a warrior society to rise up out of the Earth and throw itself in front of the juggernaut of destruction, to be antibodies against the human pox that's ravaging this precious beautiful planet." Christopher Manes, *Green Rage* (Boston, Toronto, London: Little Brown & Co., 1990), p. 84.
30. *Sierra Club v. Babbitt,* MO-91-CA-069, U.S. District Court for the Western District of Texas, Midland/Odessa Division, Order, February 1, 1993. In mid-1994, the U.S. Fish and Wildlife Service proposed to designate 20.5 million acres in thirty-three central Texas counties as critical habitat for the golden cheeked warbler. If approved, it will be the largest Critical Habitat ever. "Largest Critical Habitat in the Nation is Proposed in Texas," *National Endangered Species Act Reform Coalition Newsletter,* Summer 1994, p. 7.
31. 59 Federal Register 15366, April 1, 1994.
32. *Wild Earth* (Special Issue), "The Wildlands Project," 1992, Cenozoic Society, Inc., Canton, New York., p. 19.

David A. Russell, president of Citizens for Constitutional Property Rights, Inc., thinks that figure is low. Citing sources such as the *Florida Farm Bureau and Florida Trend* magazine, he believes plans for government-owned set-asides range from 64 percent of the state to 84 percent. Letter from David A. Russell dated September 7, 1994.

33. William Perry Pendley, *It Takes a Hero: The Grassroots Battle Against Environmental Oppression* (Bellevue, Washington: Free Enterprise Press, 1994), p. 93.

34. Ibid., pp. 171-175.

35. Ibid., pp. 109-115. Although the timber sale eventually took place, the sale cost the federal government more than it received.

36. Ibid., p. 88.

37. See, *Pozsgai v. United States*, Petition for Writ of Certiorari 93-733, Brief of Petitioners.

38. See, *Ocie and Carey Mills v. United States*, 93-2757, U.S. Court of Appeals for the Eleventh Circuit, Brief of Appellant.

39. Gore, op. cit., p. 274.

40. Pendley, op. cit., pp. 129-131.

41. Conversation with Mary Wirth, September 8, 1994. The other three counties that contain the Allegheny National Forest and the percentage of federal land ownership are Warren County (32 percent); Forest County (48 percent); and Elk County (48 percent). Ibid. This is in a state where a mere 2 percent of the land is owned by the federal government. U.S. Department of the Interior, Bureau of Land Management, "Public Land Statistics 1992," p. 5.

42. "The Wildlands Project," op. cit., inside cover. This proposal is not just about the West: "Our vision is simple: we live for the day when Grizzlies in Chihuahua have an unbroken connection to Grizzlies in Alaska; when Gray Wolf populations are continuous from New Mexico to Greenland; when vast unbroken forests and flowing plains again thrive and support pre-Columbian populations of plants and animal....

"We reject the notion that wilderness is merely remote, scenic terrain suitable for backpacking. Rather, we see wilderness as the home for unfettered life, free from industrial human intervention."

Wilderness means: "Vast landscapes without roads, dams, motorized vehicles, powerlines, overflights, or other artifacts of civilization, where evolutionary and ecological processes that represent four billion years of Earth wisdom can continue." Ibid., pp. 3-4.

43. One Eastern grassroots property rights leader was asked to give the primary difference between her community and its counterparts in the West. She responded: "The two hundred years of history of the 'takings clause' of the Fifth Amendment."

44. Along these lines, the movement to reclaim the Tenth Amendment—that all powers not delegated to the United States are reserved to the states or to the people—is also gaining support. "Colorado, Hawaii, and Missouri have passed resolutions ordering the federal government to stop passing on to them unfunded federal mandates. California and Illinois have introduced similar resolutions. New York is drafting one. Active Tenth Amend-

ment committees have been formed to consider the matter in Washington, Oregon, Nevada, Montana, and Alaska." Cal Thomas, *Washington Times*, August 24, 1994, p. A14.

The Tenth Amendment, once thought to be a "dead letter," has been revived by the decision of the *U.S. Supreme Court in United States v. Lopez*, ___ U.S. ___, 115 S.Ct. 1624, 131 L.Ed.2nd 626 (1995).

45. As discussed in Chapter 9, Secretary Babbitt refused to issue patents as required by the General Mining Law until ordered to do so by a federal court. As discussed in Chapter 3, the Clean Water Act is being used to obtain federal control over private property, rather than its intent—to protect the quality of municipal water supplies. As discussed in Chapter 2, the Forest Service under Secretary Espy managed national forests to burn, not for timber harvests.

46. "Children's fund catching up with cougar's," *Rocky Mountain News*, May 28, 1994, p. 44A. "At the end of last week, the cub had gotten $21,000; a trust fund for the children $9,000."

47. America's interest in the Middle East is all but driven by the nation's—in fact, the Western world's—dependence on its rich oil resources. Pundits, commenting on the Persian Gulf War of 1991, said we would not have been so anxious to assist Kuwait had its largest export crop been broccoli.

48. When the ski resort owner told the federal employee that there were no ponds where tadpoles could grow into frogs for miles around, the bureaucrat said, "You know that and I know that but my boss doesn't so I have to do this survey."

49. Conversation with Andrea Wojtasek, U.S. Forest Service, June 29, 1995.

50. Vice President Gore—the nation's most prominent doomsayer regarding the "greenhouse effect" and global warming—was silent regarding the Western fires.

51. In the summer of 1994, as I passed through Yellowstone National Park, I maneuvered around the incinerated tree trunks from the fires of 1988 that had fallen on the road the previous night. I later learned the electricity in the vicinity had also gone off when some of those falling trees hit power lines.

CHAPTER 2

1. Mike learned later why the Forest Service did not respond immediately. The Forest Service had received his calls, but concluded, erroneously, that the fire was in a wilderness area. At the time, the Forest Service policy had been to "let burn" all fires in wilderness areas.

2. One of Mike's colleagues in the Oregon Lands Coalition (OLC) is Jackie Lang. Jackie is rightly credited as being the reason for much of the media success enjoyed by the OLC. In September 1990, Jackie and other members of the OLC traveled to Washington, D.C., for "The Fly-In for Freedom," to walk the halls of Congress and put a human face on the distant, impersonal media story of logging in the Pacific Northwest. I asked what most surprised her about her trip to Washington.

"How uninformed most of the people are," she replied. "During a conversation with a senator's environmental l.a. [legislative assistant], I said, 'When trees die...' and he stopped me. 'What do you mean, when trees die?' he said. 'When trees die,' I replied. 'Trees die?' he said. 'I didn't know that!'"

3. The fire had destroyed more than 28,000 acres of valuable timber resources in the Wallowa Whitman National Forest, not to mention wildlife habitat. The cost of fighting that fire, including rehabilitation, exceeded $10 million and put at risk the lives of the more than eight hundred brave men and women who battled the blaze. Conversations with Mike Weidman, September 1994.

4. The first national forests were created in 1891 and were called "reserves." The 1897 Organic Act authorized commercial timber harvesting.

5. *Webster's Third International Dictionary* (Springfield, Mass.: G. & C. Merriam Company), p. 482.

6. In 1907, the name of the federal forest was changed from forest reserves to national forests to dispel the notion that federal forests were locked up. Dr. John H. Beuter, "Overview of Below-Cost Timber Sale Issue," Mason, Bruce & Girard, Inc., *Technical Bulletin* No. 90-02, November 30, 1990, p. 2.

7. 16 U.S.C. §§473-478, 479-482, 551. One court has held that the USFS "is not forbidden to consider the benefits to loggers, and hence to consumers of wood products, in deciding how to manage our national forests." *Cronin v. United States Department of Agriculture*, 919 F.2d 439, 448 (7th Cir. 1990).

8. Table 24, Federally Owned Land By Agency, Bureau and State. As of September 30, 1992, General Services Administration, at pp. 10-11. Alaska has 21.7 million acres of land for which the Forest Service is the managing agency, or 12 percent of all national forest lands. Ibid.

9. Environmentalists also oppose salvage sales. In 1991, Wendell Wood of the Oregon Natural Resources Council declared, "[W]e view logging after a fire as mugging a burn victim." *Evergreen*, January/February 1992, p. 8.

10. "Forest Service Administrative Review Regulations and Proposed Revisions," James P. Perry, assistant general counsel, Natural Resources Division, U.S. Department of Agriculture, American Bar Association Administrative Appeals and Judicial Review, May 22, 1992, p. 3. A proposal to sharply curtail such appeals generated twenty thousand comments, with the majority in favor.

11. Southwestern Regional Supervisor Larry Henson wrote in "Environmentalist Lawsuits Cost Taxpayers," *Albuquerque Journal*, September 24, 1994:
"A total of 261 appeals... were filed in the Southwestern Region (New Mexico and Arizona) in the past four years.... We estimate that about $2,350,000 has been spent to process the 261 appeals, or an average of about $9,000 each. The cost of the appeals does not take into account delays of sometimes many months for reworking the project, or the costs to communities or individuals because of delays in implementing projects."

* * *

"No matter who prevails in the appeals or the lawsuits, these remedies are costly in both time and dollars to the taxpayer. There are no special Forest Service funds for appeals or defending lawsuits, so the money comes from dollars appropriated for other purposes. For example, when millions of dollars are spent on appeals and lawsuits, those funds are unavailable for badly needed wildlife habitat and riparian improvement projects, fuelwood activities, new timber sales, and threatened and endangered species surveys."

12. Conversations with Henry Batsel on September 8, 1994. "It was awful here. Every day there were ten letters to the editor complaining about how the local environmental group FAWN (Friends Aware of Wildlife Needs) was terrible for not considering the needs of people. People had stopped spending in anticipation of the mill closure. Houses were put up for sale. People moved away. It showed the whole community how uncaring the environmentalists were that they would let this happen to our town."

13. *Sierra C.A.R.E.*, March 24, 1994, vol. 3, no. 1, pp. 1, 4, 5. On some of the timber sales, the Forest Service had even entered into contracts with the mills. Environmentalists are demanding that these contracts be withdrawn.

14. In the legislative process, what is referred to as logrolling involves making accommodations between and among various senators and members of Congress to ensure final passage of legislation. Because of the highly successful environmental lobbies in Washington, hardly a piece of federal legislation that reaches the president's desk for signature comes without several "clarifying" amendments concerning environmental protection, or at least, sensitivity.

15. 5 U.S.C. § 702.

16. 42 U.S.C. § 4321 et seq. When the NEPA was adopted, no one could possibly have objected to informed decision making. It sounded like fundamental good government. But the NEPA has become a favorite weapon of environmental extremists to stop everything. In fact, much of the litigation over the northern spotted owl was not based upon the Endangered Species Act. Rather, the lawsuits were based upon the NEPA. Environmental groups simply alleged that the USFS had not prepared the proper documents in reaching its timber harvesting decisions.

17. "Group to push for no-cut policy—Timber: The Oregon Natural Resources Council urges an end to logging of the region's federal forests," *Register Guard*, February 4, 1994, 1B.

18. When it comes to their own property, some environmentalists have another view. As Rush Limbaugh and others reported, a Sierra Club official clearcut a section of his property in northeastern Washington. Says Ken Kohli, communications director for Intermountain Forest Industry Association:

"This Sierra Club executive, the same person who has berated logging and everything associated with it for the better part of a decade, is now logging his own vacation property. He is doing this logging on a tract of land that is surrounded on all sides by a wildlife refuge. He is not only cutting timber on that land, he is also harvesting some old growth timber, the same type of trees he is suing the Colville National Forest for not protecting."

"Sierra Club Regional Director Clearcuts His Land," *GreenSpeak*, January 1994, Issue 52, p. 2.

19. William Perry Pendley, *It Takes a Hero: The Grassroots Battle Against Envi-*

ronmental Oppression (Bellevue, Washington: Free Enterprise Press, 1994), p. 189.

20. U.S. Department of the Interior, Bureau of Land Management, U.S. Department of Agriculture, Forest Service, "Draft Environmental Impact Statement on Management of Habitat for Late Succession and Old Growth Forest Related Species within the Range of the Northern Spotted Owl," 1993. Summary, S-8, under "consequence"—"a return to presettlement conditions."

21. Pendley, op. cit., p. 189.

22. Conversation with former Kootenai National Forest Supervisor Jim Rathbun, September 23, 1994.

23. George Riddle, "History of Early Days in Oregon," a series of articles in the *Riddle Enterprise*, 1920.

24. "Settlement of the Black Hills occurred at a time in ecologic history when large sections of the forest were denuded from natural causes—fires, bark beetles, and storms of various kinds." Donald R. Progulske, "Yellow Ore, Yellow Hair, Yellow Pine—A Photographic Study of a Century of Forest Ecology," *Bulletin 616*, July 1974, Agricultural Experiment Station, South Dakota State University, Brookings, SD, p. 121.

25. *Evergreen*, March/April 1994, pp. 16-17.

26. Ibid.

27. The fire in Yellowstone National Park not only burned parkland, but huge portions of the surrounding national forests as well as private land.

28. *Evergreen*, January/February, 1992, p. 5.

29. Ibid, p. 7.

30. *USA Today*, March 9, 1994, p. 8A. The University of Idaho reports: "If forest health is a statement about trees at risk of mortality from insects, diseases, and wildfires, then much of Idaho's forest land is either unhealthy or on the verge of poor health, especially in the national forests that represent two-thirds of the state's timberlands."

    Jay O'Laughlin, et al., "Forest Health Conditions in Idaho—Executive Summary," University of Idaho, *Report No. 11*, December 1993, p. 1.

31. *Evergreen*, January/February 1992, p. 10.

32. President Clinton vetoed legislation that would permit the harvesting of federal timber devastated by disease and fire.

33. Fire fighting is one of the reasons the nation's forests have become as productive as they are. Douglas MacCleery reports that the area consumed by wildfires has been reduced by more than 95 percent from the 40 to 50 million acres burned annually in the early 1900s (an area the size of Virginia, West Virginia, Maryland, and Delaware combined) to 2 to 4 million acres today. Douglas W. MacCleery, "What on Earth Have We Done to Our Forests?" *Forest Service*, p. 7.

34. Preliminary RPA Assessment Update, 1992. While much of the nation's original forest was removed to create crop lands to feed the nation, the nation's forest and farmland balance is about as it was in 1920 because of the increased ability of farmers to feed the nation, and the world, on the same amount of land. RPA Technical Report, RM-175, Forest Service, 1989.

35. New Perspectives on Managing the U.S. National Forest System, Forest Service, 1991. See also, "The Great Forest Debate," *Evergreen*, pp. 7–13.
36. *The Condition and Trends of U.S. Forests*, Forest Service, 1991.
37. *New Perspectives, 1992*; Forest Statistics, 1987.

    Much of the nation's national forests have been placed off limits. In the Pacific Northwest—the Persian Gulf of timber—the impact has been particularly dramatic. By 1970, more than 4.4 million acres of federal land had been set aside by Congress in wilderness areas, national parks, and national recreational areas. Wilderness legislation in 1976, 1978, and 1984 set aside another 2 million acres. In the 1980s, the forest planning process, required by Congress, caused the withdrawal of 9 million acres, with another 3.6 million acres being managed primarily for uses other than timber harvesting. In 1990, 1.8 million acres were withdrawn as owl habitat conservation areas. In 1991, an additional million acres were designated critical owl habitat. Thus, even before President Clinton's Option 9 "solution," 82 percent of the Pacific Northwest's federal forest land base had been set aside in areas where timber harvesting is prohibited or severely restricted.

    Says Jim Geisinger, president of the Northwest Forestry Association: "What few people realize is that we are now fighting over the last 18 percent of this region's federal forest land base [since other] dominant uses already prevail on the other 82 percent." Conversation with Jim Geisinger, September 1994.

38. Timber sold in the Clearwater National Forest has fallen from 105 MMBF in 1991 to 66.5 MMBF in 1992 and 26.5 MMBF in 1993. Forest Service Timber Program Data, Northern Idaho National Forests, compiled by Intermountain Forest Industry Association from Forest Service Timber Statistics, Accomplishment Reports, June 1994.
39. Conversation with Jim Riley, Intermountain Forest Industry Association, September 23, 1994.
40. Local expenditures by sawmill employees fell from $6.6 million to $4.6 million, while wages earned in response to the demand for goods and services fell by nearly a third. Meanwhile, Coconino County's severance tax fell from $182,881 in 1989 to $81,381 in 1992. "An Assessment of the Economic Impacts of the Kaibab Mills on Southern Utah and Northern Arizona," Southwest Center for Resource Analysis, December 1, 1992, pp. 1, 4, 16.
41. "NBC Nightly News," May 30, 1995. NBC newsman Roger O'Neil: "But then government timber sales slowed down as regulatory red tape from the Forest Service increased. Studies for clean air, clean water, recreation, wildlife. Study this, study that. Twenty-four studies in all cut the log supply in half. Then in 1993, it was cut in half again. The Mexican spotted owl, never seen in the Kaibab Forest, but photographed 120 miles away in another forest, was put on the endangered species list. That forced four more studies and more delays."
42. Conversation with Jim Matson, chairman of the Southwest Natural Resources Council, on September 23, 1994. Matson says the cutbacks are

due to four factors: restrictions because of the goshawk as well as the Mexican spotted owl; administrative appeals of timber sales; Clinton/Gore
administration manipulation of the Forest Service budget by cutting the
funds available for the sale of timber; and Vice President Gore's reinven-
tion of government, which is driving skilled career professionals out of the
Forest Service.

43. "An Assessment of the Economic Impact of the Kaibab Mills on Southern
Utah and Northern Arizona," Southwest Center for Resource Analysis,
December 1, 1992, p. 17.

44. "Northern Spotted Owl in California," *Issues and Answers*, California
Forestry Association, October 1992. As of late 1992, the aggregate timber
sale program in four California national forests—Mendocino, Shasta-
Trinity, Six Rivers, and Klamath—had dropped from 660 million board
feet to 50 million board feet.

   Forest Service policies, adopted to protect the California spotted owl,
don't only affect jobs. Jim Craine of the California Forestry Association
explains:

   "In summary, we are experiencing a loss of general forest health, a
degradation of wildlife habitat, increasing public costs, increasing fire danger and the resultant hazard to adjacent properties, a loss of recreation
potential, and a degradation of visual quality. 'Aside from that, Mrs. Lincoln, how did you enjoy the play?'"

   Memorandum from Jim Craine, dated June 10, 1994.

45. Beginning in 1983, the U.S. Fish and Wildlife Service demanded that more
and more land in the Kootenai National Forest be set aside as grizzly bear
habitat. In the words of the Forest Service, "Standards for grizzly bear management have steadily evolved.... As a result, the amount of grizzly habitat... as well as the amount of needed prescriptive guidelines have steadily
increased." Forest Service, "The Evolution of Grizzly Bear Habitat Identi-
fication and the Additional Acreage to Be Incorporated in a Kootenai Forest Plan Update," May 7, 1992, p. 3.

46. Conversation with Susan Ponce on September 8, 1994. In Wyoming's
Shoshone National Forest, the Forest Service has indicated that timber
harvest levels will have to be reduced as a result of the Yellowstone National Park fires of 1988.

47. For example, in July 1994, logging and road building equipment parked
between Libby and Eureka, Montana, was destroyed as a result of actions
by terrorists. The perpetrators were never apprehended. These criminal
acts followed the posting, in late spring 1993, of the call by the *Wild Rockies
Review*, a publication of the Earth First chapter in Missoula, Montana, to
"Burn That Dozer." Conversation with Bruce Vincent, August 31, 1994.

   Incidents of "tree spiking" (driving nails into trees scheduled for harvesting to frighten loggers and mill workers), equipment sabotage, and
other acts of environmental terrorism are too numerous to list. Until
recently, no deaths had resulted. Tragically, on April 24, 1995, Gil Murray,
executive director of the California Forestry Association, was killed by a
bomb delivered to his office.

48. Freedom of Access to Clinic Entrances Act, 18 U.S.C. § 248, et seq.
49. In *National Organization of Women, Inc., et al. v. Scheidler, et al.*, 1994, the U.S. Supreme Court held that proof of an economic motive for engaging in activities punishable under the Racketeer Influenced and Corrupt Organizations (RICO) chapter of the Organized Crime Control Act of 1970, was not necessary. Simply engaging in prohibited activities is enough: Many Westerners are exploring the possibility of using RICO against environmental terrorists. The Supreme Court has yet to address the free speech issues brought to bear under RICO.
50. The idea of increasing local spending on recreation seems to acknowledge that there is a need to spend money locally. But the benefits of such spending do not accrue to the local timber workers and their families. Further, such increased spending will not likely lure more tourists to the forest since other, more attractive recreational opportunities abound. John H. Beuter, "Overview of Below-Cost Timber Sale Issue," Mason, Bruce & Girard, Inc., Technical Bulletin No. 90-02, November 30, 1990, p. 12.
51. Says Forest Service spokesman Jack de Golia, "It's become more expensive to do environmental analyses. Harvesting in roadless areas require EIS's (environmental impact studies, which are much more costly) and the last two [EISs] we've done have ended up in court." *Montana Standard*, July 6, 1994, p. 1.
52. Brian Unnerstall of East Perry Lumber Company in Frohna, Missouri, says: "Our experience demonstrates the lie that is the so-called 'below cost timber sales.' People who oppose any timber harvesting whatsoever tie these things up in the appeals process and before the courts and force the Forest Service to spend tens of thousands of dollars defending its decisions after spending tens of thousands of dollars in environmental studies to make the decision. Then they engage in civil disobedience at the sale site and force the Forest Service to spend even more. No wonder the Forest Service can't make money on some of these sales. But if they lose money on these sales, it's the fault of these environmentalists." Pendley, op. cit., p. 113.

   The great irony, of course, especially in respect to environmental extremists who assert that they prefer recreational activities, is that timber harvest cutbacks deprive the Forest Service of the revenues that make these and other activities possible.
53. This chronology is adapted from "Where Will the Wood Come From? An Update on the Lumber Market Situation," March 9, 1993, by American Forest & Paper Association, National Association of Home Builders, National Lumber & Building Material Dealers Association, United Brotherhood of Carpenters & Joiners of America, A-1 to A-3, as well as other sources.
54. The language was referred to as the Hatfield-Adams amendment to the Interior Appropriations Bill (Section 318).
55. *Seattle Audubon Society, et al. v. Robertson, et al.*, 914 F.2d 1311 (9th Cir. 1990).
56. Contrary to popular belief, there were no owls located on any of the forty-four BLM sale sites. Since they were widely separated islands of timber surrounded by areas that had already been harvested, they could hardly be

regarded as owl habitat. Yet the FWS continued to oppose the sales, contending that each sale site might, at some time in the future, become "dispersal habitat."

57. In the state of Washington, nine hundred owl nesting sites allegedly exist, of which 587 impact private land. As a result, harvesting is restricted within 500 feet of each nest and on 6,600 to 9,700 surrounding acres. The timber lost could build 2.5 million single-family homes. Similar restrictions are being encountered in California and Oregon.

58. Larry Mason nevertheless believes there was a benefit to the Timber Summit: "Regardless, the Timber Summit, for the first time, did give us the opportunity to speak to the American people in something other than sound bites. For the first time, we were at the table and were seen as something different from environmentalists, inc. and the timber industry. You can see why the environmentalists hate us. We're the silver bullet. They can't paint us as rich timber barons. What we told Clinton and Gore that day is still true: we are problem-solvers by heritage; we can make this work, if given the opportunity. Unfortunately, in the past, we have been the first ones hurt and the last ones heard," Pendley, op. cit., pp. 189-190.

59. *Evergreen*, September/October, 1993, p. 31. The group was called the Forest Ecosystem Management Assessment Team (FEMAT). Its existence was discovered only after the Clinton plan was announced.

60. Ibid.

61. The radical nature of the document released by the Clinton team was particularly surprising. For example, the FEMAT Report, p. III-2, on Table III-1, lists the forty-eight options considered in the decision-making process—the impact of the various plans upon the owl, the murrelet, the salmon, and other wildlife. No consideration was made of the impact on people. Even more startling, item #47 was the Reed F. Noss plan, straight out of the *Wildlands Project*, whose goal is "a bold attempt to grope our way back to October 1492." *The Wildlands Project*, op. cit., inside cover.

62. Conversation with C. Larry Mason of Forks, Washington, on September 7, 1994. Larry Mason appeared before President Clinton on behalf of the timber communities of Washington State at the Timber Summit in early 1993. Larry has mastered the thousands and thousands of pages that were released in support of Clinton's Option 9. Unfortunately, the majority of the vitally important background documents are no longer available to the general public. In Larry's words, "the documents have become just like the process they are supposed to support—secretive and exclusive."

63. "This isn't rocket science," says Larry Mason. "You lose 9 direct workers and 9 indirect jobs with every million board feet of timber that isn't allowed to be harvested. The cutback is 4 billion board feet. That's 72,000 jobs, at a minimum!" Conversation with C. Larry Mason on September 7, 1994. John C. Hampton, chairman of the Northwest Forest Resource Council, said in July 1, 1993: "The employees who work in our facilities... do not want make-work projects and retraining. They want to raise their families in forest communities supported by sustained yield policies on federal forestlands."

64. In fact, the Clinton/Gore administration was considering canceling more than $310 million worth of timber contracts in the Pacific Northwest, including Idaho and Montana. While taxpayers would bear the $310 million price tag, local communities would suffer as scheduled harvests are canceled. "Logging contracts imperiled," *Missoulian*, July 10, 1994, p. 1.

65. *Evergreen*, September/October 1993, pp. 4–5.

   Environmentalists are trying to do the same thing. Writes Donald Walker, Jr: "One of the hopes I have held on to since I lost my job [as a logger] is that I could supplement our income by continuing to manage our tree farm as my father and grandfather did for so many years. But it doesn't look like this is going to pan out either.

   "Last November, I received a letter from an outfit called the Forest Conservation Council telling me that if I cut any more timber on our land it would sue me for violating the Endangered Species Act...." *Wall Street Journal*, May 15, 1992.

66. There are scientists who disagree with Option 9 but are afraid to speak out for fear of retaliation. Some have had the courage to step forward, including Dr. Chad Oliver, a professor of silviculture (the art and science of managing the forest to obtain desired structures and outputs) at the University of Washington in Seattle. Dr. Oliver believes the hands-off preservation style approach adopted by President Clinton will put the Pacific Northwest at increased risk of destruction by cataclysmic wildfire. *Evergreen*, September/October 1993, p. 7.

67. Quoted by Associated Press reporter Robert Greene. My own view of such a comment is that Chief Thomas, the "scientist," should resign so that the president can appoint a priest, rabbi, or minister to preside over such "moral decisions."

   Another aspect of the weird science of the owl is the following: "In 1972, biologist Dr. Eric Forsman located his first 59 pairs of spotted owls in Oregon. At that time he predicted, 'Within the next five years, the majority of the population may be gone.' [The latest] spotted owl counts were: 1988 about 1,500 pairs, 2,022 pairs in 1990, and 1992, 3,461." *Network News*, Oregon Lands Coalition, February 4, 1994.

68. As former Congressman Bob Smith, then ranking Republican on the subcommittee, noted later in a press release: "The administration has played this smoke and mirrors game with Oregonians long enough. The fact is their own economist says over 16 jobs will be lost for every million board feet. We are dropping four billion feet. That's 66,000 jobs lost, not the 6,000 they claim."

69. Dr. John H. Beuter, "Social and Economic Impacts of Spotted Owl Conservation Strategy," November 15, 1990, *Technical Bulletin No. 9003*, available from the American Forest and Paper Association, Washington, D.C. Even this is not enough. Two Seattle scientists report that "the president's plan exposes some mollusks to medium to high risk of extinction." They therefore favor a drastically restrictive timber plan—to cut harvest levels back to a mere 5 percent of their 1980s' rate. "Forest plan is criticized for disregarding mollusks," *Seattle Post Intelligencer*, July 16, 1993, pp. A1–2.

70. It is easy to see why the impact on local governments will be so devastating when one considers the importance of the forest products industry to Oregon. According to figures gathered from official sources by *Evergreen*, payrolls total nearly $2.25 billion (not included: self-employed independent logging or trucking contractors and wages paid to companies that sell most of their products to forest industry companies); product sales exceed $7.2 billion; and harvest and forest land taxes are more than $342 million (not included: fuel taxes, local business taxes, transportation taxes, and corporate business taxes). *Evergreen*, 1994 Fact Book, March 1994, p. 21.
71. Ibid. September/October 1991, p. 10.
72. Con Schallau, Hamilton Roddis Lecture, Department of Forestry, School of Natural Resources, University of Wisconsin–Madison, October 7, 1993, p. 7.
73. Ibid. Additional reductions could result from such issues as wetlands, so-called below-cost timber sales, riparian zones, and new forestry management practices.
74. Conor W. Boyd, et al., "Wood for structural and architectural purposes," *Wood and Fiber*, 1976, 8(1):1–72.

CHAPTER 3

1. The U.S. government brought legal action against rancher Wayne Hage of Tonopah, Nevada. If it prevails, Hage will lose his water rights. In Kanab, Utah, the federal government has served property owner Brandt Child with a cease-and-desist order effectively preventing him from using his water rights.
2. One of the Carter administration's first official acts in its War on the West was to issue a water project "hit list." The list also included Southern water projects that brought this from U.S. Senator Ernest Hollings (D-SC): "We looked closely, and we found the World Bank annual report for last year. We found some 27 pages of projects. What kind? Irrigation, dams, water projects, pork barrel in Afghanistan, if you please; a boondoggle in Brazil, if you please." *Congressional Record*, S21851 (June 30, 1977).
3. Waring & Samelson, Non-Indian Federal Reserved Water Rights, 58 Den. L.J. 783, 792 (1981) Tarlock, Protection of Water Flows for National Parks, 22 Land & Water L. Rev. 29, 44 (1986).
4. Wrote the solicitor, "Congress intended wilderness purposes to be secondary to the purposes for which the reservation on which wilderness areas are designated were originally created. As such, wilderness areas enjoy the benefits of water reserved for underlying parks, forests, or refuges but are not entitled to a separate and additional reservation of water." M-36914 (Supp. III) 96 I.D. 211, 213 (1988).
5. In 1984, the Sierra Club filed a lawsuit against the Reagan administration demanding that federal reserved water rights be declared in Colorado wilderness areas. The U.S. Court of Appeals for the Tenth Circuit dismissed the appeal, vacated the judgment of the district court, and remanded the case with directions to dismiss it "as not ripe for adjudication." *Sierra Club v. Yeutter*, 911 F.2d 1405, 1421 (10th Cir. 1990).

6. Al Gore, *Earth in the Balance: Ecology and the Human Spirit* (New York, New York: Houghton Mifflin Company, 1992), p. 112. Gore likens the California dispute to, "the conflict between Colorado and its downstream neighbors, who feel deprived of the water that would otherwise drain out of the watersheds in Colorado. The plight of so-called tail-enders—those communities far down stream from the headwaters of a water distribution system—is becoming more severe, especially where the population is growing the fastest. These arguments and others like them in the United States will be resolved through political dialogue and legal battles, although… [i]n some volatile areas of the world… these conflicts over water may not be peacefully resolved and have the potential for leading to war." Ibid., pp. 112–113.

7. A partial list includes Secretary of the Interior Bruce Babbitt, League of Conservation Voters; George Frampton, assistant secretary of Fish, Wildlife and Parks of the U.S. Department of the Interior, the Wilderness Society; David Alberswerth, assistant secretary, U.S. Department of the Interior, National Wildlife Federation; Robert Armstrong, assistant secretary, U.S. Department of the Interior, Trust for Public Lands; Bonnie Cohen, assistant secretary U.S. Department of the Interior, National Trust for Historic Preservation; Brooks Yeager, director, Office of Policy Analysis, U.S. Department of the Interior, National Audubon Society; Thomas Grumbly, assistant secretary, U.S. Department of Energy, Climate Institute; Alice Rivlin, deputy director, Office of Management and Budget, Wilderness Society; Carol Browner, administrator, Environmental Protection Agency, Citizen Action; Jean Nelson, general counsel, Environmental Protection Agency, Southern Environmental Law Center; Mary Nichols, assistant administrator, Environmental Protection Agency, Natural Resources Defense Council.

8. Fred Barnes points out that the appointment of Babbitt as secretary of the interior was itself a sign of the awesome power of environmental groups. The Clinton/Gore administration had planned to name Mayor Richard Daley of Chicago as secretary of transportation and Congressman Bill Richardson (D-NM), a Hispanic, secretary of the interior. But environmental groups objected: Richardson wasn't "green" enough; they wanted Babbitt. Clinton named Babbitt, but since he was now short one Hispanic, he couldn't name Daley to Transportation. Instead that job went to Federico Peña, mayor of Denver.

9. Wayne Hage, *Storm Over Rangeland: Private Rights in Federal Lands* (Bellevue, Wash: Free Enterprise Press, 1989), pp. 8–9.

10. Secretary Babbitt continues: "The idea of a rancher saying to the citizens of a state that 'there is not going to be any access for fishing or boating on this stream because I am going to build a fence across it and guard it with a shotgun,' is an example of why these guys are headed for extinction." The Supreme Court has noted on numerous occasions that one key aspect of private property is the right of owners to exclude others from their property. For example, *Nollan v. California Coastal Commission*, 483 U.S. 825, 831 (1987).

During the 1994 session of the Colorado State Legislature, a bill was introduced that required property owners to grant access to those wanting to fish upon their land. It never emerged from committee. Such proposals invite another question: if you can follow a stream through someone's private property, why shouldn't you be able to follow an ecosystem as well, or even a butterfly?

11. Address given at a conference entitled "Navigability: Who Owns Our Waterways?" sponsored by Continuing Legal Education Office of the Northwestern School of Law of Lewis and Clark College on November 13, 1992.

12. 58 Federal Register 68629 (December 28, 1993).

13. See the Office of Legal Counsel's June 16, 1982, memorandum, "Federal Non-Reserved Water Rights." (6 Op. Off. Legal Counsel 329 (1982)).

14. See section 7(b) of S. 2009; House of Representatives Report 838, 96th Congress, 2d Session at 20 (1980), and 104 *Congressional Record*, 11555 (1958). Furthermore, the chairman of the Senate Committee on Interior and Insular Affairs described section 4(d)(7) as a "disclaimer of any interference with State or Federal water rights" through enactment of the wilderness legislation. (Hearings on S. 174 Before the Senate Committee on Interior & Insular Affairs, 87th Congress, 1st Session at 5 (1961).)

   Environmentalists of the day agreed. Charles Collison of the National Wildlife Federation said the language guaranteed that "no claim is made to exemption from State water laws on wilderness areas." (Hearings on S. 4028 Before the Senate Committee on Interior & Insular Affairs, 85th Congress, 2d Session, Pt. 2 at 257 (1958).)

15. See, 125 *Congressional Record*, 17180 (1980). Explained the Senate Report: "Section 7 further reiterates and underscores the jurisdiction of the State of Idaho over the water resources within the wilderness area...." Senate Report No. 414, 96th Congress, 1st Session at 22 (1980).

16. The Supreme Court, having rejected one such claim already—in *United States v. New Mexico*, 438 U.S. 696 (1978)—will no doubt reject another.

17. 1991 Environmental Scorecard of Congress, signed by Babbitt, League of Conservation Voters, quoted in "Clinton's Cabinet Gets Greener," by Michael Fumento, *Investor's Business Daily*, December 28, 1992, p. 1.

18. Senator Campbell suggested that sticking with Clinton could cost Senate Democrats their jobs. "Western dissent brewing?" *Denver Post*, February 22, 1993, p. 8A. Babbitt seems to have known that. *The New Republic* reported, "Babbitt has already told Clinton the bad news about what will happen if he stays at Interior: His environmentalism will lose the Democrats the Rockies in 1996." Jacob Weisberg, "Babbitt is one of the best at finding a balance," *Rocky Mountain News*, February 24, 1993, 45, reprinted from *New Republic*. It certainly cost Clinton one Senate Democrat: Senator Campbell became a Republican.

19. Secretary Babbitt believes any state-issued water right based upon the use of water for a ranch that has federal grazing permits is subject to challenge. According to Clive Strong, Esq., chief of the Natural Resources Division of the Office of the Attorney General of the state of Idaho, Babbitt is taking that position in the Snake River Basin Adjudication now before the

Fifth Judicial District Court of Idaho, in and for the County of Twin Falls. Conversation with Mr. Strong on September 22, 1994.

20. It was just this federal requirement to comply with state water law that the Carter administration eliminated and that the Reagan administration reinstated.

21. *Congressional Record*, S14583 (October 28, 1993).

22. *Alameda Water & Sanitation District, et al. v. William E. Reilly*, "Petition for Declaratory Judgment and Other Relief," U.S. District Court Colorado, No. 91-M-2047, November 22, 1991.

23. In March 1990, the deputy regional administrator of the EPA recommended that Two Forks be vetoed. U.S. Environmental Protection Agency, Region VIII, "Recommended Determination to Prohibit Construction of Two Forks Dam and Reservoir Pursuant to Section 404(c) of the Clean Water Act," March 1990. On November 23, 1990, that is exactly what happened. U.S. Environmental Protection Agency, "Final Determination of the U.S. Environmental Protection Agency's Assistant Administrator for Water Pursuant to Section 404(c) of the Clean Water Act Concerning the Two Forks Water Supply Impoundments, Jefferson and Douglas Counties, Colorado," November 23, 1990.

24. Was there another reason for the veto, one tied to the statement by Senator Gore that questions the fairness of Colorado water remaining in Colorado? Without Two Forks, or storage projects like it, water to which Coloradans have a legal right will leave the state. *Denver Post*, April 10, 1994.

25. Moreover, the Colorado constitution guarantees that "the right to divert the unappropriated waters of any natural stream to beneficial uses shall never be denied." (Colo. Const., art. XVI, § 6.) In Colorado a water right, including a conditional water right, is a constitutionally protected property interest (*Game & Fish Commission v. Farmers Irrigation Co.*, 426 P.2d 562, 565 (1967). The U.S. Supreme Court has held the same. *Dugan v. Rank*, 372 U.S. 609, 625-26 (1963).

26. 33 U.S.C. § 1251(g).

27. 123 *Congressional Record*, 39212 (December 15, 1977).

28. 693 F.2d 156, 179 (D.C. Cir. 1982).

29. 758 F.2d 508, 513 (10th Cir. 1985).

30. "Purcell: Wyoming water development at risk: Agencies may push state to switch ranch water to cities, rather than build dams, officials fear," *Casper* [Wyoming] *Star Tribune*, May 9, 1994.

31. Peaking power is made available during peak use periods, such as during hot summer days when air conditioning units are turned on.

32. To make matters worse, utilities—from Western communities throughout Wyoming, Colorado, Utah, and Arizona—have paid more than $100 million for a host of Glen Canyon Dam environmental studies. Although these studies have not yet evaluated electricity's benefit to society, they have concluded that electricity's cost to society is from $41 million to $119 million—and that Glen Canyon recreational benefits to society come to less than $5 million.

Electricity's benefit to society, especially in the arid West, is almost incalculable. Consider the temperature ranges, for example. Utah's highest and lowest temperatures are 117 and –69°F; Colorado's highest and lowest temperatures are 118 and –61°F; and Arizona's highest and lowest temperatures are 127 and –40°F. *World Almanac and Book of Facts*, 1992 (New York, N.Y.: Pharos Book, Scripps Howard), pp. 210–211.

33. "Agency abandons dam-building mission," *Rocky Mountain News*, April 14, 1994, p. 6A.

34. "Babbitt Signs Order to Make Reclamation One of First 'Reinvented' Agencies," U.S. Department of the Interior Bureau of Reclamation News Release, April 13, 1994.

35. Already the Bureau of Reclamation is proposing policy changes that "could financially break Wyoming irrigation districts or deprive them of water they need." Two new policies involving water conservation and restricting the use of federally supplied water have Wyoming irrigators worried. "I believe they want the water," says Jack Miles, president of the Casper-Alcova Irrigation District. "I believe they want the projects back, and I believe the way they're going, they're going to get them because they're going to break us all." "BuRec rules under fire," *Rawlins Daily Times*, July 16, 1994.

36. Letter from William H. Luce, Jr., project superintendent, Fresno office (CVP), Bureau of Reclamation, U.S. Department of the Interior, dated July 16, 1993. The letter contained some startling disclosures of how the federal government determines the presence of species habitat: "Initial evaluation of lands for habitat will be by use of aerial photographs and visual border inspection. Subsequent on-site inspection will enable us to determine if species are actually present.... Lands that are not inspected by field crews will be evaluated using aerial photographs and visual border   inspection. Uncultivated parcels will likely be labelled as habitat if absence of species cannot be confirmed by inspection."

37. In order to establish a protected water right, Western water law (the prior appropriations doctrine) requires that water be applied to a "beneficial use" such as agriculture, municipal water supply, industrial use, etc. That use must be registered with the state's water authority—often called the state engineer.

38. *Denver Post*, May 15, 1994, p. 5B.

39. The Colorado Supreme Court's rejection of the attempt by Denver to develop groundwater from the aquifer that feeds the San Luis Valley "has narrowed the list of options available for supplying the long-term needs of the Front Range," *Denver Post*, May 12, 1994. Most rural Coloradans see Two Forks as far preferable to taking water from aquifers or buying up farmers' irrigation water.

40. Even the measures agreed to by the three states, wherein Colorado cities pay thousands of dollars a year to preserve and improve habitat in Nebraska, are not enough for environmental groups. They have threatened a lawsuit. "[Audubon] Society opposes Platte habitat pact," *Omaha World-Herald*, August 19, 1994.

41. According to the federal government, PACFISH is "an ecosystem-based aquatic habitat strategy" designed to "restore and conserve riparian areas

and freshwater habitat for Pacific anadromous fish." "PACFISH: Environmental Assessment on Interim Strategies for Managing Anadromous Fish-producing Watersheds—Answers to Commonly Asked Questions, March 25, 1994," U.S. Department of the Interior, Bureau of Land Management, and U.S. Department of Agriculture, Forest Service (hereinafter *PACFISH Answers*), p. 1.

PACFISH seeks to develop and implement interim strategies and long-term land management plans on "[a]ll or parts of 15 National Forests and 7 BLM Districts in 4 states." *PACFISH Answers*, p. 3. The PACFISH plan would affect California's Lassen and Los Padres National Forests and BLM's Bakerfield and Ukiah Districts; Idaho's Bitterroot, Clearwater, Nez Perce, Boise, Challis, Payette, Salmon, and Sawtooth National Forests and BLM's Coeur d'Alene and Salmon Districts; Oregon's Malheur, Ochoco, Umatilla, and Wallowa-Whitman National Forests and BLM's Prineville and Vale Districts, and Washington's Okanogan National Forest and BLM's Spokane District.

In other words, the Pacific Northwest lands that have not been regulated for the northern spotted owl will now be regulated under PACFISH.

42. Ibid., p. 7.
43. Ibid., pp. 7, 9–10. No study under the NEPA would be required, asserts the federal government, since the strategy:

"(1) is limited in time and scope; (2) would impose neither unusual risks or adverse effects on unique characteristics or resources; (3) would not produce any significant irretrievable, irreversible, or cumulative effects; and (4) would not likely cause highly controversial environmental effects (controversy in this context refers to a substantial dispute as to the size, nature, or effect of the action, rather than to opposition to its adoption)." [Ibid., p. 10.]

This is a remarkable display of arrogance. As for (1): even the government admits the plan would take "from 1 to 3 years in some watersheds, and decades in others." (Ibid., p. 9.) As for (2) and (3): everyone now admits, for example, that the forests throughout the region are unhealthy. Inability to harvest the forests yields fires and "significant... irreversible... effects." As for (4): this is the most unbelievable reading of the "controversy" aspect of the NEPA and one that ignores the intent of Congress.

44. *Congressional Record*, S5497, May 11, 1994.
45. PACFISH will result not only in reducing water use but in land lockup. For example, under PACFISH, "Interim Riparian Habitat Conservation Areas (RHCAs)" and "Key Watersheds" would be designated as set-asides for "special management attention" and "stricter management standards, guidelines, and procedures." *PACFISH Answers*, p. 6.
46. "A call upon the river" is the common phrase to indicate that an individual holding a valid water right is about to put the water to "beneficial use."
47. The Final Environmental Impact Statement (FEIS) was completed in 1980. The ground-breaking ceremonies were held on October 26, 1991. On February 29, 1992, the Sierra Club filed suit, a suit that was dropped when the government agreed to supplement the FEIS. That document was scheduled to be completed in June 1995.

48. Undated White Paper, "Four Corners Position Paper On Animas La Plata Project Phase I, Detail of Rationale in Support of Project," pp. 2–4, 8, 9. Furthermore, the Animas–La Plata project will resolve long pending water claims on the Animas–La Plata and Mancos Rivers. Ibid., p. 11.
49. Secretary Babbitt's people are already providing him the cover to oppose the project. His inspector general has recommended scrapping major portions of the project. To which Carol Knight of Senator Ben Nighthorse Campbell's office responded: "They want to renegotiate something that the tribes already negotiated in good faith. The tribes should well be sick of that." "Big cutback urged in Animas project," *Denver Post*, July 13, 1994, pp. 1 and 6A.

CHAPTER 4

1. This story sounds too good to be true. For years I thought it was an apocryphal, but poignant, illustration of the gap between East and West. Nonetheless, the late Jack Horton, born and raised in Wyoming and an assistant secretary for Land and Water of the U.S. Department of the Interior during the Nixon administration, swore it happened. As he told it years ago, the meeting took place early in the week; by Thursday, the sheepherder's comment had reached Secretary of the Interior Rogers C.B. Morton, and that Saturday, Morton related it to President Nixon.
2. A full-page advertisement in a number of national magazines tries to turn this sad reality into a draw for tourists. "One of America's most endangered species can still be found in Wyoming," proclaims the March 1993 issue of *McCall's*, above a cowboy beside a twilight campfire.
3. "Western Ranching: Culture in Crisis," Summit Films Inc., Roger C. Brown, 1055 Cottonwood Pass Road, Gypsum, Colo., 81637. This exceptionally fine video presents the debate in a clear and understandable manner. It is excellent for discussion groups, for luncheon gatherings, and for classroom use.
4. Obviously, it was not always the case. Yet it was the ranching community itself that, in response to concern over the condition of federal grazing lands, initiated reforms in 1934. Those reforms led to the Taylor Grazing Act.
5. U.S. Department of the Interior, Bureau of Land Management, "State of the Public Rangelands 1990."
6. Bureau of Land Management employee Harley Metz notes that even land rated "fair" is still valuable for the watershed it provides, for the forage available, and for its aesthetically pleasing nature. Mr. Metz points out, "[Land rated fair] is not an environmental disaster. I think it's providing for a lot of values out here that the public wants." "Western Ranching," op. cit.
7. Dr. B.E. Dahl, Texas Tech University, 1991, citing a 1990 Bureau of Land Management Report, "State of the Public Rangelands 1990." See also "Western Ranching," op. cit.
8. Ibid.
9. Ibid.
10. Ibid. At least one nationally known columnist has suggested that the cre-

ation of more urban areas on abandoned Western ranches is Secretary of the Interior Bruce Babbitt's ultimate goal. Philip M. Burgess, "Fee hike hides ominous agenda," *Rocky Mountain News*, October 19, 1993, and "'Babbittowns' will be born out of range reform," *Rocky Mountain News*, August 24, 1993. In the latter article Burgess sets forth the result of Babbitt's proposal: "[T]he year 2000 will find sprawling Babbittowns in the Old West—cow free watering holes for weekend cowboys and coastal yuppies looking for the shake-and-bake 'wilderness' experience."

11. With all of the Clintons' talk about health care, the environmental extremists within the administration threaten the very families—the ranching families—that will not burden the nation's health care system.

12. "Western Ranching," op. cit.

13. The federal fiscal year runs from October 1 through September 30 of the following year. Thus, fiscal year 1994 for the federal government began October 1, 1993, and ended September 30, 1994.

14. Conversation with Bill Myers, National Cattlemen's Association, August 31, 1994. An animal unit month (AUM) is the amount of forage eaten in a month by a cow and her calf or by five sheep.

15. *Rocky Mountain News*, September 16, 1993, p. 29A.

16. Memorandum from Kevin Sweeney, Lucia Wyman to Secretary Babbitt, Tom Collier, and Jim Baca, "Grazing Issues—One Disagreement, One Suggestion," dated June 23, 1993, p. 1. One area where the administration intended to "adjust expectations" was riparian zones—areas along streams: "Our own statistics can be used to show the range is in better shape than at any point in this century. With that in mind, we must make deliberate and public attempts to prove how bad the conditions are in many riparian zones." Ibid., p. 3.

17. Secretary Babbitt insists that he met with all interested parties in his search for middle ground. In his cover letter to the summary on Range Reform '94, Babbitt writes, "I have met with numerous groups or individuals." Yet California Cattlemen's Association Executive Vice President John L. Braly writes: "I feel we need to continue to emphasize that he has not met with industry groups or individual ranchers in every state (including California), and he has virtually ignored the national organizations." Rangeland Reform '94 Draft Environmental Impact Statement, Notes on the Executive Summary, May 6, 1994.

18. U.S. Department of the Interior's Proposed Amendment to 43 C.F.R. Parts 4, 1780, and 4100 (March 25, 1994). Said Reeves Brown, one of the Roundtable participants, "It appears that George Miller (D-CA) and Jay Hair (National Wildlife Federation) had more fingerprints on this document than the Roundtable participants." The Colorado Cattlemen's Association identified twenty-seven areas of conflict between the Roundtable and Babbitt's Range Reform. Nine of those twenty-seven are subjects on which the Roundtable had consensus. Conversation with Reeves Brown, Colorado Cattlemen's Association, September 6, 1994.

19. *Casper* [Wyoming] *Star Tribune*, May 15, 1994.

20. Shauna Hermel, "Cows won't be the only things disappearing in the West

if fair and equitable grazing fees aren't determined soon." *Beef*, May 1994, p. 15.

21. The remaining figures in percentage of ranchers going out of business followed by the annual dollar loss to the economy include Arizona: 64 percent, $36 million; California: 31 percent, $16 million; Colorado: 35 percent, $27 million; Idaho: 30 percent, $27 million; Nevada: 41 percent, $14 million; Oregon: 39 percent, $19 million; Utah: 43 percent, $24 million; Washington: 34 percent, $4 million. Ibid.

22. Environmentalists like Andy Kerr don't care. "If they want to play cowboy, they can do it on private land. It's time they grow up." "Western Ranching," op. cit.

23. U.S. Department of the Interior, Bureau of Land Management and U.S. Department of Agriculture, Forest Service, "Grazing Fee Review and Evaluation Report Update of the 1986 Final Report," April 1992, Vol. 2, App. 15.

24. Drs. Gerhard N. Rostvold and Thomas J. Dudley, "Report to Congress: New Perspectives on Grazing Fees and Public Land Management in the 1990's," Pepperdine University, June 1992 (Hereinafter: "Rostvold and Dudley"), cover letter. Rostvold and Dudley also found: "The statistical procedures fail to meet the generally accepted standards of scientific statistical inquiry. As a consequence, the conclusions drawn are of questionable validity and fail to present an acceptable basis for setting grazing fees on the public lands in the Western U.S." Ibid., p. 5.

25. Ibid., p. 7.

26. Ibid., pp. 5 and 17.

27. Rostvold and Dudley, "A Comparative Analysis of the Economic, Financial and Competitive Conditions of Montana Ranches Using Federal Forage and Montana Ranches Without Federal Grazing Allotments," Pepperdine University, July 1993, p. 4.

28. "The Value of Public Land Forage and the Implications for Grazing Fee Policy" (A Summary of the Bureau of Land Management and Forest Service Incentive-Based Grazing Fee Study, Grazing Fee Task Group), New Mexico State University, College of Agriculture and Home Economics, Las Cruces, New Mexico, December 1993, p. IV. Under recommendation is the following: "The current grazing fee, or even a lower fee, would be justified in all cases if even a minimal allowance were made for ranchers' grazing permit investments." Ibid., p. V.

  Secretary Babbitt's views on Western ranching are not shared by the men and women most knowledgeable on grazing issues: 90 percent of BLM officials and 89 percent of USFS officials agree that livestock grazing is an important conservation tool that can be used to improve the condition of the public rangeland. Furthermore, 79 percent of BLM and USFS officials agree that ranchers take good care of the land because their livelihoods depend on it. The Wirthlin Group, Public Lands Survey, February 1994, cited in *National Cattlemen*, May/June 1994, p. 17.

29. Rostvold and Dudley, pp. 9, 12, 13, 80, 81.

30. Subpart § 1784, Advisory Committees.

31. "Allowing non-resident environmentalists on these panels is blatantly unfair

and calls into question the secretary's seriousness about what he himself refers to as 'local control.' The critical decision for Mr. Babbitt is whether he is truly willing to empower communities in the West with real management authority or not. The people best suited to manage those lands are those who use and enjoy them every day." Ken Spann, of Almont, Colorado, National Cattlemen's Association Federal Lands Committee Chairman, "Rangeland Reform '94," *National Cattlemen*, May/June 1994, p. 17.

32. "It's very easy for people who do not have to put any money up to conclude that somebody else should. The permittee will have no more authority than anyone else, but he'll have a ton more [financial] responsibility." Larry Bourett, executive director, Wyoming Farm Bureau. Casper [Wyoming] *Star Tribune*, May 18, 1994. Or as Reeves Brown of the Colorado Cattlemen's Association puts it: "A chicken may have an interest in what you have for breakfast, but a pig is affected by your choice."

33. "Preserve" is neither defined nor a goal under any prior federal lands policy. Similarly, "open space" has never been a purpose of grazing lands and neither the terms "integral" nor "ecosystems" is defined or previously believed to be a purpose of managed lands.

34. In *Nollan v. California Coastal Commission*, 483 U.S. 825 (1986), the Supreme Court required a relationship between the conditions placed upon a property owner and the goal sought by the government entity.

35. *United States v. Blakely*, U.S. District Court for the District of Idaho, CR 93-038-E-EJL.

36. In *United States v. Miller*, 659 F.2d 1029 (10th Cir. 1981), the court held: "In the case at bar the United States used criminal trespass on behalf of the Indians with the intent of resolving the underlying [property] dispute. The criminal trespass statute was never designed to resolve civil property disputes. It has an unsettling effect on the parties, as well." Ibid. at 1033–34.

37. William Perry Pendley, *It Takes a Hero: The Grassroots Battle Against Environmental Oppression* (Bellevue, Washington: Free Enterprise Press, 1994), pp. 27-29.

38. See Wayne Hage, *Storm Over Rangelands: Private Rights in Federal Lands* (Bellevue, Washington: Free Enterprise Press, 1989).

39. *U.S. v. Seaman & Hage*, 94 CDOS 1637, Docket No. 93-10305 (9th Cir. 1994).

40. Conversation with Mark Pollot on September 23, 1994. *Hage v. United States*, United States Court of Claims, 91-147-OL. The decision of the attorney general of Nevada to permit the state of Nevada to be represented in a private takings case against a Nevada citizen by a national environmental group drew cries of outrage from Nevadans.

41. The view that inholders were not guaranteed right of access to their property, notwithstanding the provisions of federal law, began with the administration of President Kennedy. Despite the views of the attorney general that inholders had no such rights, the Forest Service continued, as before, recognizing those rights. During the administration of President Carter, opposition to inholder access rights began anew, culminating in what became known as the Civilette Opinion of 1980. That opinion was quick-

ly repudiated by Congress with the adoption of the access provision of ANILCA.

42. One such individual is Randolph Jenks of Luna, New Mexico. Recently, the U.S. Court of Appeals for the Tenth Circuit ruled in Mr. Jenks' favor and reversed the holding of the district court that Mr. Jenks has no access rights. *United States v. Jenks*, 22 F.3d 1513 (10th Cir. 1994).
43. *Adams v. United States*, 3 F.3d 1254 (9th Cir. 1993).
44. *Raymond Fitzgerald, et al. v. The United States of America*, CIV-94-0518-PHX-CAM, United States District Court for the District of Arizona.
45. 43 U.S.C. § 1712 (f). Prior to FLPMA, involvement was limited to those with an economic interest in the land.
46. *National Wildlife Federation, et al. v. Bureau of Land Management*, UT-06-91-1 and UT-06-93-01, Slip Op. December 20, 1993.
47. *Oregon Natural Resource Council, et al. v. Bureau of Land Management, et al.*, 129 IBLA 269, May 17, 1994.
48. *Lujan v. National Wildlife Federation, et al.*, 497 U.S. 871 (1990) and *Defenders of Wildlife, et al. v. Lujan*, U.S., 119 L Ed. 2d 351, 112 S.Ct. 2130 (1992).
49. 4 C.F.R. 4.410(a). "Any party to a case who is adversely affected by a decision of an officer of the Bureau of Land Management or of an administrative law judge shall have a right to appeal to the Board." In other words, even an "affected interest" must show that he or she is affected adversely, which appears to rise to the level of what the Constitution requires under Article III. Unfortunately, the BLM has been reticent in enforcing this clear requirement.
50. Donald K. Majors, 123 IBLA 142, May 28, 1992. In this case, the grazing permittee resided in the Colorado town of Dolores, while the individual asserting that he was an "affected interest" resided in Durango.
51. In this case, the "affected interest" was a law professor at Arizona State University in Tempe, whereas the allotment was more than 300 miles away in southeastern Utah.
52. Stu Brown letter to Mr. Ron Steward, dated April 21, 1994.
53. Conversation with Commissioner Louise Liston on September 23, 1994.
54. Reorganization is another means of achieving policy objectives. Rick Robitaille of the Petroleum Association of Wyoming is concerned about proposals to reorganize the BLM into two main divisions, one for user services, the other for ecosystem management/biodiversity. "This would effectively weaken all resource users (range, timber, mining, oil and gas) and elevate ecosystem-type activities above multiple use concepts and programs."
55. Fax memorandum from Congressman Orton, dated September 8, 1994. *Rocky Mountain News*, April 27, 1994, p. 8A. Bruce Vincent of Libby, Montana, says that those in the Forest Service with land management expertise, especially in forest health issues, have been replaced with "ologists." Conversation with Bruce Vincent, September 8, 1994.
56. Congressman Gerry Studs, says the *National Biological Survey* (NBS), has "a simple, yet awesome mission—catalog everything that walks, crawls, swims or flies around this country." *Wall Street Journal*, November 2, 1993. The NBS has recently changed its last name from "Survey" to "Service" in an

attempt to convince the public that it will "serve" landowners rather than "survey" their property.

57. "Ecosystem Protection," U.S. Environmental Protection Agency, National Performance Review, August 6, 1993.
58. Ibid., p. 3.
59. Ibid., p. 4.
60. Ibid., pp. 4, 11.
61. Ibid., p. 13. Read this barrier as "EPA knows nothing about ecosystem issues."
62. Ibid. Read this barrier as "No one knows anything about ecosystem issues." Scientifically, an "ecosystem" may be as large as the entire planet or as small as a drop of water. Secretary Babbitt says an "ecosystem" is pretty much in the eye of the beholder. "When I use a word . . . it means just what I choose it to mean—neither more nor less." Spoken by Humpty Dumpty in, *Alice's Adventures in Wonderland* by Lewis Carroll..
63. Ibid., p. 15. Read this barrier as "States are fed up with unfunded mandates and have discovered the Tenth Amendment to the Constitution."
64. Ibid., p. 16. Read this barrier as "The late Tip O'Neill was right on one thing: 'all politics is local,' regardless of what the ecosystem boundary may be."

CHAPTER 5

1. "All across the Plains, the Poppers have become as well known a couple as Donald and Ivana Trump—and about as well liked." Dayton Duncan, *Miles from Nowhere: Tales from American's Contemporary Frontier* (New York, N.Y.: Viking, 1993), p. 269.
2. Frank J. and Deborah E. Popper, *The Future of the Great Plains*, unpublished draft manuscript, p. 2.
3. As Phil Burgess of the Center for the New West says, "The Poppers may have given up on the Great Plains but the Japanese and other investors have not." Conversation on September 22, 1994. See Philip M. Burgess, et al., "A New Vision of the Heartland: The Great Plains in Transition—Overview of Change in America's New Economy," A Report to the Ford Foundation and the Aspen Institute, Center for the New West, Denver, Colo., March 1992.
4. Poppers, op. cit., p. 16.
5. 16 U.S.C. § 1531, et seq. Act Dec. 28, 1973, P.L. 93-205, 87 Stat. 884. The Poppers point to a U.S. Fish and Wildlife Service program called the "Great Plains Initiative" that seeks to "coordinate with the states and the Canadian provinces to manage wildlife and habitat on a Plains-wide basis instead of focusing only on smaller areas or single species." Perhaps understating it a bit, the Poppers call using the Endangered Species Act to engage in land-use planning over an entire region "a modest step toward the Buffalo Commons." Poppers, op. cit., 20.
6. *Congressional Record*, S25694, July 24, 1973. *Congressional Quarterly*, 1973 Almanac, p. 673.

7. Pub. L. No. 89-669, 80 Stat. 926 (1966).
8. Pub. L. No. 91-135, 83 Stat. 275 (1969).
9. H.R. Rep. No. 93-412, 93rd Cong., 1st Sess. (1973).
10. *Legislative History*, P.L. 93-205, Senate Report No. 93-307, 2990.
11. H.R. Rep. No. 93-412, 93rd Cong., 1st Sess. (1973).
12. Ibid.
13. 119 *Congressional Record*, S25674, July 24, 1973.
14. Ibid.
15. "Endangered fish may dry up river development," *Steamboat Springs Pilot*, June 9, 1994.
16. Former U.S. Senator James A. McClure reflects on what he and his colleagues envisioned: "I think we just never contemplated, in 1973, that the act would reach as far and wide as it has. I can say with some confidence that many of my colleagues would have been surprised to learn that a legal and administrative structure originally designed to protect 109 species might one day be asked to accommodate not only ten times that number of threatened species, but also potentially 4,000 or more candidate species." National Endangered Species Act Reform Coalition Newsletter, Summer 1994, p. 4.
17. *119 Congressional Record*, S25691, July 24, 1973.
18. Ibid.
19. *119 Congressional Record*, S25676, July 24, 1973.
20. Rather disingenuously, environmental groups assert that the Endangered Species Act was not what put an end to timber harvesting in most of the federal forests west of the Cascade Range. Therefore, they conclude, there is no need to change the Endangered Species Act. That is a distinction without a difference. While the environmental groups did sue under the National Environmental Policy Act and other federal laws, what they argued was that those acts had been violated because of a failure to consider impacts upon the northern spotted owl as required under the Endangered Species Act.
21. Remarkably, the pain for the people of the timber communities of the Pacific Northwest continues. With huge areas now set aside exclusively for the northern spotted owl, environmental extremists are using the marble murrelet and the salmon to further restrict the use of federal land.

    More incredibly, environmental groups have filed lawsuits to stop timber harvesting on privately owned lands. They may not need to do so since the U.S. Fish and Wildlife Service has advised state agencies that permitting timber harvesting on private lands that may cause harm to the spotted owl will expose state employees to criminal prosecution.
22. "An Endangered Species Blueprint," *National Wilderness Institute Resource*, Fall 1992, vol. III, issue 3, p. 4.
23. *Fund for Animals v. Lujan*, Civ. No. 92-800 (D.D.C. Dec. 15, 1992) (settlement agreement, ¶¶. 4–7). The Bush administration further agreed to engage in "ecosystem management." Since no one knows what in the world ecosystem management means, it is anyone's guess what such a management system will entail.

24. "Blueprint," op. cit., pp. 4–5.
25. William Perry Pendley, *It Takes a Hero: The Grassroots Battle Against Environmental Oppression* (Bellevue, Washington: Free Enterprise Press, 1994), p. 151. It is not just the economy that will suffer; 20,000 acres of refuges and 5,000 acres of private wetland will lose their water. As much as $26 million in hunting revenues will be lost. The other endangered species that utilize the wet croplands will also suffer: the swainsen hawk, the peregrine falcon, the giant garter snake, the bald eagle, and twenty-one other species.
26. Greg Ballmer, "Endangered status sought for fly," *Press-Enterprise*, Riverside, Calif., September 10, 1992, p. B-1.
27. This decision of the Forest Service is being challenged in *Mountain States Legal Foundation, et al. v. Madigan, et al.*, Civil Action No. 92-0097 (U.S. District Court for the District of Columbia).
28. *U.S. Fish and Wildlife Service v. John Shuler,* Docket Number Denver 91-2, Slip Op., March 11, 1993.
29. See, for example, discussion of PACFISH in Chapter 3.
30. See the discussion of the Owyhee Bruneau hot springsnail in Chapter 12: *Fighting Back: The Growth of Grassroots Opposition.* The effort of the people of Owyhee County to overturn the illegal listing of the hot springsnail is not only an example of outreach and working with others—the American Farm Bureau Federation, Mountain States Legal Foundation, and others were brought in to help litigate the matter—but a template for grassroots activism, organizing locally and then reaching out to others to publicize their plight. For example, both Paul Harvey and Rush Limbaugh gave ample air time to what was happening to the people of Owyhee County in the name of environmental purity.
31. *Brandt and Venice Child v. United States of America,* CIV 93-C-839W, U.S. District Court for the District of Utah.
32. "Availability of a Draft Environmental Assessment and Receipt of an Application for an Incidental Take Permit for Development in Las Vegas Valley, Clark County, NA (sic)," 56 Federal Register 10912, March 14, 1991.
33. *Four Corners Action Coalition, et al., v. Dennis Underwood, et al.*, 92-Z-341, U.S. District Court for the District of Colorado.
34. Conversation with Charles Roybal on September 23, 1994.
35. Conversation with Jim Matson, chairman of the Southwest Natural Resources Council, September 23, 1994. See "Owls win U.S. ruling over loggers," *Arizona Republic*, July 7, 1994, A1: "The ruling could place 3 million acres of Southwestern forests—an area the size of Connecticut—off-limits to logging." And more: "Spotted owl could cap oil, gas exploring—If Mexican subspecies is put on endangered list, several industries in state could be affected," *Rocky Mountain News*, May 29, 1992, p. 10.
36. For example, the U.S. Fish and Wildlife Service has designated 1,980 miles of the Colorado River and its tributaries, including portions in Colorado, Utah, New Mexico, Nevada, California, and Arizona, as critical habitat for the Colorado squawfish and a number of other fish, effective April 20, 1994, prompting a threat by a number of tribes to sue for interfering with

Indian water rights, including the Animas–LaPlata Project. "Tribes claim
feds endanger water rights," *Durango Herald*, July 11, 1994. 59 Federal
Register 13374, March 21, 1994.

37. It was not until the Endangered Species Committee (the God Squad) provision of the ESA was applied and timber communities were allowed to
participate that the media reported the presence in the fray of a third
party—the men and women of the timber-producing communities.

38. "NBC Nightly News," September 17, 1993.

39. William Perry Pendley, "Aliens and Allies," *Land Rights Letter*, Gloversville,
N.Y., January/February 1994, p. 4.

40. Fortunately, a number of entities are doing their best to bring these and
other issues involving the Endangered Species Act to light. See, for exam-
ple, "Going Broke? Costs of the Endangered Species Act as Revealed in
Endangered Species Act Recovery Plans," *National Wilderness Institute
Resource*, 1994; "An Endangered Species Blueprint," *National Wilderness
Institute Resource*, Fall 1992, Vol. III, issue 3; Ike C. Sugg, "Caught in the
Act: Evaluating the Endangered Species Act, Its Effects on Man and
Prospects for Reform," *Cumberland Law Review*, vol. 24, no. 1, 1993–1994,
pp. 1–78.

41. Even federal officials admit that what they are about has little to do with
real science. Said Marvin L. Plenert, regional director, U.S. Fish and
Wildlife Service:

"William Perry Pendley, president of the Mountain States Legal Foundation... charges in the December 28, 1993, *USA Today*, 'Science is almost
non-existent. The distinction between species and subspecies, for example,
has nothing to do with biological science but with political science.' To a
degree, Mr. Pendley is correct. It does have to do with political science.
Where I fault him is in his semantics.

"When we examine the issue of politics and biology, I think it is important that we keep our definitions straight. If you define 'politics' in the non-
pejorative sense of it being the 'balancing of competing demands,' then,
yes, our business of resource management is political by its very nature."
Endangered Species Law and Regulation Conference, Sacramento, California, February 10, 1994.

42. Dixy Lee Ray, *Trashing the Planet* (Washington, D.C.: Regnery, 1990), p.
167.

43. In making listing decisions, the government relies on a very small body of
"experts." While this can be explained in part by the narrowness of the subject, it nevertheless exposes the weakness of a system in which those who
stand to profit enormously—with contracts and consulting fees, visibility
and prestige—are the very ones who determine whether a species should
be listed by the government.

In addition, the government makes its decisions—decisions that cost
money and hurt people—based upon very little information. The National Wilderness Institute cited a host of FWS documents that demonstrated
what scanty information the agency possessed in preparing recovery plans:
"lack of information... prevents a more precise determination of the rea-

sons for the species's decline"; "little is known of the mussel's biology"; "[s]ufficient data to estimate population size or trends is lacking"; "practically no information [exists] on the life history, population levels, and habitat requirements for this species." "Going Broke," op. cit., p. 25.

44. Dr. J. Gordon Edwards, "The Endangered Species Act," San Jose State University, undated and unpublished manuscript, p. 5.

From whom does the FWS get proposed listings? From petitioners like Stephen McCabe, who proposed the listing of three insects in the Santa Cruz mountains of California because: "My goal is to protect the habitat in the Ben Lemend sand hills. The best route at present is to try to get individual species listed and by doing that get protection for the habitat." "Expert bugged by proposed listing," *Santa Cruz* [California] *County Sentinel*, June 27, 1994, p. A1.

45. 16 U.S.C. § 1532 (16).

46. Listing of the wolf under the Endangered Species Act allows environmental extremists to demand that the wolf be "recovered," that is, returned to its "range." 16 U.S.C. § 1533(f) Today, efforts to "recover" the wolf are underway in eighteen states. For example, the U.S. Fish and Wildlife Service has placed the wolf in Yellowstone National Park, central Idaho, and northwestern Montana. See U.S. Department of the Interior, Fish and Wildlife Service, "The Reintroduction of Gray Wolves to Yellowstone National Park and Central Idaho—Final Environmental Impact Statement," 1994.

47. The listing of the murrelet is currently being challenged. *Northwest Forest Resource Council, et al. v. Babbitt*, Civil No. 93-1579, U.S. District Court for the District of Columbia, Complaint for Declaratory and Injunctive Relief. The complaint quotes the U.S. Fish and Wildlife Service: "Marbled murrelets spend the majority of their lives on the ocean, and come inland to nest although they visit some inland stands during all months of the year." (57 *Federal Register* 45328, October 1, 1992).

48. Conrad Istock and Peter A. Strittmatter, "The Biological Situation of the Mt. Graham Astrophysical Study Area in Light of the Second Biological Opinion Rendered by the USFWS, July 14, 1988," unpublished, August 1988, p. 1. As to the reasons for the actions being taking by the Fish and Wildlife Service, Istock and Strittmatter venture: "[I]t is hard to believe that the main purpose of [the FWS] report is to help the squirrel. A more likely goal seems to be that of stopping the observatory. Having found no good environmental reason for rejecting the UA proposal, the Opinion invents one through unreasonable and arbitrary restrictions on public use and access." Ibid., p. 4.

49. A lawsuit by the city of Las Vegas and others, challenging both the scientific basis for the listing as well as its economic impact upon Clark County, was unsuccessful. *City of Las Vegas, et al. v. Lujan, et al.*, Memorandum Order, No. 89-2216 (D.D.C. August 24, 1989), Slip Op., p. 6. Affirmed, *City of Las Vegas, et al. v. Lujan, et al.*, 891 F.2d 927 (D.C. Cir. 1989).

50. 16 U.S.C. § 1539(a) (1988). See, in general, *Searching for Consensus and Predictability: Habitat Conservation Planning Under the Endangered Species Act of*

1973, Robert D. Thorton, 21 Envtl. L. 605 (1991). The National Wilderness Institute's review of 306 recovery plans revealed that more than 60 percent (184) called for "large scale habitat purchases." "Going Broke?" op. cit., p. 28.

51. Even the popular press has begun to question such plans. *U.S. News & World Report* (October 4, 1993) noted: "But in fact such plans—aimed at preserving entire ecosystems rather than individual species—rarely provide politically or scientifically tidy solutions to regional conflicts.... [T]he schemes please few parties in practice.... They are also expensive.... The issue of how much land is enough is often complicated by the fact that planners don't know how many members of the species remain or where they live.... Even if scientists have a pretty good fix on population, however, they often know very little about a species' biology and the ecosystem in which it dwells."

52. "Availability of a Draft Environmental Assessment and Receipt of an Application for an Incidental Take Permit for Development in Las Vegas Valley, Clark County, NA" (sic), 56 *Federal Register* 10912, March 14, 1991.

53. The thirty-year plan under which building could take place in the entire Las Vegas Valley has not yet been developed or approved. In the summer of 1994, the FWS announced a one-year extension of the original permit until July 31, 1995, and its expansion from 22,352 to 30,352 acres. At the same time, the size of the tortoise habitat set-aside will be increased by 140,000 acres. "Incidental Take Permit for Desert Tortoises in Las Vegas Valley and Boulder City Extended for One Year," *U.S. Fish & Wildlife Service News Release*, dated July 29, 1994.

54. Such demands have a chilling effect upon other economic activity. For example, in order to diversify from its dependence on forestry, Libby, Montana, is considering a ski hill. If the government wants $8 million for a twenty-year mine using a mere 500 acres, what will it demand from Libby for a fifty-year ski operation spread over 5,000 acres?

55. 16 U.S.C. § 1534. In *Sweet Home Chapter of Communities for a Great Oregon, et al. v. Babbitt, et al.*, 17 F.3d 1463 (D.C. Cir. 1994), the Court saw that acquisition, not regulation, was the means chosen by Congress for the protection of species upon private lands: "The ESA pursues its conservation purposes through three basic mechanisms: (1) a federal land acquisition program (citation omitted); (2) the imposition of strict obligations on federal agencies to avoid adverse impacts on endangered species (citation omitted); and (3) a prohibition on the taking of endangered species by anybody.

"The legislative history reflects this balance, and confirms the intention to assign the primary task of habitat preservation to the government." Ibid., p. 1466.

56. The government's ability to engage in such an abuse of the Endangered Species Act was denied by a federal court of appeals. In *Sweet Home Chapter of Communities for a Great Oregon, et al. v. Babbitt, et al.*, op. cit., the U.S. Court of Appeals for the District of Columbia held that "habitat modification" cannot be defined as "harm" under the ESA. The court found it particularly significant that Congress had declined to include such language in

the 1973 act: "Congress's deliberate deletion of habitat modification from the definition of 'take' strengthens our conclusion." Ibid., p. 1467.

On June 29, 1995, the Supreme Court, by a 6 to 3 decision, reversed, holding that the FWS's definition of "harm" as including "habitat modification" on private land was "reasonable." *Babbitt, et al. v. Sweet Home Chapter of Communities for a Great Oregon, et al.* ___ U.S. ___, ___ L.Ed. 2d ___, ___ S.Ct. ___ (June 29, 1995).

57. 16 § 1533 (d).
58. Between 1967 and 1993, the federal government spent only $253 million to acquire land for listed species protection, a tiny fraction of the amount appropriated by Congress from the Land and Water Conservation Fund, which is now running at $900 million a year.
59. "Going Broke?" op. cit., p. 2.
60. Ibid., p. 18.
61. Professor William McKillop of the University of California at Berkeley calculated that the increased cost of unemployment compensation that resulted from President Clinton's Option 9 exceeded $745 million. Ibid., p. 22.

CHAPTER 6

1. The National Park Service includes (1) Natural Areas (National Parks, National Monuments, National Preserves, National Environmental Education Landmarks, and Registered Natural Landmarks); (2) Recreation Areas (National Parkways, National Recreational Areas, National Seashores, National Lakeshores, National Scenic Trails, National Scenic Riverways, and National Wild and Scenic Rivers); and (3) Historical Areas (National Historic Sites, National Historical Parks, National Memorials, National Military Parks, National Battlefield Sites, National Cemeteries, and National Historic Landmarks). Index of the National Park System and Affiliated Areas as of June 30, 1977 (GPO, 1977).
2. U.S. Department of the Interior, Bureau of Land Management, "Public Land Statistics 1992," p. 5.
3. U.S. Department of the Interior, National Park Service, "Briefing Statement," February 9, 1994, p. 1.
4. "Issues on Aircraft Overflights of National Parks," Air Access Coalition, submitted at National Park Service Workshop, Flagstaff, Arizona, March 16–18, 1994, p. 4. Approximately 800,000 people took air tours of the Grand Canyon in 1993: 30 percent, or 240,000, were elderly (fifty years and older); 7 to 12 percent were legally handicapped; 20 percent had health or physical limitations.
5. Ibid.
6. Yellowstone Park Act: United States Statutes at Large, 17, p. 32., March 1, 1872.
7. Ibid.
8. I am indebted for much of this analysis to the ground-breaking and prescient work of the late Don Hummel: *Stealing the National Parks: The*

Destruction of Concessions and Public Access (Bellevue, Wash.: Free Enterprise Press, 1987). A lawyer as well as builder, owner, and operator of several national park concessions, his love of the parks dates from his early days as a ranger at Grand Canyon National Park. But he loved the people he served even more. Anyone who cares about parks and people should read his book.

9. National Park Service Act: Public Law No. 64-235, August 25, 1916. The act is usually referred to as the National Park Service Organic Act.

10. Conservation is defined as "the wise utilization of a natural product" in *Webster's Third New International Dictionary*, 1969.

11. U.S. Department of the Interior, National Park Service, "Yellowstone National Park Master Plan," 1976.

12. Hummel, op. cit., p. 2. What is "unnecessary?" Privately run facilities strive mightily to satisfy visitors in order to stay in business. When the facilities are run by the U.S. government, which does not need to satisfy the customer, the facilities will quickly become "unnecessary," and the National Park Service and its environmental extremist allies will have a self-fulfilling prophecy.

13. Ibid.

14. The Stanford Research Institute reported that the overwhelming majority of the American people do not want overnight hotel and lodge facilities in the national parks closed. *Stanford Research Institute, The Concession System in United States National Parks: Background, Services Performed, Public Attitude Toward, and Future Considerations, Executive Summary*, SRI Project ECC-4268 (Menlo Park, Calif.: January 1976).

15. Hummel, op. cit., p. ix.

16. The wide open spaces of the West, as well as the size of the parks of the West, make concessions inside the parks a necessity.

17. Concessions Policy Act, 16 U.S.C. § 20 et seq. Congress also expressly provided that the return to the federal Treasury was "subordinate to the objectives of protecting and preserving the areas and of providing adequate and appropriate services for visitors at reasonable rates," 16 U.S.C. § 20b(d).

18. Hummel, op. cit., p. 16. The El Tovar Hotel in Grand Canyon National Park, the Glacier Park Lodge, Le Conte Lodge in the Great Smokey Mountains, the Ahwahnee in Yosemite National Park, Crater Lake Lodge, Death Valley's Furnace Creek Inn, the Lake Crescent Lodge in Olympic National Park, and the Chateau at Oregon Caves National Monument were all built by the free enterprise system.

19. *New York News World*, March 10, 1983, quoted in Hummel, op. cit., p. 4. Removing all vehicles from the valley floor of Yosemite National Park has long been an objective of the park purists.

20. Conversation with Allen Howe, August 31, 1994.

21. Letter from Michael V. Finley, superintendent of Yosemite National Park, to Jesse Brown, dated April 7, 1994. In an attached cover letter Finley notes: "Secretary of the Interior Babbitt has also reviewed the letter and is supportive of the National Park Service position." Finley is now superintendent of Yellowstone National Park. On taking his new post he remarked, "I believe the only way we can protect a national park in

today's environment is to work beyond park boundaries—work with our neighbors and look at the larger picture." *Denver Post,* May 28, 1994, p. 11B.

22. Ironically, while the Concession Policy Act of 1965 has been attacked and all but abandoned, the statute enacted a few months earlier has been praised and promoted. Hummel reports that the final congressional hearings on what became the Wilderness Act of 1964 and the Concessions Policy Act of 1965 occurred within less than forty days of each other in 1964. These measures "gained support from many of the same legislators and administrators." Hummel, op. cit., p. 219.

23. Hummel, op. cit., p. 243.

24. U.S. Department of the Interior, *The National Parks: Index,* 1993.

25. Gene Coan, ed., *Sierra Club Political Handbook: Tools for Activists* (San Francisco, Calif.: Sierra Club, 1979), p. 35.

26. Hummel, op. cit., pp. 249-250.

27. In the past, if park service employees held such views, those views remained unexpressed; such advocacy was left to environmental extremists. As Micah Morrison reports regarding the Greater Yellowstone Coalition (GYC), an assemblage of major environmental groups allied "to protect Yellowstone": "The GYC played an important role in the political ecology of the Yellowstone area. Organized, articulate, aggressive, expansionist—it flanked the mostly middle-of-the-road liberals of the Park Service to the left. It could say and do what the Park Service could not. It lobbied. It sued." Micah Morrison, *Fire in Paradise: The Yellowstone Forest and the Politics of Environmentalism* (New York, N.Y.: Harper-Collins, 1993), p. 34.

28. U.S. Department of the Interior, National Park Service, "National Parks for the 21st Century: The Vail Agenda," Report and Recommendations to the Director of the National Park Service, 1992, p. 20. It seems we can't just glory in a beautiful sight anymore. We must be filled with National Park Service-style "meaning."

29. Ibid., p. 21.

30. In Yosemite National Park in California, I have stood at the foot of massive and towering sequoias, alone in the moonlight at 2:00 A.M., hearing only the sound of the wind through the trees.

   In Hawaii Volcanoes National Park, I have walked across lava that was still hot, stood at the edge of the ocean and watched the red hot river, streaming only inches beneath my feet, spew into the sea.

   In Rocky Mountain National Park in Colorado, I have passed over the tundra high atop Trail Ridge Road, feeling one could be no higher, and looked around to see even more majestic snow-covered peaks above.

   In Mount Rainier National Park in Washington, I have seen the majesty of snow-covered Mount Rainier shining pink in the reflected glory of a setting sun.

   In all of those places, I felt something special and was greatly moved. Millions of Americans have had and will continue to have similar experiences. Yet there are other ways to see the nation's parks and other experiences for which the parks are valuable.

31. Conversation with Bruce Vincent on September 6, 1994.

32. Conversation with concessioner George Crump on May 9, 1994.

33. Ibid.

34. The cafeteria is not the only thing the National Park Service has closed down. For a number of years George Crump ran a nursery for small children. Although Crump lost more than $30,000 a year on the nursery, he was willing to do so for the sake of the visitors. In April 1993, the National Park Service decided it needed the building where Crump ran his nursery and put him and the nursery out. Today, says Crump, his former nursery is "filled with junk."

35. Some years back, Rex Walker offered a horseback ride over the Continental Divide on a trail once used by the Ute Indians. The National Park Service, citing inadequate funds to maintain the trail, closed it. Millions for acquisition, mere pennies for operation and maintenance.

36. Conversation with Rex Walker on May 23, 1994.

37. Those involved in tourism in Colorado think that is exactly what is happening. "They're trying to put me out of business," says Mike O'Boyle, owner of Eagle Tree Tours in Grand Junction, Colorado, regarding the quadrupling of entrance fees charged by national parks. Debbie Kovalik, director of the Grand Junction Visitor and Convention Bureau, thinks the fee increases will cut tour bus activity by 20 percent a year, costing the local area more than $5.6 million. *Denver Post*, April 11, 1994.

38. National Park Index 1985 (GPO, 1985).

39. National Park Service & Forest Service, "Vision for the Future: A Framework for Coordination in the Greater Yellowstone Area, Draft," August 1990, p. 1-3.

40. Ibid., pp. 3-7 and 3-25.

41. Morrison, op. cit.

42. *Parker Land and Cattle Company, Inc., v. United States of America*, No. 91-CV-0039-B, Findings of Fact and Conclusions of Law, June 5, 1992, pp. 22-23. Declared the federal judge: "It was unreasonable for these agencies (the National Park Service and the U.S. Fish and Wildlife Service) to do nothing more than commission studies in light of the fact it was their actions in managing the wildlife which dramatically increased the transmission of the disease. The least they could have done was to cooperate wholeheartedly with the state in its vaccination program. Thus, the FWS and NPS have acted negligently in managing the wildlife, in that they each have failed to take an active role in eliminating the brucellosis problem in the elk and bison which are under their control."

43. U.S. Department of the Interior, Fish and Wildlife Service, "The Reintroduction of Gray Wolves to Yellowstone National Park and Central Idaho—Final Environmental Impact Statement," 1994. Since wolves have a range of up to 500 miles, it is not just Yellowstone National Park's rural neighbors who may have a close encounter with the "wild." "[S]tudies have shown that long-range dispersals of up to 500 miles by individual wolves occur regularly." *Alaska's Wolves—Supplement to Alaska's Wildlife*, January/February 1992, p. 5. (A 500-mile circle with Old Faithful as its center easily reaches Denver,

Colorado; Salt Lake City, Utah; Burns, Oregon; Spokane, Washington; Bismarck, North Dakota; and Pierre, South Dakota.)

44. "Proposed Change to Colorado Regulation No. 3—Regulatory Consideration for Protection of Class I Wilderness and National Parks," unsigned, undated, two-page document, likely from Forest Service, April/May 1994.

45. U.S. Department of the Interior, Office of Inspector General, "Audit Report: Department of the Interior Land Acquisitions Conducted With the Assistance of Nonprofit Organizations," Report No. 92-I-833, May 1992, pp. 4-5.

46. Ibid., p. 9.

47. Ibid., pp. 16-19. Even when the government did make an appraisal to determine fair market value, it was done months and even years before the sale, rendering its worth highly questionable. In all, the inspector general concluded that, on sixty-four federal purchases with a fair market value of $44 million, the American people lost $5.2 million. Ibid., p. 5.

48. One of the reasons the federal government does so is because it is a huge money maker for the land trusts. Some of the land trusts have admitted as much. According to documents accompanying a press release issued by The Trust for Public Land, "Sixty percent of TPL's operating income comes primarily from its land sales to government." Trust for Public Land, "Land Protection Group Calls DOI Report 'Biased,'" June 5, 1992, p. 4.

49. In a panel on which I appeared in Austin, Texas, a spokesman for The Nature Conservancy (TNC), Tom Wolf, admitted that nearly 90 percent of the land bought by TNC in Texas ended up in federal hands. Others have reported the same thing. "Why we cannot buy our way out of environmental dilemmas," *Los Angeles Times*, July 21, 1991, p. M2.

50. Rural counties, in which the vast majority of the land is owned by the federal government, cannot afford to lose any more land from the tax rolls. County official after county official has advised me on how devastating the loss of even one parcel is to the ability of the county to function.

    Local governments in the West are particularly hard pressed because of unfunded federal mandates, wherein federal laws impose unreasonable and very expensive standards upon local government. The city of Cheyenne, Wyoming, must spend $25 million over the next five years to meet federal environmental mandates. The entire budget for the city of Cheyenne for one year is only $22 million. In October 1993, the mayor of Cheyenne joined with forty-three other Wyoming mayors in a letter to President Clinton and the Wyoming congressional delegation demanding an end to unfunded federal environmental mandates.

51. Office of Inspector General, op, cit., p. 25.

52. Memo from Troy Timmons, legislative director, Congressman Dan Schaefer, October 26, 1994.

53. Mr. Brookes' seven-part series of columns began on January 17, 1991, and ran through January 29, 1991, in the *Washington Times*.

54. Ostensibly, the NNLP was established under the authority of the Historic Sites Act of 1935, 16 U.S.C. §461, et seq. However, the Historic Sites Act speaks only of a "prehistoric or historic district, site, building, structure, or

object...." 16 U.S.C. §470w. The word "natural" is nowhere to be found in the Historic Sites Act. Citing the Historic Sites Act, federal regulations define a National Natural Landmark as any area "within the boundaries of the United States... that contains an outstanding representative example(s) of the nation's natural heritage, including terrestrial communities, aquatic communities, landforms, geological features, habitats of native plant and animal species, or fossil evidence of the development of life on earth." 36 CFR Ch. 1 (July 1, 1992 Edition) § 62.2.

55. William Perry Pendley, *It Takes a Hero: The Grassroots Battle Against Environmental Oppression* (Bellevue, Washington: Free Enterprise Press, 1994), p. 123.

56. Ibid.

57. In 1989, a landowner in Idaho discovered that the National Park Service, without the landowner's knowledge or permission, had proposed that his property be designated as a National Natural Landmark. As a result, federal officials refused to issue permits or to take actions requested by the landowner. To make matters worse, it appears the proposed designation took place at the request of a private citizen who then used the National Park Service's listing of the property as grounds for attempting to prevent the issuance of various permits and other authorizations to the landowner. Letter from W.F. Ringert to director, National Park Service, February 18, 1992.

CHAPTER 7

1. "Bill to Halt Growth at Rocky Mountain Park," *Denver Post*, May 3, 1994, p. 3B. Colorado Senator Brown protested: "Wilderness designation of 91 percent of the park would tend to restrict the recreational opportunities in the park.... We ought to be looking for ways to expand recreational opportunities in the park, not reduce them."

2. The Wilderness Act, P.L. 88-577; 78 Stat. 890, "Definition of Wilderness" (1964) at 1014.

3. Many extreme wilderness advocates, living in the most privileged, pampered, and prosperous society in the history of the world, eschew the wherewithal that makes their lifestyles possible. Through the use of surrogates, the "sins" of modernity—that is, their own personal distance from the "natural" world that they revere—have been expiated.

4. 16 U.S.C. §§ 1131-1136.

5. Don Hummel, *Stealing the National Parks: The Destruction of Concessions and Public Access* (Bellevue, Wash.: Free Enterprise Press, 1987). pp. 285–286.

6. In 1973, the Forest Service initiated a process called "Roadless Area Review and Evaluation (RARE)," which led to a variety of wilderness proposals. In 1977, the Forest Service announced a new study called RARE II to add more roadless areas to the 1,449 already in existence. Terry S. Maley, *Handbook of Mineral Law*, Revised Second Edition, MMRC Publications, Boise, Idaho, 1979, p. 109. The process of studying roadless areas for designation as wilderness has never stopped.

7. 43 U.S.C. § 1782(a). During the Carter administration, the BLM was

unable to study large portions of Western land under its jurisdiction for wilderness designation because the areas were already honeycombed with roads and therefore not "roadless." So Carter's BLM simply redefined roads. Throughout the West, wherever a road got in the way of making an area "roadless," the BLM called the road a "way."

8. Forest Service chart, "States with National Wilderness Preservation System Areas," December 1992.
9. The breakdown is as follows:

States with National Wilderness Preservation System Areas
December 1992
(Includes USFS, BLM, NPS & USFWS)
(thousands of acres)

States	Total Acres of State	BLM	USFS	NPS	USFWS	Total	%
AZ	72,668.0	1,405.0	1,345.0	443.7	1,343.4	4,537.1	6.2
CA	100,206.7	13.0	3,921.0	1,990.0	0.1	5,924.1	5.9
CO	66,485.7		2,587.0	55.6		2,642.6	3.9
ID	52,933.1	0.8	3,960.2	43.2		4,004.2	7.5
MT	93,271.0	6.0	3,371.6		64.5	3,442.1	3.6
NV	70,264.3	6.4	798.0			804.4	1.1
NM	77,766.4	128.0	1,388.0	56.4	39.9	1,612.3	2.0
OR	61,598.7	15.7	2,079.0		0.5	2,095.2	3.4
UT	52,696.9	26.6	774.0			800.6	1.5
WA	42,693.8	6.9	2,571.4	1,678.2	0.8	4,257.3	10.0
WY	62,343.0		3,080.4			3,080.4	4.9
	752,927.6	**1,608.4**	**25,875.6**	**4,267.1**	**1,449.2**	**33,200.3**	**4.4**

Chart from U.S. Forest Service

10. *Public Land Statistics 1992*, op. cit., p. 5.
11. Office of Governmentwide Real Property Relations, op. cit., p. 11.
12. Ibid.
13. Ibid.
14. Ibid.
15. Ibid.
16. In 1992, U.S. Senator Jim McClure (R-ID) and Governor Cecil Andrus hammered out a tough bipartisan solution to Idaho's wilderness debate. When language was added for hard release, the Wilderness Society labeled the 2 million plus-acre bill "antiwilderness" and killed it.
17. Consideration of lands for wilderness designation continues unabated as a part of federal planning requirements.
18. *Public Land Statistics 1992*, op. cit., p. 58.
19. Ibid.
20. Ibid. More than 9.169 million were deemed "suitable," 16.104 million

declared unsuitable. The states with the most "suitable" lands include California (2.263 million acres, or 13 percent of BLM lands), Utah (1.952 million acres, or 9 percent of BLM lands), Nevada (1.877 million acres, or 4 percent of BLM lands), and Oregon (1.278 million acres, or 8 percent of BLM lands).

21. Ibid.

22. George F. Leaming, Ph.D., "The Adverse Economic Impacts of Wilderness Land Withdrawals in Utah," Western Economic Analysis Center, Marana, Arizona, January 1990, p. 3.

23. Ibid.

24. U.S. Senator Ben Nighthorse Campbell (R-CO) once faulted environmental extremists for their lack of understanding of Western problems and for their unwillingness to compromise on the issue of wilderness.

25. Congresswoman Maloney's proposed legislation will designate, as wilderness, lands managed by the Forest Service. When she was asked, during a congressional hearing, if she had discussed her legislation with the chief of the Forest Service, Jack Ward Thomas, she asked, "Who is Jack Ward Thomas?" Joint Hearings before the U.S. House of Representatives Subcommittee on Specialty Crops and Natural Resources (Agriculture Committee) and Subcommittee on Environment and Natural Resources (Merchant Marine and Fisheries), May 4, 1994. Conversation with Bruce Vincent, September 1, 1994.

26. This same legislation was introduced by Congressman Peter Kostmayer— a favorite of the environmental movement. Mr. Kostmayer's legislation went nowhere, as did his political career. In 1992, he was defeated for reelection, in large part because of the grassroots efforts of working men and women from the Pacific Northwest who traveled to his district to campaign against him.

27. Even Governor Cecil Andrus, one-time hero to the environmental movement when he was secretary of the interior during the Carter administration, opposed the Kostmayer bill.

28. Yet another example is the effort of federal officials to use the proximity of wilderness to restrict air quality-related activities in distant cities, as mentioned in Chapter 6. An even more serious threat to the West, through the use of parks and other set-asides, is the park protection act proposed by Congressman Bruce Vento (D-MN), legislation that would place "buffer zones" around parks, wilderness areas, and even privately owned national natural landmarks.

29. As Alice Menks of Madison, Virginia, reports, "Every time the National Park Service talks about 'threats' to the park, they are talking about the use of private property anywhere close to the park." See Pendley, op. cit., pp. 159-164.

30. The Washington State Wilderness Act (WSWA) provides, in relevant part: "Congress does not intend that designation of wilderness areas in the State of Washington lead to the creation of protective perimeters or buffer zones around each wilderness area. The fact that nonwilderness activities or uses can be seen or heard from areas within the wilderness shall not, of itself, preclude such activities or uses up to the boundary of the wilderness area."

Washington State Wilderness Act of 1984, Pub. L. 98-339, §9, 98 Stat. 299, 305 (1984).

31. *Northwest Motorcycle Association v. U.S. Department of Agriculture, et al.*, Civil Action No. CS-91-0403-JLQ, Defendants' Memorandum of Law in Opposition to Plaintiff's Cross-Motion for Summary Judgment, U.S. District Court for the District of Washington, pp. 30-31.

32. The district court judge wrote: "[I]f an activity is prohibited, in part, for reasons other than the possible effect that activity will have on an adjoining Wilderness area, it is not an impermissible buffer zone under the Wilderness Act.... Therefore... the Wilderness Act does not prevent the Forest Service from considering the Wilderness classification of adjoining land as *a* factor in developing the Land and Resource Management Plan for the non-wilderness area." (emphasis in original) *Northwest Motorcycle Association v. U.S. Department of Agriculture, et al.*, op. cit., pp. 30-31.

Under the judge's ruling, it is unclear what proportion of the Forest Service's decision to close nonwilderness lands to multiple-use activities may be due to the adjacent wilderness before that decision conflicts with Congress' "buffer zone" language.

33. Letter from Richard A. Ferraro, reviewing officer, deputy regional forester, to Roger F. Dierking, dated February 12, 1990.

34. *Millard County, Utah v. The United States of America*, CIV 93-C-591J, United States District Court for the District of Utah, Order date May 2, 1994.

35. This lack of understanding is aggravated by the fact that few outside the West realize what real "wilderness" is. See, for example, the discussion in Appendix C regarding the Walt Disney Wilderness Lodge "[t]ucked into a wilderness area... a natural oasis that's just a stone's throw from a world of extraordinary Disney attractions."

36. A fitting close to any discussion of wilderness took place recently in New Mexico. There, a fourteen-year-old Illinois boy scout was separated from his troop in the Pecos Wilderness. For more than twenty-four hours, the Forest Service refused to permit a helicopter to land to bring him to safety. "We made a call according to our Wilderness Act. I guess some people can perceive it as a bad call," said a Forest Service spokesperson. Such misplaced priorities are made even more interesting by the nature of the wilderness experience enjoyed by the young lad. "To while away the hours, [he] read a Star Wars novel. He also had a Walkman stereo, on which he listened to comedy tapes by George Carlin and Dennis Leary and a taped book by Garrison Keillor." "Boy rescued after 3 days in the Pecos," *Santa Fe New Mexican,* July 16, 1994, p. A-1.

37. 16 U.S.C. § 1271, et seq.

38. Fact Sheet received from the Niobrara/Missouri National Scenic Riverways, O'Neill, Nebraska, September 7, 1994. The Niobrara Scenic River Act, Public Law 102-50, 1991.

39. 16 U.S.C. § 1274(b) and 1277(a).

40. 43 U.S.C. § 1711.

41. National Historic Preservation Act, 16 U.S.C. § 470(w)(5) (1988). The BLM has calculated that between 3 million and 5 million cultural resources

properties are on federal lands. See J. Muhn and H.R. Stuart, *Opportunity and Challenges: The Story of BLM, 203* (September 1989), citing John G. Douglas, BLM, Washington, D.C. See also the Antiquities Act of 1906, 16 U.S.C. §§ 431-433 (1988), and the Archaeological Resource Protection Act of 1979, 16 U.S.C. 471 (1988).

42. "Public Land Statistics 1992," U.S. Department of the Interior, Bureau of Land Management, Vol. 177, September 1993, p. 55. The number of ACECs and their total acreage for the ten Western states are as follows: California: 112 areas, 937,714 acres; Utah: 41 areas, 911,420 acres; Oregon: 104 areas, 514,325 acres; Idaho: 65 areas, 505,438 acres; Wyoming: 31 areas, 493,860 acres; Colorado: 41 areas, 387,780 acres; Arizona: 33 areas, 305,581 acres; New Mexico: 58 areas, 258,906 acres; Nevada: 7 areas, 134,236 acres; and Montana: 5 areas, 38,328 acres. No ACECs were listed for the state of Washington in which the BLM has exclusive jurisdiction over a mere 333,510 acres. Ibid., p. 6.

The BLM also reports that since 1986 it has used ACEC guidelines to designate Research Natural Areas (RNAs), which are lands to be managed primarily for research and educational purposes. As of 1992, there were 84 RNAs totalling 169,893 acres in six Western states.

43. Ibid.
44. Ibid.
45. This program, which is conducted primarily by the National Park Service, is explored in some detail in Chapter 6.
46. Ibid., pp. 54, 55. Public Land Statistics does not indicate the amount of private land that has been included in NNLs. That information is likely available from state BLM offices. More than 69 percent of the NNL acreage is in the states of California and Idaho.
47. So obscure is the *E. Penlandii* that it is extremely difficult to identify and, once located, almost impossible to differentiate from other similar plants.
48. See, for example, the letter from the Elko County commissioners challenging Forest Service plans. Letter from Ernie Hall, chairman, Board of County Commissioners, Elko County, to Gary Reynolds, regional forester, Forest Service, dated March 31, 1992.
49. *Evergreen*, March/April 1994, p. 6.

CHAPTER 8

1. As others have noted before, every soft energy path—geothermal, wind energy, solar power—becomes a hard energy path once one starts down that road. In the end, environmental groups oppose most means of generating energy. For example, on the Big Island of Hawaii, environmental groups sued to stop the development of geothermal power because, among other things, it would anger the fire goddess Peli. *Wao Kele O Puna, et al. v. Waihee, et al.*, Civil Action No. 91-3553-10, Circuit Court of the First Circuit, Hawaii.

In Montana, a proposal to generate energy with windmills drew the fire of environmental extremists. See, "Critics: Wind power plan endangers birds," *Denver Post*, March 15, 1992, 1C, where an official of the U.S. Fish and Wildlife Service threatened: "...I can tell them that if their [windmills] kill threatened or endangered species, then, adjudicative action will be taken." Ibid., at p. 7C.

2. In early 1981, the U.S. Geological Survey planned to approve an application for permit to drill (APD) for a gas well in northwestern Wyoming. Since the lease had been issued years earlier, the only question was how to protect environmental values. That was the rub. The lease tract was 17 miles southeast of Jackson, Wyoming. As a deputy assistant secretary in Reagan's Department of the Interior, I briefed the Wyoming delegation. Before I returned from Capitol Hill, all three members of the delegation had called Secretary Watt with their views: revoke the lease!

The next day, at a meeting in the Oval Office, Watt told Reagan of the need to revoke the lease. "Why?" asked Reagan. "Three reasons," Watt said, "Wallop, Simpson, and Cheney." "Jim," Reagan said, "those who don't want us to search for energy will always oppose us regardless of what we do. Tell the company to drill and pray for a discovery."

In the end there was no need for prayers. The company withdrew its application and abandoned the search for natural gas near Jackson. Today, the homes there are heated with electricity generated by hydroelectric facilities or from propane trucked in from southwestern Wyoming. The newest bumper sticker in Jackson reads: "Turn Off The Lights, Save A Fish," out of concern for the water needs of the salmon.

3. An excellent book on this issue has been written by former Secretary of the Interior and Secretary of Energy Donald Paul Hodel and Robert Dietz, *Crisis in the Oil Patch* (Washington, D.C.: Regnery, 1994).

4. U.S. Department of Energy, Energy Information Administration, "Short Term Energy Outlook," August 1994, Table 7, p. 24. By comparison, in 1973, during the nation's first energy crisis, American dependence on foreign sources was 34.8 percent. U.S. Department of Energy, Energy Information Administration, "Monthly Energy Review 1994," Table 3.1A, pp. 60–61.

5. An article in the *Oil & Gas Journal*, January 31, 1994, reported that "oil imports averaged a record 49.4 percent of consumption in the U.S.... The decline in U.S. crude production dates back to the mid-1980s, when congressional moratoriums on offshore drilling began to be felt and crude oil prices took a dive."

6. Testimony of Terry Belton before the U.S. Senate Energy and Natural Resources Committee, April 14, 1994.

With falling production comes falling federal revenues. From 1980 through 1985, oil royalties from onshore federal lands amounted to over $3 billion, or $513 million annually. From 1986 to 1992, oil royalties from the same lands dropped by 47 percent to $1.6 billion, an average annual loss of $285 million. Ibid.

7. Responding to what he calls "the wholesale lockup of new energy prospects on public lands," Ken Derr, CEO of Chevron Oil Corporation, says, "I would love to spend more money looking for oil in the United States. But how long are you going to keep banging your head against the wall?" "Getting Pushed Out of America," *Fortune*, September 5, 1994, p. 117.

8. Belton, op. cit. The U.S. Geological Survey's estimate for the West's oil and gas potential does not include the gas reserves from unconventional sources such as tight sands and coal bed methane.

9. *Mountain States Legal Foundation v. Andrus*, 499 F.Supp. 383, 386 (D. WY) 1980, (Andrus).

10. Contrary to popular belief, oil and gas "deposits" do not lie in big pools in the ground. In fact, they are trapped in porous deposits between and among the solid matter in which they are found.

11. *Conner v. Burford*, 848 F.2d 1441, 1450, n. 21 (9th Cir. 1988), (Conner).

12. The wilderness process was referred to as RARE II (Roadless Area Review and Evaluation) and involved 2,919 roadless areas encompassing more than 62 million acres. On May 2, 1979, the Carter administration recommended that 631 areas totalling more than 15.5 million acres be designated as wilderness and that 322 areas totalling 10.8 million acres be studied further. Andrus, op. cit., 499 F. Supp. pp. 387-388.

13. At the time it was estimated that the two areas contained as much as 209 million barrels of oil and 6,409 billion cubic feet of natural gas. Andrus, op. cit., 499 F.Supp. p. 387.

14. Andrus, op. cit., 499 F.Supp. pp. 386, 392.

15. 42 U.S.C. § 4332(2)(C). The NEPA was adopted to ensure that when the federal government proposed "major Federal actions significantly affecting the quality of the human environment," a "statement" would be prepared.

16. Conner, op. cit., 848 F.2d p. 1443.

17. *Park County Resource Council, Inc., et al. v. U.S. Department of Agriculture*, 817 F.2d 609, 612-613 (10th Cir. 1987), (Park County).

18. Conner, op. cit., 848 F.2d p. 1444.

19. Ibid., 848 F.2d. p. 1455.

20. An environmental assessment (EA) is the precursor to a full-blown environmental impact statement (EIS). If the EA reaches a "finding of no significant impact" (FONSI), no EIS need be prepared. Ibid.

21. Ibid.

22. Ibid.

23. "[I]ncomplete information about post-leasing activities does not excuse the failure to comply with the statutory requirement of a comprehensive biological opinion using the best information available." Conner, op. cit., 848 F.2d p. 1454. The court held that "the FWS [Fish and Service] could have determined whether post-leasing activities in particular areas were fundamentally incompatible with the continued existence of the species." Ibid. In the midst of 1.3 million acres, the questions occur, what "post-leasing activities" and what "particular areas"?

24. Conner, op. cit., 848 F.2d p. 1462.

25. Ibid.

26. Park County, op. cit., 817 F.2d pp. 612-613.

27. Ibid.

28. Ibid.

29. The Court of Appeals for the Ninth Circuit also includes Alaska and Hawaii.

30. Chief Justice Rehnquist defines the term thus: "[A] petition for certiorari is, stripping away the legal verbiage, a request to the Supreme Court to hear and decide a case that the petitioner has lost either in a federal court of appeals or in a state supreme court." William H. Rehnquist, *The Supreme Court: How It Was, How It Is* (New York, N.Y.: Quill/William Morrow, 1987), p. 263.

31. A conflict did appear to exist between the Conner decision and an earlier, landmark decision of the U.S. Supreme Court. In a very similar case, the U.S. Supreme Court held that the mere issuance of oil and gas leases in the Outer Continental Shelf did not trigger the requirement for further study. The reason for not requiring expanded study and review was clear: "At the lease sale stage [such review] is, at best, inefficient, and at worst impossible: Leases are sold before it is certain if, where, or how exploration will actually occur." *Secretary of the Interior v. California*, 464 U.S. 312, 343, 344, 338-39, 342 (1984).

    One of the judges who decided Conner saw the same problem:

    "[A]ll that the agency has done in selling the 'leases' is conveyed priorities in submitting plans for development of these tracts; it has not obligated itself to approve any of these plans. As such, the leasing stage under the terms of the leases before us is as discrete a stage as that mandated by the OCSLA." See *Secretary of Interior v. California*, 464 U.S. 312, 104 S.Ct. 656, 670, 78 L.Ed.2d 496 (1984). *Conner v. Burford*, op. cit., 848 F.2d at 1463 (Wallace, concurring in part and dissenting in part).

32. *Sun Exploration and Production Company, et al. v. Lujan*, 489 U.S. 1012 (1989).

33. The final nail in the coffin of Western oil and gas leasing was working its way through the federal courts, one regarding leasing near the Bob Marshall Wilderness Area in west central Montana. Fewer than twenty leases had been issued in a 42,000-acre area with "high potential for the development of natural gas resources." *Bob Marshall Alliance, et al. v. Hodel*, 852 F.2d 1223, 1226 (9th Cir. 1988). Some of the leases contained NSO provisions while others contained stipulations permitting restrictions on surface-disturbing activity. All of the leases contained provisions prohibiting activities that would violate the Endangered Species Act. Nonetheless, environmental groups sued, contending that the leases violated the NEPA and the ESA.

    The district court agreed and ordered the leases set aside. On appeal, the U.S. Court of Appeals for the Ninth Circuit upheld the district court's holding, referencing its earlier decision in *Conner v. Burford*. On remand, following an unsuccessful request for review by the U.S. Supreme Court, the district court vacated all of the oil and gas leases. The search for gas near the Bob Marshall Wilderness Area was over.

34. Unlike the General Mining Law of 1872, under which private citizens can search for, locate, and develop minerals if lands are not closed to mining, under various federal laws, oil and gas leases are issued solely at the discretion of the federal land managers. Federal officials have total discretion over whether to search for energy in a particular area, or the manner in which and when that search may be conducted. Thus, as a result of the

opposition of environmental extremists to oil and gas leasing, more and
more land has been put off limits.

35. Belton, op. cit., p. 4, and "Overview of BLM Onshore Oil & Gas Program," Rocky Mountain Oil and Gas Association, Denver, Colorado,
March 18, 1994.

The reason for the incredible decline is directly related to the National Environmental Policy Act, and the abuse of that process by environmental groups through appeals and litigation. The Forest Service, fearing
litigation, concluded that the existing forest plans could not serve as leasing decision documents. As a result, new supplemental environmental
impact statements were prepared for oil and gas leasing on all but two of
the forty-one forests in the Northern, Rocky Mountain, and Intermountain Regions.

36. Belton, op. cit., p. 3.

37. Ibid., p. 4.

38. Conversation with Richard T. Robitaille on May 23, 1994.

39. Oil and gas are not the only energy commodities that draw lawsuits by
environmental groups. A proposal to lease a billion tons of coal in
Wyoming's Powder River Basin was the subject of years of litigation by
several environmental groups that ended only recently. "Interior rejects
Powder River mine appeal," *Casper Star Tribune*, May 25, 1994.

40. Belton, op. cit., pp. 4, 5.

Forest Service and Bureau of Land Management officials have taken
increasingly to demanding a full-blown environmental impact statement
(EIS) simply out of fear of litigation. Since the federal government does
not have the money or the ability to complete the study on a timely basis,
operators seeking prompt decisions must pay third parties to perform EISs
at a cost of between $100,000 and $600,000.

Often an Environmental Assessment (EA) would meet all of the
requirements of federal environmental law. Since an EA can be completed
for $50,000 and finished in three to six months, it offers a much more effi-
cient alternative. However, even an EA is often beyond the reach of the
federal government's financial and human resources; operators are being
asked to bear this burden.

41. Ibid.

42. While the Forest Service is the land-managing agency for national forest
lands such as those in the Bridger-Teton National Forest, the Bureau of
Land Management is the agency responsible for leasing rights to explore
for and develop the oil and gas resources beneath the forest. The Forest
Service does have primary responsibility for making recommendations for
specific proposed lease sales and for performing the environmental analysis under the NEPA.

43. Belton, op. cit., p. 6. A similar situation is taking place in two other Rocky
Mountain States.

In Utah, the Bureau of Land Management determined, after years of
study and public hearings, that 1.9 million out of a total of 3.2 million acres
met the criteria for wilderness designation. Environmental groups object-

ed, asserting that an additional 2.5 million acres of wilderness should be designated. In response to their demands, Congressman Maurice Hinchy (D-NY) sponsored legislation to create that amount of wilderness. As a result of an order from Secretary Babbitt, no leasing is occurring on these lands, even though they are not part of a wilderness study area.

In Montana, the BLM agreed with an environmental group not to lease areas that might be subject to seasonal lease stipulations until a supplemental wildlife environmental impact statement could be completed regarding wildlife. Not only has the study not begun, there is currently no funding available for it. Ibid.

44. In Utah, for example, the BLM is preparing an "Ecoregion Plan" for the entire southern part of the state, involving five or six resource areas—one of which extends into Colorado—and covering about 15 million acres, an area the size of West Virginia. Belton, op. cit., p. 8.

45. Ibid.

46. Yet another area in which the EPA could seriously injure the Western oil and gas industry is through the Resource Conservation and Recovery Act (RCRA). Although Congress exempted drilling muds and certain other oil and gas related materials from the hazardous waste provisions of RCRA— since these materials are covered by other state and federal statutes—the EPA continues to threaten action. The Independent Petroleum Association of America points out that under additional RCRA regulations 80 percent of oil and gas wells will be shut in and the nation will lose 13 percent of its domestic production. How fragile this important industry is is startling. As of April 1994, employment in the oil and gas extraction industry had declined by 22,500 workers from November 1993. IPAA Briefing paper, dated June 7, 1994.

47. Dr. Larry Squires, of Hobbs, New Mexico, is challenging the EPA's claim that his lands are "waters of the United States." Dr. Squires is represented by Mountain States Legal Foundation. *Laguna Gatuna v. Browner, et al.*, CIV 93-0772-JC, United States District Court for the District of New Mexico, Order dated April 8, 1994.

48. Ibid.

49. The BLM decreed: "Construction of above-ground electrical facilities shall be required to incorporate designs that discourage or prevent their use as hunting perches by species that prey on black-footed ferrets (e.g., birds of prey)." *BLM Application for Permit to Drill (APD) Draft Stipulation*, p. 3.

50. The shock waves in Casper's oil and gas industry continue. In May 1994, Amoco and Marathon announced plans to eliminate 135 jobs. *Rocky Mountain News*, May 14, 1994, p. 54A. Moreover, notes the *Denver Post*, September 25, 1994, "Since Amoco closed [its Casper] refinery... the Denver area has been short of refining capacity...." And "construction on [a new pipeline from Texas] has stopped south of Denver" because a Colorado county denied the pipeline its permit.

51. Another home-grown source of opposition to economic activity includes state-funded law schools. *USA Today* reports: "University of Wyoming law professor Mark Squillace was criticized by logging families for challenging

a timber sale in the Medicine Bow National Forest. They claim he is closing an industry that helps pay his and other state employees' salaries." *USA
Today*, July 20, 1994, p. 9A.

52. State Senator Mike Enzi (R-Gillette), during his tenure on the Appropriations Committee, sought to have the Wyoming Game and Fish Commission appear before the committee to disclose its budget. Members of the
commission declined, saying, "That's our money. We don't have to discuss
it with you." Conversation with Enzi on September 7, 1994.

53. Conversation with Richard T. Robitaille on September 9, 1994.

54. 58 *Congressional Record* 7510 (1919), quoted in Andrus, op. cit., 499 F. Supp.
at 392.

CHAPTER 9

1. Act of May 10, 1872 (17 Stat. 91) 30 U.S.C. § 21, et seq.
    Ironically, while the creation of Yellowstone National Park is justly
praised as a far-sighted and beneficial act by a thoughtful Congress, the
General Mining Law has been excoriated as, at best, a short-sighted statute
that has outlived its usefulness, or, at worst, an abominable tool of the
"rape, ruin, and run boys." It was then-Secretary of the Interior Cecil
Andrus, former governor of Idaho, who coined the phrase.

2. Today, mining contributes significantly to the economy of the West.
According to a survey conducted in 1992, the hard rock mining industry
had the following impact upon Western states:

State	# Directly Employed	Average Salary	Indirect Gross Revenue (*)	Mining Revenue
AZ	13,996	$29,297	340,629,859	3,060,218,000
CA	14,332	$35,606	219,026,995	2,722,343,000
CO	7,560	$38,680	126,112,346	405,315,000
ID	2,971	$28,120	55,148,680	344,185,000
MT	4,819	$29,149	61,276,488	573,781,000
NV	12,979	$31,985	535,927,506	2,625,554,000
NM	7,829	$28,219	10,771,365	1,078,038,000
OR	1,834	$24,457	38,443,057	220,609,000
UT	6,908	$32,492	534,357,519	1,234,669,000
WA	3,782	$30,269	32,584,962	473,381,000
WY	9,208	$34,085	25,918,174	934,338,000

   Chart supplied by the American Mining Congress, Washington, D.C.
Column 1 is from statistics compiled by the Mine Safety and Health
Administration. Column 2 is from Western state employment bureaus.
Column 3 is from information gathered by the Direct Impact Company,
based on figures submitted by thirty mining companies producing hard
rock minerals in the West. Column 4 is from U.S. Bureau of Mines State
Mineral Summaries, 1992.

3. *Nevada Miner,* March 1994, p. 12. Nevada leads the nation in gold mining with over 70 percent of the total gold production and 11 percent of world gold production. Nevada also leads the nation in the production of silver, barite, mercury, and magnetite. Nevada also produces copper, lithium carbonate, gypsum, limestone, and specialty clays. *Nevada Miner,* February 1994, p. 12, citing the Nevada Division of Minerals.

4. The term "Great Terrain Robbery" comes from a one-sided, fatally flawed analysis of the General Mining Law that appeared in the *Reader's Digest.*

5. U.S. Senate Committee on Energy and Natural Resources, Subcommittee on Mineral Resources, May 4, 1993, p. 90.

6. "U.S. Mineral Vulnerability: National Policy Implications," a report prepared by the Subcommittee on Mines and Mining of the Committee on Interior and Insular Affairs of the U.S. House of Representatives, 96th Congress, 2nd Session (November 1980) at 64.

7. See generally George F. Leaming, Ph.D., "The Copper Industry's Impact on the Arizona Economy—1992," Western Economic Analysis Center, April 1993.

8. Under the GML, once the individual has made a discovery, he or she can stake a claim to it and then record that claim with both the Bureau of Land Management and the county of the state in which it is found. The claim, or "location," is protected against all others, under the legal doctrine of *pedis possesso.* That is, the location is safe from the adverse claims of all but the U.S. government, which can, at any time, challenge its validity. Such challenges most often allege that a "valuable" discovery has not been made. The test to determine if a discovery has been made is the "prudent man rule": "where minerals have been found and the evidence is of such a character that a person of ordinary prudence would be justified in the further expenditure of his labor and means, with a reasonable prospect of success, in developing a valuable mine...." *Castle v. Womble,* 19 L.D. 455 (1894). *Maley, Handbook of Mineral Law,* Revised Second Edition (Boise, Idaho: MMRC Publications, 1979), pp. 212–219.

9. Maley, p. 194. Maley defines "patent" as "[a] government deed; a document that conveys legal title of public lands to the party to whom the patent is issued." Ibid., p. 455. It is during the process of examining the patent application that the federal government most often challenges the validity of the discovery.

10. Since 1781, 288 million acres of federal land have been given to private parties as agricultural homesteads while 94 million acres have been given to railroads as land grants. But since 1872, only 3 million acres—an area smaller than one county in Nevada—have been patented under the General Mining Law. U.S. Department of the Interior, Bureau of Land Management, "Public Land Statistics 1992," p. 4.

11. If ever there was a case for not writing into statute current cost figures, this is it. No doubt, in 1872, $2.50 was a reasonable amount for conveying title, but today $2.50 would not cover the cost of sending the documents to Washington, D.C., for review.

12. U.S. Bureau of Land Management study of Mineral Patenting Costs in

Nevada, April 9, 1992. The minimum costs for patenting are as follows:

Mineral Survey

Cost of survey (per 20-acre claim)	$ 2,000
Cost of survey approval (first claim)	750
Application filing fee	250
Preparation of application by attorney	6,500

Includes title search, title opinion, preparation and filing of application, preparation and filing of final proofs and statements with BLM for issuance of first half Final Certificate.

Mineral Report

Consulting geologists report fee	$ 2,500
Publication of Legal Notice	300
Payment of Purchase Price	100
Required Improvements	500
Drilling/Geological work to prove discovery	25,000
Total for Mineral Survey and Report	**$37,900**

13. *New World News*, Crown Butte Mines, Inc., December 1993, p. 3.
14. For example: Clean Air Act, 42 U.S.C. §§ 7401 to 7642; Clean Water Act, 33 U.S.C. §§ 1251 to 1387; Comprehensive Environmental Response, Compensation, and Liability Act of 1980, 42 U.S.C. §§ 9601 to 9675; Emergency Planning and Community Right-to-Know Act of 1986, 42 U.S.C. §§ 11001 to 11050; Endangered Species Act of 1973, 16 U.S.C. §§ 1531 to 1544; Federal Land Policy and Management Act of 1976, 43 U.S.C. §§ 1701 to 1784; National Environmental Policy Act of 1969, 42 U.S.C. §§ 4321 to 4370b; National Forest Management Act of 1976, 16 U.S.C. §§ 1600, 1611 to 1614; Safe Drinking Water Act of 1976, 16 U.S.C. §§ 330f to 300j-11; Toxic Substances Control Act, 15 U.S.C. §§ 2601 to 2692; Uranium Mill Tailings Radiation Control Act of 1978, 42 U.S.C. §§ 7901 to 7942.
15. The discussion of Viceroy Resource Corporation's Castle Mountain Mine is taken from three sources: Uldis Jansons, "Finding Gold Is Just the Beginning: One Company's Experience with Permits," *Minerals Today*, December 1992; Lynn A. Pirozzoli and James S. Pompy, "Implementing an Award Winning Reclamation Plan at Castle Mountain Mine," *California Geology*, November/December 1992; and the following documents from Viceroy Resource Corporation: Annual Report 1993; "The Financial Post Environment Awards for Business 1992"; Castle Mountain Gold Mine Fact Sheet.
16. The EIS contains a laundry list of environmental mitigation measures, including, but not limited to, a $2 million Environmental Enhancement Fund to be used in the East Mojave National Scenic Area; the upgrading of an existing country road (at a cost of $330,000); replacement of plastic claim posts (at a cost of $80,000); free van service to minimize traffic to the site; purchase of previously mined clay pits (at a cost of $500,000); and use of enclosed solution storage tanks (at a cost of $400,000).

17. It was the lure of gold that first brought white men into the upper Yellowstone region. As early as 1875, ore was being smelted in the area. In 1882, the Crow Indian Reservation was reduced in size and the property in the Cooke City area was put into the public domain to permit creation of the New World Mining District, following which there was a rush to the area. By 1952, gold production in the area helped to make Park County the third highest gold-producing area in Montana. Information obtained from a series of documents made available by Crown Butte Mines, Inc., Missoula, Montana.

18. "Public will halt plan to mine near park, group says," *Rocky Mountain News*, May 16, 1994, p. 12A.

19. Leaming, "The Copper Industry's Impact on the Arizona Economy—1992" op. cit., pp. i and 1.

20. Ibid., p. 7. In fact, a large part of the copper exports went to purchasers in the Far East, thus helping to offset imports from that region. Ibid.

    America produces 94 percent of the copper that it uses annually. Obviously, the ability to mine domestically available ores, such as copper, offsets the need to import minerals such as columbium, manganese, chromium, and others not available in the United States. U.S. Bureau of Mines, "Mineral Commodity Summaries 1994," pp. 3 and 54–55.

21. Ibid. Arizona, although the nation's largest copper producer, is not the only state with copper mines.

22. Today, thirteen copper mines produce 95 percent of the U.S. output of copper and copper concentrates; nine lead mines produce all of the nation's primary lead; twenty-five gold mines produce 75 percent of the nation's gold; and twenty-five zinc mines and ten iron mines produce 99 percent of the nation's output of those valuable resources. Compare these paltry figures to the nation's 606,890 oil wells or 257,279 gas wells or 2,915 coal mines. Statement of Robert J. Muth, vice president of Government and Public Affairs, ASARCO Inc., before the Subcommittee on Mining and Natural Resources, Committee on Interior and Insular Affairs, U.S. House of Representatives, June 20, 1991, unpublished, pp. 3–4.

23. *Public Land Statistics, 1992*, Bureau of Land Management, U.S. Department of the Interior, Volume 177, September 1993, p. 5.

24. Denver International Airport (DIA) sprawls over more than 34,000 acres, one-fifteenth the land used by all the metal mines in the country.

25. Testimony of Douglas C. Yearley, chairman, president, and chief executive officer, Phelps Dodge Corporation, before the Subcommittee on Energy and Mineral Resources of the Committee on Natural Resources, U.S. House of Representatives, March 11, 1993, p. 4. Even if environmental extremists should never fly in commercial aircraft, they live in houses. Each new home in the United States used 430 pounds of copper. Ibid.

26. "U.S. Minerals Vulnerability: National Policy Implications," Subcommittee on Mines and Mining of the Committee on Interior and Insular Affairs of the U.S. House of Representatives, November 1980, p. 5.

27. Ibid., p. 63. According to the report, six different mining companies explored the Keystone lead-zinc-silver mine on Mount Emmons before the

August 1977 discovery of "the world's fourth largest deposit of molybdenum, valued at more than $7.5 billion. The outer edge of this deposit is less than 200 feet beyond the workings of the old base-metal mine." Ibid.

28. Ibid., pp. 63–64. According to the report, "[P]rior to discovery of the Troy (Spar Lake) copper-silver deposit by Bear Creek Mining Company geologists in 1963, the area had been studied by both state and federal geologic teams with no apparent recognition of its mineral potential. Two additional copper-silver deposits, one located within sight of a paved road, have since been discovered in the same area. Not only had two competent geologic survey agencies failed to locate these subtle shows of mineralizations, but so had several other major exploration companies."

29. Unpublished memorandum entitled, "Stillwater Project," signed by J.D. Mancuso, president, Minerals Business Unit, Pittsburg & Midway Coal Mining Company, June 29, 1992.

30. "The geological uniqueness of mineral deposits is even better exemplified by a rule-of-thumb that the average mining company can stay in business if it makes one significant discovery every 20 to 30 years." *U.S. Minerals Vulnerability,* op. cit., p. 58. To put it another way, out of each one thousand rock mineral prospects identified through initial reconnaissance, only eighty will merit extensive drilling, only eighteen (1.8 percent) will be brought into production, and only seven (0.7 percent) will return enough revenue to recover the investment. Such a reality led the Public Land Law Review Commission to acknowledge nearly a quarter century ago: "Mineral deposits of economic value are relatively rare and, therefore, there is little opportunity to choose between available sites for mineral production.... [Hence] development of a productive mineral deposit is ordinarily the highest economic use of land."

    "One Third of the Nation's Land," report to the president and to Congress by the Public Land Law Review Commission, 1970, p. 122.

31. "Final Report of the Task Force on the Availability of Federally Owned Mineral Lands," U.S. Department of the Interior, 1977, p. 48.

32. "U.S. Minerals Vulnerability," op. cit., p. 60.

33. Ibid. Perhaps as bad, in the committee's view, such land lockup was "aggravated by the total lack of interest within the executive [branch] for specifically determining the availability of public lands for mineral development." Ibid.

34. Courtland L. Lee, "Lack of Access Makes Mining Law Reform Irrelevant: An Update of Federal Land Availability for Hardrock Mining," *American Mining Congress Journal,* Vol. 80, No. 8, August 1994, p. 1. "All together, more than 410 million acres—62 percent of all our public lands—are virtually unavailable for mineral exploration and development."

    The ability of miners to hold onto their claims has also decreased sharply. Under the 1994 Budget Reconciliation Act, claimholders are now required to pay an annual $100 holding fee on each and every mining claim. According to the U.S. Department of the Interior, since this was first imposed, 75 percent of all claimants have dropped their claims. Thus the number of mining claims has fallen from 1.2 million in 1991 to 325,000 claims today. "Mining claims on the wane," *Rocky Mountain News*, May 19, 1994, p. 50A.

35. *New York Times*, February 21, 1994. Redford seems to have special contempt for gold mining. Yet some 21 percent of the gold produced in the United States is used in the electronics industry, since 95 percent of all electrical contacts in computers and integrated circuits must be gold plated.

36. Meg Greenfield, "The Word's Too Big," *Newsweek*, April 30, 1990, p. 80.

37. Although "abandoned mines" and "superfund sites" may be evidence of past abuses reflecting a time when the nation had other priorities and interests, they are not evidence of any deficiency in current law. Abandoning mines and the activities that turn areas into superfund sites are strictly forbidden and vigorously regulated. For example, it is illegal to abandon mine sites. Resource Conservation and Recovery Act, 42 U.S.C. §§ 6901 et seq., 6973 (1988). The Environmental Protection Agency can order miners as well as those who mined in the past to clean up a location that poses an imminent hazard to human health and the environment. 42 U.S.C. § 6973 (1988).

38. For example, the GML sets the fee at which mining claims are to be acquired at $2.50 an acre. As already seen, mining companies are paying much more than $2.50 an acre. Nonetheless, everyone agrees that this outdated provision should be changed and that the mining claimant should pay fair market value for the surface estate being acquired.

   Another oft-cited example is that while federal law prohibits the use of claims for residential, recreational, or other purposes not related to mineral development, no current provision of federal law precludes the use of patented mining claims for developers or other speculators to obtain patents for any use other than mining. Everyone wants to close this legislative loophole.

   Similarly, Western mining advocates support legislation to ensure that if states have no reclamation requirements, reclamation will be mandated. Currently federal law and all Western states mandate reclamation.

39. Michael Brown and Marci Anderson, Esq., "What the U.S. Can Learn from Other Nations About Hardrock Mineral Royalties," Gold Institute, March 1993.

40. John D. Leshy, "The Mining Law: A Study in Perpetual Motion," Resource for the Future, Washington, D.C., 1987, p. 366.

41. U.S. Department of the Interior, "Economic Implications of a Royalty System for Hardrock Minerals," August 16, 1993.

42. Stephen D. Alfers and Richard P. Graft, "Economic Impact of Mining Law Reform," Davis, Graham & Stubbs and Coopers & Lybrand, Denver, Col., January 28, 1992, unpublished study.

   Environmental extremists assert that destruction of the General Mining Law will generate jobs. Yet once the U.S. mining industry is gone there will be no one to pay for the reclamation work such advocates plan. Even if those jobs were available, how do they compare with mining jobs? The answer is not well, as is seen in a comparison between operations and reclamation performed by Coeur Thunder Mountain, Inc.:

	Operations	Reclamation
Years:	1985 to 1990	1990 to 1993
Employees:	110 direct full time	4–10 full time/seasonal
Salary:	$34,000 annual	$12,500 full time/seasonal
Payroll:	$3.7 million	$75,000 to $80,000
Jobs:	Long-term	Limited transitional
Hiring:	75 percent local	Mixed
Capital:	$16 million	$1.0 to $1.3 million
Costs:	$14 million annual	$110,000 annual
Taxes:	$165,000 annual	No taxes except sales

43. The impact of a royalty is best seen in a study performed by Dr. John L. Dobra of Reno, Nevada. Examining the long-run total cost of production of gold over the entire expected productive lives of twenty-two major U.S. properties, Dr. Dobra calculated that the mines possessed 70 million ounces of gold. At the current price of gold, only 45 million ounces (of the 70 million ounces available) could be produced at a profit. The addition of an 8 percent royalty, however, would mean that only 20 million ounces (of the 70 million ounces available) could be produced at a profit. "In other words," Dr. Dobra reports, "as a result of the royalty the amount of gold that can be produced at a profit at these 22 operations falls by more than 50 percent." John L. Dobra, Ph.D., letter to Michael Brown, dated July 2, 1992, p. 1.

44. Fact Sheet from J.D. Mancuso, president, Minerals Business Unit, Pittsburg & Midway Coal Mining Company, June 29, 1992.

45. Donald Paul Hodel and Robert Deitz, *Crisis in the Oil Patch* (Washington, D.C.: Regnery Publishing, Inc., 1994).

46. U.S. Department of Justice attorneys see the citizen suit provision of various mining proposals as "an open invitation to sue the Secretary [of the Interior] at any time." Unsigned letter from Acting Assistant Attorney General M. Faith Burton to Director Leon E. Panetta, p. 7. The same attorneys indicate that under various mining law proposals the "United States could be liable for countless millions of dollars in damages for the taking of private property, and it could face a volume of litigation requiring years to resolve." Ibid., p. 3.

47. One incentive to sue is the fees available to those who bring "citizen suits." For example, lawsuits over the northern spotted owl netted environmental groups more than a million dollars. "Lawyers in spotted owl case seek fees," *Register-Guard*, August 4, 1994, pp. C-1 and 2.

48. 56 *Federal Register* 5099, October 9, 1991. Legal commentators view such regulations as an indication that federal officials "contemplate citizen enforcement as a fundamental component of the enforcement program...." Dean R. Massey, David A. Bailey, Laurie L. Korneeffel, "Citizen Suits: The Litigation Threat of the 1990s," 39 Rocky Mt. Min. L. Inst., 1-16 (1993).

49. Bruce Fein, "Citizen Suit Attorney Fee Shifting Awards: A Critical Examination of Government-'Subsidized' Litigation," *Law and Contemporary Problems*, vol. 47, no. 1, Winter 1984, pp. 223–224.

50. Nancie G. Marzulla, "David v. Goliath? Environmentalists, government,

two Goliaths, hand in hand," *Phoenix Gazette*, December 4, 1993.

51. Some argue that citizen suits are needed to goad reluctant regulators into court. Not so! Congress, with its broad and exacting oversight responsibilities, is quite capable of putting officials on the hot seat over any alleged failure to enforce environmental laws.

52. In 1994, eight Western governors weighed in regarding the General Mining Law with a letter to President Clinton asking that he "offer [his] support" for "reasonable and fair reform legislation" that would "encourage the viability of the industry, and continue recognition of mining as one of the legitimate multiple uses of the public lands." Western Governors' Association letter to William Jefferson Clinton, dated February 3, 1994. The following governors signed the letter: Bob Miller (NV), Michael O. Leavitt (UT), Marc Racicot (MT), Mike Sullivan (WY), Fife Symington (AZ), Bruce King (NM), Pete Wilson (CA), and Roy Romer (CO).

53. *Marathon Oil Company, et al. v. Lujan, et al.*, 937 F.2d 498 (10th Cir. 1991) and *Larsen v. Lujan*, Civil Action No. 91-C-393J, Slip Op., July 28, 1992, U.S. District Court for the District of Utah.

54. *Barrick Goldstrike Mines, Inc. v. Bruce Babbitt, Secretary, U.S. Department of the Interior, et al.*, Case No. CV-N-93-550-HDM(PHA). Magistrate's Report and Recommendations dated January 14, 1994. District Judge's Order Adopting Magistrate Judge's Report and Recommendation dated March 21, 1994.

55. Prepared Statement of Bruce Babbitt, Secretary of the Interior, Before the Subcommittee on Mineral Resources Development and Production, Committee on Energy and Natural Resources, U.S. Senate, March 12, 1993, p. 5. Babbitt made similar remarks before the U.S. House of Representatives on March 11, 1993, and the National Press Club on April 27, 1993.

56. *Barrick Goldstrike Mines, Inc. v. Babbitt, et al.*, Case No. CV-N-93-550-HDM(PHA), Report and Recommendation of U.S. Magistrate Judge, January 18, 1994, pp. 17–19.

57. "Proposed Fiscal Year 1995 Budget Requests for the Department of the Interior and the Forest Service," Hearing before the Committee on Energy and Natural Resources, United States Senate, February 24, 1994, p. 52.

58. Letter to Secretary of the Interior Bruce A. Babbitt from U.S. Senators Malcolm Wallop (R-WY), Robert F. Bennett (R-UT), Larry E. Craig (R-ID), and Harry Reid (D-NV), dated March 24, 1994.

59. "There's no reason for mining to take shortcuts to swindle the public out of royalties we know are coming." "Babbitt terms mining lawsuits a 'legal swindle'," *Rocky Mountain News*, June 2, 1994. This is what Babbitt is calling a "swindle": Babbitt refuses to obey the law; a mining company sues asking that he be required to obey the law; a federal judge orders Babbitt to obey the law.

CHAPTER 10

1. Letter from Connie Wood, president, Libby Area Chamber of Commerce, December 12, 1991.

2. *Lake County Examiner,* September 3, 1992, p. 1. Kerr's jab at the pride of
   the cattlemen of eastern Oregon was made with a two-edged knife, since
   barbed wire is not only an indispensable implement on ranches but the historical symbol of private property.
3. *Denver Post,* February 14, 1993, pp. 1G and 4G. Also mentioned as Colorado "towns that people drive through—not to—nine months of the
   year": Fairplay, Ouray, and Walden.
4. Robert Redford, "The gold in our hills," *New York Times,* February 21,
   1994.
5. "Long commutes take toll on family life," *Rocky Mountain News,* September 4, 1994, p. 13A.
6. Bruce Vincent, founder of Communities for a Great Northwest, often
   begins his speeches this way:
      "Have any of you ever been to Libby, Montana? On purpose? Did you
   buy a major appliance while you were there? You know tourism is our
   future. Times are so tough at home, I'm sure we could find someone to
   weld a freezer to your bumper if you wanted to take one home."
7. Bill Walsh, Memorandum, Arcata Redwood Company, 1986, pp. 1–2. The
   Sierra Club proposal would have included 77,000 acres of privately owned
   lands.
8. Statement of John Saylor, representative from Pennsylvania, *Congressional
   Record,* September 12, 1968, H8587.
9. Walsh, op. cit., p. 3.
10. Ibid., p. 4.
11. "The Redwoods," National Park Service, U.S. Department of the Interior,
    September 15, 1964. In a 1966 follow-up report the National Park Service
    reduced its estimate of the five-year growth in tourism to 950,000. Walsh,
    op. cit., p. 8.
12. Ibid., p. 3.
13. Ibid., p. 5. Unemployment in the area rose to 15 percent. The increased
    harvesting from the Six Rivers National Forest did not take place. Instead
    of increasing by 37 million board feet, as promised, the annual cut fell by
    96 million board feet between 1969 and 1976. The annual cut on the Six
    Rivers National Forest has fallen even further from the 1976 days. Harvest
    volumes have fallen from 195 MMBF in 1990, to 42 MMBF in 1993. Let-
    ter from George A. Lottritz, Natural Resources Staff Officer, Six Rivers
    National Forest, Forest Service, dated May 25, 1994.
14. Walsh, op. cit., p. 6.
15. Ibid., p. 9. Also revealed in National Park Service figures: the average visit
    lasts less than an hour and the year-to-year growth in visitor hours is less
    than 3 percent.
16. Ibid., p. 9, citing National Park Service and California Department of
    Parks and Recreation studies.
17. Gloria Zuber, president of the Orick Chamber of Commerce, Testimony
    before the Subcommittee on National Parks, U.S. House Interior and
    Insular Affairs Committee, Eureka, Calif., April 13, 1977. Orick resident
    Donna Hufford says: "I can't tell you our exact unemployment rate but I

can tell you that our elementary school is 90 percent AFDC [Aid to Families with Dependent Children], which shows that unemployment is rampant. The park sure didn't help for employment purposes. The people with
money to invest who were involved in timber moved away and their money
went with them." Conversation with Donna Hufford, September 24, 1994.
18. How do environmental extremists feel about the tiny towns that border on
the national parks? Scott Reed, National Audubon Society board member,
told the Idaho Conservation League:
    "[T]he greatest environmental disaster coming out of the Yellowstone
Park fire was its failure to burn up [the town of] West Yellowstone. In the
fierce competition between Wyoming and Montana for the ugliest town,
West Yellowstone is the easy winner. What a wonderful thing it would have
been to reduce all that neon clutter and claptrap to ashes."
    Micah Morrison, *Fire in Paradise: The Yellowstone Fires and the Politics of
Environmentalism* (New York, N.Y: Harper-Collins, 1993), p. 69.
19. Walsh, op. cit., pp. 10, 12.
20. Congressman Don H. Clausen, *Congressional Record*, February 9, 1978, H870.
Professor of Forestry Emanuel Fritz agreed and argued against the expansion:
    "The Redwood National Park, created in 1968, was to cost
$92,000,000, a figure provided in the bill. Up to the present it has cost
more than $172,000,000, and $109,000,000 is still to be collected. Total
final cost: $281,000,000 for something not needed.
    "The proposed expansion of the same park to 48,000 acres is estimat-
ed to cost another $359,000,000! If the cost history of the first acquisition
is a good guide for guessing what the expansion will cost, it will be nearer
$450,000,000 for another 'something' not needed. If the Burton bill is
passed and the president signs it, it will be the biggest rip-off yet."
    Emanuel Fritz, Testimony before Subcommittee on Parks and Recre-
ation of the U.S. House of Representatives Committee on Energy and
Natural Resources, U.S. Senate, September 6, 7 and October 5, 1977, pp.
568, 570.
21. Walsh, op. cit., pp. 13–14.
22. Ibid., pp. 14–15. Dr. Gerald Partain, chairman of the Department of
Forestry, Humboldt State University, noted the impact of park expansion
on the taking of private land: "Let me give you an example of what could
be done with the 48,000 acres you want to preserve and rehabilitate. Private industry can provide any necessary rehabilitation and produce enough
timber to build 3,885 homes per year forever. It could provide direct permanent employment for 380 people just in harvesting and lumber or plywood production." Dr. Gerald Partain, Testimony before Subcommittee
on Parks and Recreation of the U.S. Senate Committee on Energy and
Natural Resources, September 6, 7, and October 5, 1977, p. 285.
23. Linda Billings, Washington representative, Sierra Club, Testimony before
Subcommittee on Parks and Recreation of the U.S. Senate Committee on
Energy and Natural Resources, September 6, 7, and October 5, 1977, p.
157. Why hadn't tourism boomed following the 1968 creation? The park
was "ecologically unsound and disjointed." If only that were fixed, "then

the tourism boom would finally occur." Walsh, op. cit., p. 16. The U.S. government was similarly bullish: "Tourism is going to be a growth industry for that area, particularly with the expansion of the park." Energy and Natural Resources Committee, op. cit., p. 365, testimony of Harold W. Williams, deputy assistant secretary for Economic Development, Department of Commerce.

24. Energy and Natural Resources Committee, op. cit., p. 106.

25. Walsh, op. cit., pp. 12, 16.

26. Ibid., p. 18, based upon National Park Service numbers.

27. Ibid.

28. Ibid., p. 19.

29. U.S. Department of the Interior, Fish and Wildlife Service, "The Reintroduction of Gray Wolves to Yellowstone National Park and Central Idaho: Final Environmental Impact Statement" ("Wolf EIS"), May 1994, Chapter 7, p. 10. Of course, wolves will roam a lot farther than that. The range of the wolf is 500 miles, which, from Yellowstone National Park alone, could take it all the way past Denver to Colorado Springs, Colorado. "[S]tudies have shown that long-range dispersals of up to 500 miles by individual wolves occur regularly." *Alaska's Wolves—Supplement to Alaska's Wildlife*, January/February 1992, p. 5.

30. "Wolf EIS," op. cit., pp. 4–24. Paul Hoffman, executive director of the Cody Chamber of Commerce, says, "If it means eliminating 60 jobs at Cody Lumber with a $1 million-a-year payroll to get a 10 percent increase in tourism, I don't think you can say that translates into economic benefits." "Feds: Wolf return means big boost in tourist money," Associated Press, undated.

31. Even more ludicrous is the manner in which the FWS has performed the cost/benefit analysis. According to the FWS, which always undervalues the impact of its actions on economic activity, the loss to the hunting industry ranges from $394,000 to $879,000 while the loss to the livestock industry ranges from $1,888 to $30,470. Yet those costs are insignificant compared to what the FWS calls the "economic existence value" of wolves in the Yellowstone area: $6.6 to $9.9 million! Just what is "existence value?" According to the FWS, it is "the value a person associates with the knowledge that a resource exists, even if that person has no plans or expectations of ever directly using that resource." "Wolf EIS," op. cit., pp. 4–25, 26. With this type of cost/benefit analysis, Westerners will always lose.

32. The FWS already admits that portions of the park will have to be placed off limits to visitors. "Wolf EIS," op. cit., pp. 4–17.

33. Mark Obmascik, "Wolves should bring respect for nature back to the West," *Denver Post*, May 7, 1994, p. B1. Mr. Obmascik might want to share his thoughts with the families of an eighteen-year-old Evergreen, Colorado, man and a California woman; both were killed by mountain lions while jogging near their homes.

34. *Denver Post*, August 18, 1991.

35. Conversation with Mr. Brandt Child, June 10, 1992. Mr. Child has been given a cease-and-desist order prohibiting him from using his land. Although he believes that the order is illegal and that the government has

no authority over his land, a federal court has ruled that he cannot challenge the jurisdiction of the U.S. government unless he violates the cease-and-desist order, thereby risking millions of dollars in fines and jail time. *Brandt and Venice Child v. United States of America*, CIV 93-C-839W, U.S. District Court for the District of Utah, Slip Op., May 6, 1994.

36. George F. Leaming, Ph.D., "The Adverse Economic Impacts of Wilderness Land Withdrawals in Utah," Western Economic Analysis Center, Marana, Arizona, January 1990, p. 3.

37. John Keith, et al., "Characteristics and Expenditures of Users of Selected Wilderness Areas in Southern Utah: Some Preliminary Results," Department of Economics, Utah State University, Logan, Utah, pp. 4, 13, 18–19.

38. Dr. Thomas Michael Power, "Wilderness, Timber Supply, and the Economy of Western Montana," *Wild Montana*, Montana Wilderness Association, May 1989, p. 4.

39. Keith, op. cit., p. 14.

40. Miners and timber workers earn some of the highest working wages in the country. It takes a lot of tourist-based service jobs to replace the loss of a mill worker.

  A study done in northeastern Oregon concluded that the elimination of so-called "below cost timber sales" would cost nearly 2,000 timber jobs in three counties, causing a loss of $56 million in earnings. "[T]o replace lost timber earnings [Wallowa-Whitman National Forest] recreation has to increase nearly 28 times." M. Henry Robison, Ph.D., and Jon Freitag, "The Economic Impact to Local Communities of Eliminating the Wallowa-Whitman National Forest Timber Program," Robison and Associations, Moscow, Idaho, January 1994, pp. v and vi.

41. The Forest Service based part of its decision upon the cost involved, disregarding the more than $500,000 it had received. In addition, it asserted that the adjacent wilderness area—Mount Evans was designated as wilderness except for the summit and the paved road corridor to the peak—made the Crest House discordant. Then, in a slight of hand with the numbers, the Forest Service asserted that tourist visits had not dropped following the Crest House fire. They had!

42. *Mount Evans Company, et al. v. Madigan, et al.*, Civil Action No. 91-F-617, U.S. District Court for the District of Colorado, 4th Environmental Assessment, Appellant's Appendix, p. 72.

43. Letter from Wilfred S. Davis, forest ranger, to Wm. Thayer Tutt, president, Mount Evans Company, July 23, 1941.

44. "Federal Government Losing Millions by Not Minding the Concessions Store," Investigative Staff Report of Senator William S. Cohen, May 16, 1994.

45. Conversation with John F. Imler, director of Government Affairs, California Travel Parks Association, March 9, 1992.

CHAPTER 11

1. For a thoughtful and thorough discussion of each of these six words and their historical origin and legal definition, see Mark K. Pollot's outstanding work, *Grand Theft and Petit Larceny: Property Rights in America* (Pacific Research Institute, 1993), pp. 91–129.
2. Richard A. Epstein, *Takings, Private Property and the Power of Eminent Domain* (Cambridge, Mass.: Harvard University Press, 1985), p. 16.
3. Legal Tender Cases, 12 Wall 457, 551 (1871).
4. *Northern Transportation Co. v. Chicago*, 99 U.S. 269 (1879).
5. Epstein, op. cit., p. 63. Pennsylvania Coal Company, 260 U.S. 293, 393 (1922). Two other commentators said the decision "cast the longest shadow of any Fourteenth Amendment interpretation ever issued." Davis and Glicksman, "To the Promised Land: A Century of Wandering and a Final Homeland for the Due Process and Taking Clauses," 68 *Oregon Law Review* 393, 414 (1989).
6. *Pennsylvania Coal Co. v. Mahon*, 260 U.S. at 415, 412–413.
7. Ibid., p. 415.
8. Ibid., p. 416. Furthermore, "If [the city's] representatives have been so shortsighted as to acquire only surface rights, without the right of support, we see no more authority for supplying the latter without compensation than there was for taking the right of way in the first place and refusing to pay for it because the public wanted it very much." Ibid., p. 415.
9. 505 U.S., 120 L.Ed. 2d 798, 112 S.Ct. 2886 (1992).
10. Ibid., 120 L.Ed. 2nd at 807. Lucas planned to build a home for his family on one lot and a home for resale on the other. Lucas's lots were separated by an intervening lot upon which was located a home built in the early 1980s. In addition, there were homes on either side of his lots, including one home built in 1975. *Lucas v. South Carolina Coast Council*, Petitioner's Brief on the Merits, p. 3.
11. S.C. Code Ann. § 48-39-250(6) (Supp. 1990).
12. Ibid., 120 L.Ed. 2d at 808.
13. Ibid., 120 L.Ed. 2d at 808-809. The trial court held that the South Carolina Act had "deprive[d] Lucas of any reasonable economic use of the lots, …eliminated the unrestricted right of use, and rendere[d] them valueless." Ibid., p. 809. The trial court's holding was determinative since the loss of all "economic use" makes the "taking" indisputable.

    Rarely, in the seventy years following Mahon, has the Court addressed the question of what is "just compensation," focusing instead on whether a taking has occurred. As to the proper test, Professor Epstein suggests that "the ideal solution is to leave the individual owner in a position of indifference between the taking by the government and the retention of the property." Epstein, op. cit., p. 182. The Supreme Court held in *Olson v. United States* that the owner of condemned property must be placed "in as good a position pecuniarily as if his property had not been taken. He must be made whole but is not entitled to more. It is the property and not the cost of it that is safeguarded by state and federal constitutions." 292 U.S. 246, 255 (1934).

14. *South Carolina Coastal Council v. Lucas*, 304 S.C. 376, 379, 383, 404 SE2d 895, 896, 899 (1991), citing inter alia, *Mugler v. Kansas*, 123 U.S. 623, 31 L.Ed. 205, 8 S.Ct. 273 (1887).

15. Petitioner's Brief on the Merits at 9. Technically, Mr. Lucas filed a Petition for Certiorari from the Supreme Court of South Carolina.

16. *David H. Lucas v. South Carolina Coastal Council*, 91-453, Official Transcript Proceedings before the Supreme Court of the United States, March 2, 1992, p. 30.

17. Ibid., p. 27.

18. "A prohibition simply upon the use of property for purposes that are declared, by valid legislation, to be injurious to the health, morals, or safety of the community, cannot, in any just sense be deemed a taking or an appropriation of property." *Muglar v. Kansas*, 123 U.S. 623, 668-669, 31 L.Ed. 205, 8 S.Ct. 273 (1887). "Muglar was only the beginning in a long line of cases." Dissent, *Lucas v. South Carolina Coastal Council*, 120 L.Ed. 2d p. 833.

19. Official Transcript, op. cit., p. 35.

20. Chief Justice Rehnquist and Justices White, O'Connor, and Thomas joined in Justice Scalia's opinion. Justice Kennedy filed a concurring opinion. Justices Blackmun and Stevens dissented in separate opinions. Justice Souter filed a statement indicating that he would have dismissed the writ of certiorari. Lucas, op. cit., 120 L.Ed. 2d at 799–800.

21. Ibid., p. 812.

22. Ibid.

23. Ibid., pp. 813–14. "As we have said on numerous occasions, the Fifth Amendment is violated when land use regulation 'does not substantially advance legitimate state interests *or denies an owner economically viable use of his land*.'" (emphasis added by *Lucas* court) (citing *Agins v. Tiburon*, 447 U.S. 255, at 260, 65 L.Ed. 2d 106, 100 S.Ct. 2138 (1980)).

    The Court also signaled a willingness to revisit the Court's decision in Penn Central: "For an extreme—and, we think, insupportable—view of the relevant calculus [of the loss of all economically beneficial use of the land in question], see *Penn Central Transportation Co. v. New York*...." *Lucas*, op cit., 120 L.Ed. 2d at 813, note.

24. Ibid., pp. 816–871.

25. Ibid., p. 820.

26. Ibid.

27. Ibid., quoting *Curtin v. Benson*, 222 U.S. 78, 86, 56 L.Ed. 102, 32 S.Ct. 31 (1911).

28. *Sic utere tuo ut alienum non laedas*: use your own property in such a manner as not to injure that of another. Henry C. Black, *Black's Law Dictionary* (Minn.: West Publishing Co., 1951), p. 1551.

29. *Lucas*, op. cit., p. 822–823. Despite the favorable results, Lucas leaves four questions unanswered: (1) what does the Court mean by total destruction of value? (2) what is the subject property when the Court speaks of total deprivation of value of the property? (3) when does government regulation diminish the value? and (4) what is the scope of state nuisance law that will excuse government from having to pay compensation?

30. Bachman S. Smith III, attorney for the South Carolina Coastal Council, quoted in *Washington Post*, July 17, 1993, p. E1. Also reported in *Reader's Digest*, August 1994, pp. 97, 98.

31. *Goldblatt v. Hempstead*, 369 U.S. 590, 594 (1962). Noted the Court, "There is no set formula to determine where regulation ends and taking begins."

32. *Penn Central Transportation v. City of New York*, 438 U.S. 104 (1978).

33. 480 U.S. 470 (1987).

34. Ibid., p. 506. There were two glimmers of light in the Court's opinion, both in footnotes. Footnote 16 suggests a level of scrutiny higher than judicial deference in examining statutes. Footnote 20 appears to reject a broad police power exception, noting that the exception is really a nuisance exception. Ibid., pp. 487 and 492. See also Pollot, op. cit., p. 144.

35. *Williamson County Planning Commission v. Hamilton Bank*, 473 U.S. 172 (1985).

36. The three decisions decided on ripeness grounds included *San Diego Gas & Electric v. City of San Diego*, 450 U.S. 621 (1981), *Williamson Planning Commission v. Hamilton Bank*, 473 U.S. 172 (1985), and *MacDonald, Sommer & Grates v. Yolo County*, 477 U.S. 340 (1986). The two decided on substantive grounds, but later referenced as ripeness examples, included *Penn Central Transportation v. City of New York*, 438 U.S. 104 (1978), and *Agins v. City of Tiburon*, 447 U.S. 255 (1980).

37. *McDonald*, 477 U.S. at 348 (1986). Analyzing the requirements set forth in Williamson Planning Commission and Yolo County, two commentators concluded: "[C]laimants seeking to improve property could now obtain substantive federal judicial review of the constitutionality of a denial only after the appropriate body had reached a final, negative decision on all possible development schemes, unlikely in the normal handling of owner-initiated requests, and all state judicial remedies had been exhausted." Davis and Glicksman, op. cit., p. 433.

38. David and Glicksman, op. cit., at 432. Justice Souter declined to join the majority on ripeness grounds in Lucas. Instead he filed a "statement," asserting that his preference was to "dismiss the writ of certiorari... as having been granted improvidently." *Lucas*, op. cit., 120 L.Ed. 2d at 851.

39. *First English Evangelical Lutheran Church v. County of Los Angeles*, 482 U.S. 304 (1987).

40. Ibid., p. 307.

41. Ibid., pp. 321–322.

42. Justice Brennan conceded as much in *Penn Central*: "A 'taking' may more readily be found when the interference with property can be characterized as a physical invasion by government, [citation omitted] than when interference arises from some public program adjusting the benefits and burdens of economic life to promote the common good." *Penn Central*, op. cit., 438 U.S. at 124. Note that Justice Brennan wrote of invasion "by government." Note also the inherent conflict between "adjusting the benefits and burdens of economic life to promote the common good," and "forcing some people alone to bear public burdens which, in all fairness and justice, should be borne by the public as a whole." *Armstrong v. United States*, 364

U.S. 40, 49 (1960).

43. 483 U.S. 825 (1987). The Court had taken the same position five years earlier in *Loretto v. Teleprompter Manhattan CATV Corp.*, 458 U.S. 419 (1982):
"A permanent physical occupation [is] a taking to the extent of the occupation, without regard to whether the action achieves an important public
benefit or has only minimal economic impact on the owner." Ibid., pp.
434–435. The Court found such a "permanent physical occupation" even
though the item in question was a mere one and one-half cubic feet in size.
"In any event these facts are not critical: whether the installation is a taking does not depend on whether the volume of space it occupies is bigger
than a breadbox." Ibid., p. 438, note 16.

44. *Nollan*, op. cit., 483 U.S. at 832. Justice Scalia dismissed Justice Brennan's
dissent that the public easement sought to be imposed upon the Nollans'
property was not a taking but "a mere restriction on its use." Wrote Justice
Scalia, "[T]o use words in [this] manner… deprives them of all their ordinary meaning [since] 'the right to exclude [others is] ["]one of the most
essential sticks in the bundle of rights that are commonly characterized as
property.["]'" Ibid., p. 831.

45. Ibid., pp. 834, 837.

46. Ibid., pp. 841. Justice Scalia and others are most concerned when the government, which establishes the purposes, is the one that benefits from
"avoidance of the compensation requirement." For example, heightened
scrutiny "is of particular importance… where the Government has a direct
pecuniary interest in the outcome of the proceeding." *U.S. v. Good*,
___U.S. ___, 114 S.Ct. 492, 502, 126 L.Ed.2d 490 (1993). Further, "[a]s we
have recognized in the context of other constitutional provisions, it makes
sense to scrutinize governmental action more closely when the State stands
to benefit." *Harmelin v. Michigan*, 501 U.S. 957, 111 S.Ct. 2680, 2693 note
9 (1991).

47. Epstein, op. cit., p. 112. Continues Epstein, "The other side of the proposition, that the state can act only to control nuisances, is far more controversial."

48. *Penn Central*, op. cit., 438 U.S. at 144 (Rehnquist, J., dissenting).

49. *Keystone*, op. cit., 480 U.S. p. 491, note 20.

50. *Lucas*, op. cit., 120 L.Ed.2d p. 823, 822.

51. Ibid., pp. 822, 817–819, and quoting *Nollan*, op. cit., U.S. 824 p. 834.

52. This is the approach of the Court regarding other rights accorded constitutional protection. Discussing the regulatory "means" chosen by the federal government to control public nuisances, Professor Epstein criticizes
the failure of the Supreme Court to view the Fifth Amendment guarantee
of "private property" with the same protective concern conferred upon the
First Amendment guarantee of "free speech." Justice Scalia appears
inclined to treat property on an equal basis with other fundamental rights.
In fact, as shown below, Chief Justice Rehnquist used such language in his
opinion in *Dolan*.

53. *Dolan v. City of Tigard*, Brief for the United States as Amicus Curiae Supporting Respondent, U.S. Supreme Court, October 1993, No. 93-518. In

Notes 295

the Clinton/Gore administration's brief on the merits, the solicitor general urged the Court to adopt a requirement that the property owner show that the land-use restriction is "a subterfuge for imposing otherwise unconstitutional conditions...." "Brief for the United States as Amicus Curiae Supporting Respondent," p. 21. Justice Scalia responded, "[T]hat's an awful burden to put on the... small individual property owner...." *Dolan v. City of Tigard*, 93-518, Official Transcript Proceedings before the Supreme Court of the United States, March 23, 1994, p. 50.

54. Brief for the United States, p. 21.
55. Petitioner's App. A-11 n.8.
56. Mrs. Dolan—and David Lucas before her—were supported with amicus briefs by a host of conservative public interest legal foundations.
57. A recent missive from environmental groups described the takings issue as one of an "unholy trinity." The other two are federally "unfunded mandates" and "cost/benefit amendments" (risk assessment). Eric Olson, Natural Resources Defense Council, March 4, 1994, memo to John Adams, Peter Barie, Jay Hair, Fred Krupp, Jane Perkins, and Carl Pope.
58. *Dolan v. City of Tigard*, Brief for the National Audubon Society as Amicus Curiae Supporting Respondent, U.S. Supreme Court, October 1993, No. 93-518, p. 3.
59. Ibid., p. 8.
60. The Chief Justice was joined by Justices O'Connor, Scalia, Kennedy, and Thomas. Justice Stevens filed a dissenting opinion in which Blackmun and Ginsburg joined. Justice Souter filed a separate dissenting opinion. *Dolan v. City of Tigard*, 512 U.S., 129 L.Ed. 2d 304, 305, 114 S.Ct. 2309 (1994).
61. Ibid., 129 L.Ed. 2d at 317.
62. Ibid., 320. While the Court did not require a "precise mathematical calculation," it did mandate "some sort of individualized determination" that "quantif[ies] its findings... beyond [a] conclusory statement [that there is a nexus]...." Ibid., at 320, 323.
63. Ibid., 320.
64. Ibid., 321.
65. Ibid., 323, quoting *Pennsylvania Coal*, op. cit., 260 U.S. at 416.
66. *Whitney Benefits v. United States*, 752 F.2d 1554 (Fed. Cir. 1985), 18 Cl. Ct. 394 (Cl.Ct. 1989), 926 F.2d 1169 (Fed. Cir. 1991).
67. 926 F.2d 1169, at 1178.
68. *Florida Rock Industries, Inc. v. United States*, 21 Cl.Ct. 161, 164 (1990).
69. Ibid, 167, 176.
70. *Loveladies Harbor, Inc., v. United States*, 21 Cl.Ct. 153, 159 (1990).
71. Ibid., 160-161. Attorneys fees and costs were to be assessed in subsequent proceedings.
72. *Flotilla, Inc. v. State of Florida*, Manatee County Circuit Court, Florida, Case No. 90-2356, Feb. 2, 1993.
73. *Christy v. Hodel*, 857 F.2d 1324 (9th Cir. 1989), cert. denied, 490 U.S. 1114 (1989).
74. *Moerman v. State of California*, Petition for Writ of Certiorari to the Court of Appeals, State of California, First Appellate District, Division One, U.S.

Supreme Ct., Oct. Term 1993. The failure by the U.S. Supreme Court to hear a case does not mean that the Court necessarily agrees with the decision below. As to the elk situation in Mendocino County, it is anticipated that it will give rise to yet another takings case.

75. *Armstrong v. United States*, 364 U.S. 40, 49 (1960).

76. *Hage v. United States*, United States Court of Claims, 91-147-OL. As proof of the fear environmental extremists have of the takings clause, a host of environmental groups sought to intervene in the *Hage* case. That effort was denied, as was the extraordinary attempt by the attorney general of Nevada to be represented in federal court by the National Wildlife Federation.

77. Dr. B.H. McDaniels of El Paso, Texas, filed a lawsuit against the U.S. government under the Federal Tort Claims Act.

78. *U.S. v. Gerbaz, et al.*, Civil Action No. 89-M-554, U.S. District Court for the District of Colorado.

79. Much of this discussion appeared originally in William Perry Pendley, *It Takes a Hero: The Grassroots Battle Against Environmental Oppression* (Bellevue, Washington: Free Enterprise Press, 1994).

80. Pendley, op. cit., pp. 148–149.

81. Source, American Farm Bureau Federation, April 18, 1994. The Arizona statute was repealed by initiative in 1994. The Arizona State Legislature is in the process of adopting new "takings" legislation.

CHAPTER 12

1. "Report on the Wise Use Movement," *Wilderness Society*, second printing, revised March 1993, inside front cover.

2. Ibid. George Frampton is now serving as assistant secretary of Fish, Wildlife and Parks of the U.S. Department of the Interior.

3. Ibid., p. 2.

4. Ibid., p. 46.

5. Ibid., pp. 14–15.

6. Ibid., pp. 34–35. In fact, according to a 1990 Times Mirror study, quoted in the report, 58 percent of the American people believe "government regulation of business usually does more harm than good"; 62 percent of the American people believe "the federal government controls too much of our daily lives"; and 77 percent of the American people think "the federal government should run only those things that cannot be run at the local level." *Times Mirror Magazines*, National Environmental Forum Survey, "Natural Resources Conservation: Where Is Environmentalism Headed in the 1990s?" Poll conducted by the Roper Organization in June 1992. Ibid, p. 35.

7. Ibid., p. 37.

8. Ibid., pp. 2, 4–5, 37, 39. The report's authors were particularly complimentary of the movement's leaders: "The national leaders of Wise Use have known each other for a long time. They share a common ideology, set of values and long-term goals. While they do not control the grassroots and are at some level competitors, their shared sense of purpose, expertise

and information gives them the ability to influence the movement. Absent the development of major schism within the movement, it is likely that their power at the grassroots will grow." Ibid., p. 10.

9. Ibid., p. 58.

10. Ibid., p. 59.

11. No Western advocates of a balanced approach to environmental issues were invited to the conference. In fact, during Session 26, the speaker asked anyone associated with anti-environmental groups to identify himself or herself and presumably be ushered out.

Subsequently, even though audio recordings of the entire conference were available, my attempt to purchase them was rejected on the grounds that "you can't get the tape since you weren't there." Other individuals were able to obtain copies of the audio recordings that are the source of the quotes contained in the text.

12. Environmental Grantmakers Association, 1992 Fall Retreat, Session 26: "The Wise Use Movement: Threats and Opportunities," p. 2.

13. Ibid., p. 4.

14. ABC News "Nightline" #3329 Air Date: February 24, 1994, transcript, p. 1. Said Mr. Koppel: "A few weeks ago, Mr. Gore called to draw our attention to some of the forces, political and economic, behind what he would regard as the anti-environmental movement. The vice president suggested that we might want to look into connections between scientists who scoff at the so-called greenhouse effect, for example, and the coal industry. There was also a connection, he said, to the Reverend Sung Myung Moon's group, and with Lyndon Larouche's organization. I told the vice president we'd do two things. We'd look into whatever his staff gave us, and that if we did anything on the story, I would explain to you how it was that we came to be doing it in the first place." Ibid.

15. Arnold and Gottlieb, op. cit., p. 299.

16. Ibid., pp. 592, 616, citing Environmental Data Research Institute.

17. Ibid., pp. 595-601.

18. Report on the Wise Use Movement, op. cit., inside front cover.

19. Says Bruce Vincent, "Do you know how they tell a good bear from a bad bear? A bad bear has bells in its poop."

20. The heroic story of Bruce Vincent and more than fifty others who have gone from innocent bystanders to victims to heroic activists is set forth in William Perry Pendley, *It Takes a Hero: The Grassroots Battle Against Environmental Oppression* (Bellevue, Washington: Free Enterprise Press, 1994).

21. "Handout—Elements of An Appeal," Montana Wilderness Association, (undated), 2 pages.

22. "Workin' Man (Nowhere To Go)" not only expresses the frustration of the Western timber worker, but is a fight song as well.

Country Singer Hoyt Axton, who has a place between Hamilton and Darby, saw the trucks going by, found out what was going on, and took his band to Darby to perform an all-day concert. The song most requested was "Workin' Man."

23. Conversations with Bruce Vincent, spring and summer 1994.

24. According to Bruce Vincent, Senator Baucus denied that such an offer was ever made. When Bruce Vincent made the statement in text during congressional testimony, Senator Baucus interrupted, "Bruce, I didn't say that!" Bruce said, "Max, Dave [Erickson] keeps saying it's true; one of you is lying."

25. Even the far-off *New York Times* carried an advertisement that called the effort to stop the "Accords" the "Chainsaw Massacre."

26. The Sweet Home Chapter of Communities for a Great Oregon was the lead plaintiff in a ground-breaking decision before the U.S. Court of Appeals for the District of Columbia Circuit, in which the court struck down U.S. Fish and Wildlife Service regulations that attempted to regulate activity on private lands. The court held that the term "harm" in the Endangered Species Act did not include "habitat modification." *Sweet Homes Chapter of Communities for a Great Oregon, et al. v. Bruce Babbitt, et al.*, 17 F.3d 1463 (D.C. Cir. 1994).

27. The "Fly in for Freedom" is now an activity of Alliance for America that has hundreds of groups nationwide. Much of what the alliance first did was patterned after the incredible successes of the Oregon Lands Coalition.

28. Pendley, op. cit., pp. 223–229.

29. Bill Grannel, "Green extremism fuels grass-roots 'people' campaign," unpublished article, dated April 5, 1994.

30. These include, in Wyoming, the Shoshone National Forest and the Bridger-Teton National Forest; in Idaho, the Targhee National Forest and the Caribou National Forest; and in Montana, the Gallatin National Forest, the Custer National Forest, and the Beaverhead National Forest. The YNP is not the only national park in the area. The Grand Teton National Park sits just to the south of the YNP and includes the Grand Teton Mountain Range west of Jackson, Wyoming, as well as the John D. Rockefeller Memorial Parkway.

31. Not all of these USFS-managed lands are included in what the federal government calls the Greater Yellowstone Area (GYA) or the Greater Yellowstone Ecosystem. Of the land in these forests, 9.1 million acres are included, added to 2.6 million acres of national parks and nearly a million acres of other federal lands. In addition, 4.8 million acres of private land, .8 million acres of Indian Reservations, and .7 million acres of state land are included in the GYA. National Park Service and Forest Service, "Vision for the Future: A Framework for Coordination in the Greater Yellowstone Area—Draft," August 1990, pp. 1–3.

32. See Chapter 6 for a description of the YNP's "let burn" policy and its effect on the park's neighbors. See also Alton Chase, *Playing God with Yellowstone: The Destruction of America's First National Park* (New York, N.Y.: Harcourt Brace Jovanovich, 1987), as well as Micah Morrison, *Fire in Paradise* (New York, N.Y.: HarperCollins, 1993).

33. The Wyoming groups included the Wyoming Stockgrowers Association, the Petroleum Association of Wyoming, allied with the Rocky Mountain Oil and Gas Association, the Wyoming Mining Association, the Wyoming Farm Bureau, and the Wyoming Heritage Society.

34. The Idaho organizations involved included the Idaho Farm Bureau Federal, the Idaho Cattle Association, the Idaho Woolgrowers, and others.
35. The Montana organizations included in the campaign were the Montana Mining Association, the Montana Farm Bureau, the Montana Petroleum Association, the Montana Wood Products Association, the Montana Trail Vehicle Riders Association, the Montana Stockgrowers Association, and others.
36. George F. Leaming, Ph.D., "The Adverse Economic Impacts of Wilderness Land Withdrawals in Utah," Western Economic Analysis Center, Marana, Arizona, January 1990, p. 3.
37. Pendley, op. cit., pp. 141–143.
38. Currently, between three hundred and five hundred counties have adopted some form of the Catron County ordinance. Conversation with Ruth Kaiser of the National Federal Lands Conference, September 2, 1994.
39. In 1989, Mountain States Legal Foundation was the first to designate communities "endangered" as a result of federal policies and lawsuits.
40. *Mountain States Legal Foundation, et al., v. Madigan, et al.*, Civil Action No. 92-0097, U.S. District Court for the District of Columbia.
41. *Douglas County et al., v. Lujan, et al.*, 801 F. Supp. 1470 (Ore. 1992). The county asserted that the agency's recovery plan for the northern spotted owl violated the National Environmental Policy Act, which requires that an environmental study be prepared before a recovery plan is implemented.
42. *Millard County, Utah v. The United States of America*, CIV 93-C-591J, U.S. District Court for the District of Utah.
43. *Bruneau Hot Springsnail Briefing Book*, prepared by Idaho Farm Bureau, Bruneau Valley Coalition, 1993.
44. Ibid.
45. The Bruneau Valley Coalition was aided in its legal efforts by the American Farm Bureau Federation as well as a supportive amici curiae brief filed by Mountain States Legal Foundation on behalf of the Idaho Trail Machine Association, the Gem State Hunting Association, and the Idaho Orienteering Association.
46. See columnist Paul Harvey, "Idaho's Jurassic Park in miniature," syndicated nationwide, September 1993.
47. *Idaho Farm Bureau Federation, et al., v. Babbitt, et al.*, CIV 93-0168-E-EJL, Order of December 14, 1993 (ID. 1993).
48. Report on the Wise Use Movement, op. cit., p. 59.

APPENDIX B

1. Source: American Forest and Paper Association, 1111 19th Street, N.W., Suite 700; Washington, D.C. 20036; 202-463-2700; Fax 202-463-5180. For more information, contact the American Forest and Paper Association or your state forestry association.
2. Source: National Cattlemen's Association, 1301 Pennsylvania Avenue, N.W., Suite 300; Washington, D.C. 20004; 202-347-0228; Fax 202-638-0607; P.O. Box 3469; Englewood, Colorado, 80155; 303-694-0305; Fax

303-694-2851. Contact the National Cattlemen's Association or your state stockgrowers association. Also, American Sheep Industry Association, 6911 South Yosemite Street, Englewood, Colorado 80112, 303-771-3500. Contact the American Sheep Industry Association or your state woolgrowers association.

3. Source: National Mining Association; 1130 17th Street, NW, Washington, D.C. 20036-4677; 202-463-2625; Fax 202-463-6152. Contact the NMA or your state mining association.

4. Source: Rocky Mountain Oil and Gas Association (RMOGA); 1775 Sherman Street, Suite 2501; Denver, Colorado 80203; 303-860-0099; Fax 303-860-0310; and Independent Petroleum Association of Mountain States (IPAMS), 518 17th Street, Suite 620, Denver, Colorado, 80202; 303-623-0987; Fax 303-893-0709. Contact RMOGA or IPAMS or your state oil and gas, independent oil and gas, or petroleum association.

APPENDIX C

1. The Wilderness Act, P.L. 88-577; 78 Stat. 890.
2. Recently, I saw an advertisement in an inflight magazine for a stay at Disney's Wilderness Lodge:

    Answer the call of the wild with a Delta flight to Disney's Wilderness Lodge, the luxurious new resort at Walt Disney World in Florida. Tucked into a wilderness area on the shores of a large lake, the hotel is a majestic monument to the National Park lodges of the great Northwest.... Fly Delta to a natural oasis that's just a stone's throw from a world of extraordinary Disney attractions.

    "*SKY*" *Magazine*, Delta Airlines, April 1994, p. 105.

    With a "wilderness" featuring a "luxurious new resort" and a "hotel [that] is a majestic monument to the National Park lodges of the great Northwest," all just a "stone's throw from [modern] attractions," why do Westerners oppose the designation of more "wilderness?" Why indeed?

3. Of the 73.238 million acres managed by the National Park Service, 52.891 million acres, or 72 percent is in Alaska. Figures are as of September 30, 1992. Table 24, Federally Owned Land by Agency, Bureau and State, as of September 30, 1992, General Services Administration, pp. 14–15.

4. Ibid. California figures do not include the California Desert bill passed by the Senate late in 1994. That legislation adds nearly 3 million acres to the National Park System. Some states outside the West do have large parks: Florida has 2.1 million acres and Texas has 1 million acres in parkland set-asides. Ibid.

5. Table 24, Federally Owned Land by Agency, Bureau and State, as of September 30, 1992, General Services Administration, pp. 14–15.

6. Ibid. Unlike most federal agencies, the Fish and Wildlife Service has its largest holdings outside the Mountain West, the largest of which include Alaska (76.4 million acres), Minnesota (3.5 million acres), and Michigan (1.1 million acres). Ibid.

7. Ibid., pp. 14–15. The Bureau of Land Management has responsibility for

92,741,651 acres in the state of Alaska. Ibid., p. 14.
8. Ibid., pp. 14–15.
9. Ibid.
10. "Public Land Statistics—1992," U.S. Department of the Interior, Bureau of Land Management, p. 5.
11. Table 24, Federally Owned Land by Agency, Bureau and State, as of September 30, 1992, General Services Administration, at pp. 10–11. Alaska has 21.7 million acres of land for which the Forest Service is the managing agency, or 12 percent of all national forestlands. Ibid.
12. Ibid.
13. "Public Land Statistics—1992," U.S. Department of the Interior, Bureau of Land Management, p. 5.
14. Ibid.
15. Ibid. A relatively small amount of Western land is managed by a number of other federal agencies, including the U.S. Department of Energy (707,501 acres—72 percent of which is located in Idaho); U.S. Department of Agriculture Agricultural Research Service locations (324,084 acres); and the U.S. Army Corps of Engineers (95,776 acres).

Index

Absaroka-Beartooth Wilderness Area, 146
Access rights, 79
ACECs. *See* Areas of critical environmental concern
Activism, 214-215
Administrative Procedure Act, 33
Affected interests, 80
Air quality, 111-112
Air tours, 100-101
Alar, 10
Alaska National Interest Lands Conservation Act, 79
Amicus curiae brief, 80, 180
Amoco Oil Refinery, 138
Ancient Forest Rescue, 39
Andrus, Cecil, 162
ANILCA. *See* Alaska National Interest Lands Conservation Act
Animas–La Plata water project, 63-64
Anti-environmental movement, 190
APD. *See* Application for a permit to drill
Appeals, 31-32
Application for a permit to drill, 133
Arbuckle Wilderness, 225-226
Arcata, California, 160
Areas of critical environmental con-
cern, 124-125, 149
Arizona: copper industry, 147-148
Arizona Farm Bureau, 185
Arleigh, Isley, 29
Arnold, Ron, 204
Arthur, Ivan, 81
Audubon Society, 180

Babbitt, Bruce: biological survey, 98; *de facto* moratorium,155-156; disregard for General Mining Law, 20; Straw Man Memo, 72-73; water law speech, 63-64; water rights attack, 52-55
Baggs, Wyoming, 69
Banjo Sheep Company, 64
Barbee, Robert, 163
Barrick Goldstrike Mines, 155
Baucus, Max, 196
Beach Front Management Act, 171-174
Beaty's Butte case, 80
Beaverhead National Forest, 10
Beuter, John H., 45-46
Bierstadt, Albert, 166-167
Bighorn National Forest, 39
Biological survey, 98
Bitterroot National Forest, 193

Blackwood, Jeff, 36
BLM. *See* Bureau of Land Management
Blue Mountains, Oregon, 36
Blue Ribbon Coalition, 203
Bob Marshall Wilderness Area, 130-131
Bonneville Power Association, 63
Bridger–Teton National Forest, 135, 136
Brookes, Warren, 113
Brower, David, 14–15
Bruneau hot springsnails, 207-209
Bruneau Valley Coalition, 208
Buffalo Commons, 85-86
Buffer zones, 17, 122
Bumpers, Dale, 150
Bureau of Indian Affairs, 227
Bureau of Land Management: affected interest challenge, 80; amount of landholdings, 227-229; federal grazing lands, 69-76; National Conservation Areas, 125; oil and gas leases, 133; PACFISH, 61-63; *Public Land Statistics 1992*, 124; regulation allowing enforcement of federal laws, 76-77; restriction of oil and gas development, 138; timber sale program, 42; wilderness study, 119
Bureau of Land Management Organic Act, 117
Bureau of Mines, 227
Bureau of Reclamation, 60, 92, 227
Bush Administration: dam releases ordered, 59; influence on "God Squad," 43; water rights action, 56; wilderness designations, 124

California: timber harvesting lawsuits, 89. *See also specific areas*
California Cattlemen's Association, 80
California Department of Fish and Game, 183-184
California spotted owl, 38, 43
Callahan, Debra, 190-191
Campbell, Ben Nighthorse, 55

Canal Fire, 29
Carlsbad Caverns, 108-109
Carter Administration, 120, 131
Catron County Ordinances, 206
Center for the Defense of Free Enterprise, 204
Center for the New West, 86
CGNW. *See* Communities for a Great Northwest
Charleston County, South Carolina, 170-171
Cheyenne Frontier Days, 159
Child, Brandt, 165
Children, 211-213
Chinook salmon, 62-63
Christian Science Monitor, 199
Church, Frank, 54
Citizen lawsuits, 153-155
Civil disobedience, 39
Clark County, Nevada, 91
Clean Air Act, 138
Clean Water Act, 20, 32, 53, 57-58, 65, 137
CLEAR. *See* Clearinghouse on Environmental Advocacy and Research
Clear-cut, 11
Clearinghouse on Environmental Advocacy and Research, 191
Clearwater National Forest, 37-38
Clinton Administration: conservation duty, 96; ecosystem management, 136; forest policy, 37; takings cases, 179; Timber Summit, 42-43
Coalition for Balanced Environmental Planning, 192
Colorado: Mount Evans, 166-168. *See also specific areas*
Colorado Department of Game and Fish, 71
Colorado River, 59
Colorado River Storage Projects Act, 59
Colorado Roundtable, 72
Colorado squawfish, 92
Colorado's Front Range, 60
Columbia River, 62-63
Committee on Renewable Resources

for Industrial Materials, 47
Communities, 213
Communities for a Great Northwest, 195-197
Communities for Great Oregon, 197
Concessions, 103-105
Concessions Policy Act of 1965, 104
Confusion Range, 120
Conner v. Burford, 134
Conservation, 30
Conservation duty, 96
Cook, Adena, 203
Cooke City, Montana, 146
Cooper & Lybrand, 151
Copper industry, 147-148
Coronado National Forest, 94
Corps of Engineers, 50, 59, 63
Corridors, 17
Council on Environmental Quality, 89
Cowboys, 7
Coyotes, 67-68
Craig, Larry, 63
Crapser, Bill, 193
Crescent Beach, 161-162
Crest House, 167-168
Critical Habitat One area, 38, 90, 192
Critical habitats, 17
Crown Butte Corporation, 145-147
Crown Butte Mines, 143-144
Crump, George, 109
Cushman, Chuck, 203–204
Custer National Forest, 136

Dams, 59
Darby Lumber Mill, 193
de facto moratorium, 155-156
De-roading, 126
Denver, Colorado, 56-57
Department of the Interior: amount of landholdings, 227; draft recovery plan, 42; water rights, 51-52
Desert tortoise, 91, 95-96, 145
Desert Tortoise Management Zone, 95
DF&G. *See* California Department of Fish and Game
Dolan v. City of Tigard, 179-181
Domenici, Pete, 73

DTMZ. *See* Desert Tortoise Management Zone
Dupuyer, Montana, 12
Dwyer, William, 41–42

EA. *See* Environmental assessment
Earth Day, 11
Earth in the Balance, 14, 52
Eastern-style wilderness, 17
Ecosystem management, 136
Ecosystem Protection program, 82-83
Edwards, J. Gordon, 93
Edwards Aquifer, 16-17
Eggelston, Ed, 196
EISs. *See* Environmental impact statements
Eldorado National Forest, 31-32
Ellen, Bill, 17
Employees, 213-214
Endangered Species Act: citizen lawsuits, 32; effect on oil and gas development, 131-133; effect on timber industry, 41-42; environmental groups objectives, 8; history of, 86-98; self-defense provision, 12; takings litigation, 182-183; as threat to ranchers, 82; water rights and, 60
Endangered Species Committee, 42
Endangered Species Conservation Act, 87
Endangered Species Preservation Act, 86-87
Environmental assessment, 132
Environmental Grantmakers Association, 190–191
Environmental impact statements, 132, 144
Environmental litigation, 9-10
Environmental organizations: financial resources, 13; litigation power, 9; objectives, 7-8; relationship with federal government, 9
Environmental Protection Agency: citizen lawsuits, 154;
Ecosystem Protection program, 82-83; restriction of oil and gas development, 137; water rights, 56-57

EPA. *See* Environmental Protection Agency
Epstein, Richard A., 169-170
Erickson, Dave, 196
ESA. *See* Endangered Species Act
Espy, Mike, 20
Etienne, Joanne, 198
Evergreen, 126
Executive Order 12630, 185
Extinction, 87

Farmers Home Administration, 208
Federal grazing lands, 69-76
Federal Land Policy and Management Act, 80, 117, 124
Federal mining law, 7
Fein, Bruce, 154
Fenton, David, 10
Fifth Amendment, 169
Finney, Joan, 129
First English Evangelical Lutheran Church v. County of Los Angeles, 176
Fish and Wildlife Service: amount of landholdings, 227; effect on timber industry, 41, 43; grassroots opposition, 208-209; grizzly bear killing, 12; as threat to ranchers, 82, 93-95
Flathead National Forest, 131-132
Florida Rock Industries, Inc. v. United States, 182
FLPMA. *See* Federal Land Policy and Management Act
"Fly in for Freedom," 198
FmHA. *See* Farmers Home Administration
Foreign oil, 128-129
Forest fires, 24-25
Forks, Washington, 33
Fox, Michael W., 15
Frampton, George, 187
Francis, Edwin A., 167
Fredonia, Arizona, 38
Friends of Earth, 102
Frye, Helen, 42
Fuel buildup, 27, 29
FWS. *See* Fish and Wildlife Service

GABs. *See* Grazing Advisory Boards and Councils
Gallatin National Forest, 131-132
Gas supersaturation, 63
General Management Plans, 107
General Mining Law, 20, 141-156
Geothermal Steam Act of 1970, 127-128
Gerbaz ranch, 49-51, 184
Gerber, Grant, 204-205
Gillette, Wyoming, 67
Glacier National Park, 108
Glacier Peak Wilderness Area, 122
Glen Canyon Dam, 59
Glen Canyon National Recreational Area, 81
Glenn–Colusa Irrigation District, 89-90
GML. *See* General Mining Law
"God Squad," 42, 199-200
Gold deposits, 144-145
"The Gold in Our Hills," 150
Goldblatt v. Hempstead, 174
Gore, Al: *Earth in the Balance*, 14; reinventing government campaign, 60; water rights issue, 52
Goshawk, 125-126
Government-owned land, 8
Graber, David M., 15
Grand Canyon National Park, 99-101
Grannel, Barbara, 200-201
Grannel, Bill, 200-201
Grants Pass, Oregon, 194
Grassroots opposition, 187-209
Grattet, Paul M., 61
Grazing Advisory Boards and Councils, 75
Grazing Fee Task Force, 75
Grazing fees, 72-75
Grazing lands, 69-76
Great American Desert, 5
Great Northwest Log Haul, 193-194
Great Plains, 85-86
"The Great Terrain Robbery," 150
Greater Yellowstone Ecosystem, 110, 146
Greber, Brian, 45

Greeley, Colorado, 60-61
Green River Resource Area, 135
Green sales, 32
Greenfield, Meg, 150
Grizzly bears, 12, 14, 38, 90, 192

Habitat conservation plans, 95
Habitat modification, 96
Habitat One area. See Critical Habitat One area
Hage, Wayne, 53, 77-79, 184, 205-206
Hard release, 119
Harney County, Oregon, 6
Heicher, Bill, 71
High Country Stable Corporation, 109-110
Himmel, Pete, 32
Hirons, Tom, 197
Hocker, Philip M., 142
Holmes, Oliver Wendell, 170
Hoosier National Forest, 17
Hoosier Ridge RNA, 125
Humane Society of the United States, 15
Humphrey, Hubert, 54
Hydroelectricity, 59

Incidental take permits, 95
Indicator species, 125-126
Inholders, 77
Integral vistas, 111
Interagency Scientific Committee, 45
International Woodworkers of America, 42-43
ISC. See Interagency Scientific Committee
Isle of Palms, 170-171
Istock, Conrad, 94

Jack Ward Thomas Report, 41, 45
Jamison, Cy, 42
Jeopardy opinion, 95
John D. and Catherine T. MacArthur Foundation, 191
Johnson, Met, 81-82, 206-207
Johnson, Valerie, 197-200

Kaibab mills, 38
Kaiser, Ruth, 205-206
Kanab ambersnail, 91, 165
Kanamine, Linda, 36
Kane, Pennsylvania, 18-19
Kane County, Utah, 18-19
Kangaroo rat, 93
Kansas Independent Oil and Gas Association, 129
Kerr, Andy, 158
Keystone Bituminous Coal Association v. DeBenedictis, 175
Killian, Mark, 206-207
The Kootenai Accords, 196-197
Kootenai National Forest, 32, 196
Kootenai Valley, Montana, 20, 36
Kootenai Wildlands Alliance, 196
Koppel, Ted, 191
Krulitz, Leo, 51-52
Krulitz Opinion, 51-52
Kunzman, John, 197-198
KWA. See Kootenai Wildlands Alliance

Lagoon Creek, 162
Lake City, Colorado, 115-116
Lake Koocanusa, 158
Lakeview, Oregon, 158
Land acquisition program, 96, 112-113
Land lockup, 22
Land-use planning, 57
Lang, Jackie, 199
Las Vegas, Nevada, 95-96
Lava Butte, Oregon, 34
Lawson, Billie, 46
Lawsuits: citizen lawsuits, 153-155; timber harvesting, 88-89, 92
League of Conservation Voters, 55
Leaming, George F., 165-166
Leasing and land-use planning system, 152-153
Leshy, John D., 54, 151
Lewis and Clark National Forest, 130
Libby, Montana, 157-158, 192
Lincoln County, Montana, 95
Liston, Louise, 81, 206
Litigation power, 9

Little Snake River, 64-65
Litton, Martin, 102
Loggers, 14, 19
Lolo National Forest, 196
London Metal Exchange, 149
Longs Peak, 116
Loveladies Harbor, Inc. v. United States, 182
Lucas, David H., 18, 170-174
Lucas v. South Carolina Coastal Council, 170-174
Lujan, Manuel, 59, 105, 155
Lyman, Ivan, 81
Lyndon B. Johnson grove, 162

MacWilliams Cosgrove Snider, 187
Maloney, Carolyn, 121
Managed forests, 29
Manning, Dick, 206
Marbled murrelet, 43
Mason, C. Larry, 33-34, 44
Master Plans, 107
McDaniels, B. H., 184
McDonald, Sommer & Frates v. Yolo County, 175
Media, 214
Merchant Marine and Fisheries Committee, 87
Mexican spotted owl, 38, 92
Mich-Cal, 32
Michigan Wilderness Act, 123
Military reservations, 229
Millard County, Utah, 120
Miller, Cecil, 185
Mills, Ocie, 18
Mineral Leasing Act of 1920, 140
Mineral Policy Center, 142
Mines and Mining Subcommittee, 127-128
Mining, 141-156, 221-222
Mining law, 7
Missoula, Montana, 195
Mitigation, 95-96
Moerman, Robin R., 183-184
Mojave Desert, 144
Montana: population density, 4; temperature records, 5. *See also specific*

areas
Montana Department of State Lands, 146
Montana Wilderness Association, 192
Mount Evans, 166-168
Mount Graham, 94
Mountain States Legal Foundation, 50, 200
Mountain Ute Indian Tribe, 63-64
MRACs. *See* Multiple Resource Advisory Councils
MSLF. *See* Mountain States Legal Foundation
Multiple Resource Advisory Councils, 75
Multiple Use Land Alliance, 203-204
Multiple Use Strategy Conference, 204
Murkowski, Frank, 142
MWA. *See* Montana Wilderness Association

NACo. *See* National Association of Counties
National Association of Counties, 206
National Biological Survey, 82, 98
National Conservation Areas, 125
National Environmental Policy Act, 33, 56, 131-133
National Federal Lands Conference, 205-206
National forests, 30
National Inholders Association, 203–204
National Marine Fisheries Services, 63
National Natural Landmarks Program, 113-114, 125
National Park Service, 15, 99-114, 227
National parks: concessions, 103-105; environmental groups' objectives, 8; restrictions, 22
National Wild and Scenic Rivers System, 123-124
National Wilderness Institute, 97
National Wilderness Preservation System, 149
National Wildlife Federation, 10

National Wildlife Federation v. Gorsuch, 58
Native Americans, 34, 63-64
Natural Resources Defense Council, 10
Nature Conservancy, 76, 81
Navajo Indian Reservation, 92
NCAs. *See* National Conservation Areas
Nelson, Gaylord, 88
NEPA. *See* National Environmental Policy Act
New West, 54-55
New World Mine, 145-147
Newkirk, Ingrid, 15
NFLC. *See* National Federal Lands Conference
NMFS. *See* National Marine Fisheries Services
NNLs. *See* National Natural Landmarks Program
No net job loss policy, 43
No surface occupancy, 132
Nollan v. California Coastal Commission, 176-177
Noranda Mining Corporation, 95-96
North America Wilderness Recovery Project, 19
Northern Rockies Ecosystem Protection Act, 121
Northern spotted owl, 41-47
Northwest Timber Compromise, 41, 198
NPS. *See* National Park Service
NRDC. *See* Natural Resources Defense Council
NSO. *See* No surface occupancy
Nuisances, 177-179
NWI. *See* National Wilderness Institute

Obermiller, Fred, 70
Obmascik, Mark, 164-165
Observatories, 94
O'Conner, Sandra Day, 172
OCS. *See* Outer Continental Shelf
Office of Management and Budget, 72

Oil and Gas Journal, 128
Oil and gas resources, 21-22, 128-140, 222-223
OLC. *See* Oregon Lands Coalition
Olympic National Forest, 34
Omak, Washington, 195
O'Neil, Roger, 92
Option 9 decision, 33, 45
Oregon: timber harvesting lawsuits, 89. *See also specific areas*
Oregon & California Lands Act, 44
Oregon Lands Coalition, 28, 198-200
Organic Act, 30
Orick Chamber of Commerce, 162
Ortega, Ernest, 109
Orton, Bill, 82
Osborne photograph, 34
O'Toole, Pat, 65
Outer Continental Shelf, 153
Overthrust Belt, 129-130
Owyhee County, Idaho, 91, 208-209

PACFISH, 61-63
Pacific Legal Foundation, 184
Panguitch, Utah, 38
Park County, Colorado, 125
Parks. *See* National Park Service; National parks; *specific parks*
Parrish, Connie, 102
Paseneaux, Carolyn, 203
Patents, 143
Payson, Arizona, 38
Penn Central Transportation v. City of New York, 174-175
Pennsylvania Coal Company v. Mahon, 170
People for the Ethical Treatment of Animals, 15
People for the West, 201
Pepperdine University, 74
Petersen, Jim, 126, 194-195
Petroleum Association of Wyoming, 135
Pew Charitable Trusts, 191
Pinchot, Gifford, 30
Platte River, 56-57
Poison 1080, 67

"Polluters' Protection Act," 185
Popper, Deborah, 85-86
Popper, Frank, 85-86
Population density, 4
Portland, Oregon, 197
Power, Tom, 166
Pozsgai, John, 17-18
Presettlement conditions, 33-35
Private Property Protection Act, 185
Property rights protection statute, 19
Public Land Statistics 1992, 124
Public Law Statutes, 125

Rahall, Nick Joe, 150
Ranching: facts, 219-221
Rangeland Reform '94, 73, 75
Rathdrum, Idaho, 195
Ray, Dixy Lee, 93
Reach of the river, 50
Reagan Administration: oil and gas leases, 131; Takings Implication Assessment, 185
Recreational lands, 22-23
Red-cockaded woodpecker, 97
Red squirrel, 94
Redford, Robert, 159
Redwood National Park, 160-163
Rehnquist, William, 175, 178, 180-181
Reilly, William K., 56-57
Reinmuth, James, 46
Reinventing government campaign, 60
Reno, Janet, 54
"Report on the Wise Use Movement," 187-209
Research Natural Areas, 125
Rigby, Idaho, 77
Ripeness, 175
Riverside County, California, 90
Riverside Irrigation District v. Andrews, 58
RNAs. *See* Research Natural Areas
RNP. *See* Redwood National Park
Roaring Fork River, 49-51
Robertson, Dale, 193
Robitaille, Rick, 135
Rockefeller Foundation, 191
Rocky Mountain National Park, 109-110
Rocky Mountain Region, 129

Roosevelt National Forest, 61
Rosario Resort, 190
Rovig, Dave, 168
Royalties, 151
R.S. 2477, 123

Salmon, 61-63, 91
San Antonio, Texas, 16-17
San Juan Island, 190
San Juan National Forest, 39
San Juan Resource Area, 135
Sandstone Dam, 64-65
Santini, Jim, 127
Scalia, Antonin, 172-173, 177-179
Schneider, Stephen, 93
Section 318, 198
Self-initiation, 143
Shawnee National Forest, 17, 40
Sheridan, Wyoming, 59
Shoshone National Forest, 131, 133, 136
Shuler, John E., 12, 14
Sierra Club, 14, 102, 162-163
Sierra Club Political Handbook, 107
Sierra Nevada Mountains, 31, 38, 43
Silver Fire Complex, 194
Silver Fire Roundup, 195
Single use set-asides, 8
Sinkholes, 137
Six Rivers National Forest, 160, 163
Skaggs, Dan, 116
Ski resorts, 22
Skinner, Quentin, 70-71
Smith, Bob, 36
Snails, 165, 207-209
Snake River, 62-63
Solidarity Celebration, 195
South Carolina: Beach Front Management Act, 171-174. *See also specific areas*
South Carolina Coastal Council, 171
Southern Ute Indian Tribe, 63-64, 80
Species, 93
Spilling, 62-63
Spotted owls, 31, 38, 41-47, 92
Squires, Larry, 137
St. Croix, Indiana, 198

Steinberg, Saul, 3
Stevens, Ted, 87-88
Stillwater Complex, 152
Stimson Lumber Company, 197
Straw Man Memo, 72
Sullivan, Mike, 65
Sun, Kathleen, 71-72
Surface Mining Control and Reclamation Act of 1976, 181
Sweet Home, Oregon, 197
Sweetheart lawsuits, 154
Sweetwater County, Wyoming, 5
Sylvania Wilderness, 123
Symington, Fife, 185
Synar, Mike, 79

Takings, Private Property and the Power of Eminent Domain, 169-170
Takings Clause, 169-186
Takings Implication Assessment, 185
Tall Tree grove, 163
Tarr, Ralph W., 52
Temperature records, 5
Thomas, Jack Ward, 45
"Threats and Opportunities," 190-191
Tigard, Oregon, 179-181
Timber: below-cost timber sales, 39-40; environmental groups objectives, 7; environmental impediments to harvesting, 21; facts, 217-219; growth, 37; harvesting litigation, 88-89, 92; national forests, 30
Timber Dollars, 199
Timber Summit, 42-43
Tonopah, Nevada, 78
Tourism, 7, 157-168
Trashing the Planet, 93
Trenk, Peggy Olson, 203
Tule elk, 183-184
Twin Lakes Reservoir, 59
Two Forks dam, 56-57
Udall, Morris K., 103
Umatilla National Forest, 36
United Brotherhood of Carpenters and Joiners of America, 42-43
Unsuitability designations, 155-156
Upper Basin States, 59

U.S. Court of Appeals for the Ninth Circuit, 79
U.S. Forest Service: amount of land-holdings, 228-229; buffer zones, 122; de-roading, 126; decision appeals, 31-32; federal grazing lands, 69-76; forest neglect, 27-28; Mount Evans, 167; Mount Graham observatory, 94; PACFISH, 61-63; Research Natural Areas, 125; timber sale program, 31-32
U.S. Geological Survey, 129, 143, 227
USFS. *See* U.S. Forest Service
USGS. *See* U.S. Geological Survey
Utah: Wilderness Study Areas, 119-120. *See also specific areas*
Utah Association of Counties, 120, 165
Ute Indian Tribe, 92

Vail, Colorado, 107-108
Vail Agenda, 107-108
Valid existing rights, 122-123
Viceroy Resource Corporation, 144
Vincent, Bruce, 32-33, 160, 192-198, 207
Vision Document, 110, 202-204

W. Alton Jones Foundation, 190-191
Walker, Rex, 109-110
Walking Box Ranch, 145
Wallop, Malcolm, 58
Wallop amendment, 57-58
Wallowa Whitman National Forest, 27-29
Washington: timber harvesting lawsuits, 89. *See also specific areas*
Water resources, 7
Water rights, 51-52, 121-122
Water storage facilities, 60-61
Watt, James, 104
Weber, Ray, 69-70
Weidman, Mike, 27-28
Wenatchee National Forest, 122
Western Council of Industrial Workers, 42-43
Western Economic Analysis Center, 165

Western Environmental Trade Association, 203
Western Interstate Region, 206
Western States Coalition, 206-207
Western States Public Lands Coalition, 200
Wetlands violations, 17-18
Wheeler Peak, 159
White, Byron, 183
Whitney Benefits, Inc. v. United States, 181
Wildcatters, 129
Wilderness Act of 1964, 51-52, 54, 106, 117
Wilderness designation: description, 116-126; grassroots organizations, 195-200; misperceptions, 225-226
Wilderness Impact Research Foundation, 204-205
Wilderness Report, 102
Wilderness Society, 88, 102, 187, 191, 209
Wilderness Study Areas, 119-120
The Wildlands Project, 19
Wildlife, 70

Williams, Harrison, 88
WIR. *See* Western Interstate Region
Wise Use Movement, 187-209
Wolves, 164
World Forestry Center, 197
Writ of certiorari, 133
WSAs. *See* Wilderness Study Areas
Wyoming: oil and gas operations, 135-136; population density, 4; temperature records, 5. *See also specific areas*
Wyoming Game and Fish Commission, 138-139
Wyoming Public Lands Council, 203

Yellowstone National Park: creation of, 101, 141; fires, 35; Vision Document, 202-204; wolves, 164
Yellowstone National Park Act, 102
Yellowstone Vision Document, 202-204
Yeutter, Clayton, 9-10
YNP. *See* Yellowstone National Park
Yosemite National Park, 104-106

Zilly, Thomas, 41